Celal Nuri

Celal Nuri

Young Turk Modernizer and Muslim Nationalist

York Norman

I.B.TAURIS
LONDON • NEW YORK • OXFORD • NEW DELHI • SYDNEY

I.B. TAURIS
Bloomsbury Publishing Plc
50 Bedford Square, London, WC1B 3DP, UK
1385 Broadway, New York, NY 10018, USA
29 Earlsfort Terrace, Dublin 2, Ireland

BLOOMSBURY, I.B. TAURIS and the I.B. Tauris logo are
trademarks of Bloomsbury Publishing Plc

First published in Great Britain 2021
This paperback edition published 2023

Copyright © York Norman, 2021

York Norman has asserted his right under the Copyright, Designs and
Patents Act, 1988, to be identified as Author of this work.

For legal purposes the Acknowledgments on p. viii constitute an
extension of this copyright page.

Series design by Adriana Brioso
Cover image: Celal Nuri Bey (1881–1938) illustration, circa 1910s.
(© Chronicle / Alamy Stock Photo)

All rights reserved. No part of this publication may be reproduced or
transmitted in any form or by any means, electronic or mechanical, including
photocopying, recording, or any information storage or retrieval system,
without prior permission in writing from the publishers.

Bloomsbury Publishing Plc does not have any control over, or responsibility for,
any third-party websites referred to or in this book. All internet addresses given
in this book were correct at the time of going to press. The author and publisher
regret any inconvenience caused if addresses have changed or sites have
ceased to exist, but can accept no responsibility for any such changes.

A catalogue record for this book is available from the British Library.

A catalog record for this book is available from the Library of Congress.

ISBN: HB: 978-0-7556-1720-3
PB: 978-0-7556-4357-8
ePDF: 978-0-7556-1721-0
eBook: 978-0-7556-1722-7

Typeset by Integra Software Services Pvt. Ltd.

To find out more about our authors and books visit www.bloomsbury.com
and sign up for our newsletters.

*Dedicated to my mother, Jane Marie Norman,
and my late father, Jack Roy Norman*

Contents

Acknowledgments · viii

1 Celal Nuri's Life and Work: Introductory Remarks · 1
2 On Politics · 21
3 The Nationalities Problem · 39
4 Vulgar Materialism and Islam · 65
5 Women, Family, and Society · 81
6 Turkish Language Reform · 103
7 Conclusion · 125

Notes · 130
Bibliography · 182
Index · 197

Acknowledgments

I have a huge debt of gratitude for all of those who have helped me bring this book project to a successful conclusion. First and foremost I would like to thank Birsen Bulmuş for her enormous generosity in translating all of the French materials I have used in this book to English. Brad Finger has spent a great deal of time twice editing the entire manuscript. John Abromeit, Nikolai Antov, Kimberly Hart, and Albert Michaels have all read significant portions of the manuscript and/or proposal and have provided key feedback and suggestions that I have incorporated in this book. I have also benefited greatly from all the organizers and participants of the various conferences I presented papers on Celal Nuri, including the 2018 Great Lakes Ottomanist Workshop at the University of Chicago, the Ottoman Empire and World War I Workshop in Sarajevo Bosnia in 2012, and the 2015 and 2018 New York State Association of Europeanist Historians Annual Conferences at St. John Fisher's College and St. Francis College. I also appreciate the Near and Middle Eastern Civilizations Department at the University of Toronto for inviting me for a special paper presentation in 2013.

Support from my colleagues at the History and Social Studies Education Department at SUNY Buffalo State has been vital to completing the book, particularly from my chair Andrew Nicholls. The sabbatical the department gave me in Fall 2014 was all important to research conducted in Turkey for this project. A prior visit in Summer 2009, funded with the help of a Multi-Country Research Fellowship from the Council of American Overseas Research Centers and a Summer Travel Grant by the Institute of Turkish Studies, was also critical to this effort.

Thanks also are due to all the libraries, archives, and websites involved in providing me the materials I have needed. The Turkish archives I accessed include the Prime Minister's Ottoman Archives, State Library, Atatürk Library, and Islamic Research Center in Istanbul, and the Prime Minister Republican archives, and National Library in Ankara. The research libraries I used in the United States and Canada include Binghamton University, The Library of Congress, New York Public Library, The Ohio State University, Princeton University, Stanford University, the University at Buffalo, the University of

California, Berkeley, the University of California, Los Angeles, the University of Chicago, and the University of Toronto.

A special thanks go to Susan Jaworski and all the library staff at Buffalo State for providing material from interlibrary loan and our own collection.

I also benefited greatly from innumerable purchases from the various second-hand booksellers of Turkey. Much of this material was purchased online via Nadirkitap.com

I would also like to thank Rory Gormley, my book editor, and Yasmin Garcha, his editorial assistant, for their time, patience, and understanding for processing my book proposal and manuscript. The two anonymous reviewers whom they chose provided me with extremely helpful suggestions, which, I believe, made the book far stronger than it was previously. I am grateful to new teachers who freely impart their knowledge even though I have had no personal or institutional connection to them.

Note on the use of Turkish names and surnames: European-style surnames were only used after the passage of the 1934 Turkish Surname Law (*Soyadı Kanunu*). I have used Turkish surnames sparingly because most of this study deals with events from 1909 to 1926. In general, I have only used the surname when I introduce a Turkish historical figure the first time in a chapter. I have given the surname in brackets immediately after the first and middle name, that is, Celal Nuri (İleri). The exception to this rule is Mustafa Kemal (Atatürk), the founder of the Republic of Turkey. In his case I use the name Mustafa Kemal when discussing him up to 1933, and Atatürk anytime after. I have also used the surname Atatürk when referring to him to times both before and after passage of the Turkish Surname Law.

1

Celal Nuri's Life and Work: Introductory Remarks

A New Era

The Istanbul newspapers' announcement on the morning of July 24, 1908, that Sultan Abdülhamid II would reconvene the Ottoman Parliament after thirty years of inactivity and autocratic rule was a pivotal moment in the history of his empire. The sultan, faced with a small-scale, but menacing insurrection in Macedonia, decided the night before to placate the rebels, an assorted group of disgruntled young army officers and local Albanian militias.[1] The army officers, associated with a clandestine political society, the Committee of Union and Progress (CUP), became instant heroes throughout the southern Balkan and Aegean provinces and the affluent quarters of Istanbul, as they were seen as having inaugurated a new period of "liberty, fraternity, equality, and justice."[2] The various opponents of Abdülhamid II—among them liberals, minorities, intellectuals, junior-level military officers, and administrative officials—all cheered. Their hopes for better governance took on a variety of contradictory forms. Many Armenian, Greek, Arab, and Albanian subjects supported a liberal vision of decentralized government and greater individual religious and political liberties, believing that the only way for the empire to survive was to satisfy the needs of its minorities. Their stress would be on reinvigorating the parliament and the constitutional order to be more inclusive of these concerns.[3]

At first the CUP was partially sympathetic toward the liberals, believing that their policies might convince the European powers to forestall further intervention into Ottoman affairs. Indeed, the initial 1908 rebellion had been sparked at least in part by the June 1908 Reval meeting between Czar Nicholas II and King Edward VII, at which the Russians and British agreed to push for autonomy in the Ottomans' Macedonian provinces under international supervision.[4] Many of the most active participants in the revolt were Balkan Muslims.[5]

A second revolt, this time against the CUP, took place on the night of April 12–13, 1909 (known as the "March 31 Incident" because of the Ottoman Rumi calendar in use at the time). This uprising, which began in the Taşkışla barracks near Beyoğlu, Istanbul, was largely led by conscripts and non-commissioned officers. They marched to the parliament building in the capital with the support of Muslim seminary (*medrese*) students, guildsmen, and other conservative circles. In addition to denouncing the CUP, they also demanded the dismissal of the grand vizier and two other key ministers, as well as the replacement of a number of CUP officers, deputies, and the president of the parliament. They likewise called for the restoration of Islamic law, as well as amnesty for themselves. The grand vizier and ministers resigned, and the rebels took over Istanbul until April 24, when the CUP helped lead a counter-coup with the "Action Army" (*Hareket Ordusu*), whose core support came from units from Thrace and Macedonia. Once back in control, they executed the Dervish Sheikh Vahdeti, the alleged spiritual leader of the uprising, banned the Muhammadan Union, the political and religious organization he represented, and forced Abdülhamid II to step down from the throne.[6]

This uprising convinced the CUP that they were particularly vulnerable. They feared religious conservatives might follow the footsteps of Sheikh Vahdeti and rally the majority of Ottoman Muslims against the CUP, and restore Abdülhamid II as an autocratic sultan/caliph.[7] Equally disconcerting for the CUP were the liberals, who were also likely involved in the 1909 uprising. The liberals apparently hoped to use the conservative mob as popular means to displace the CUP in favor of their own supporters.[8]

This crisis was compounded by Ottoman territorial losses from 1908 up until the First World War. Bulgaria's declaration of independence from the Ottoman Empire on October 5, 1908, was followed the next day by two further blows: Austro-Hungary formally annexed Bosnia-Herzegovina and the Cretan assembly resolved that the island be united with Greece. On September 29, 1911, Italy declared war on the Ottomans and invaded Libya the next month. In October 1912, an alliance of Balkan Christian nations, including Bulgaria, Montenegro, Serbia, and Greece, attacked the Ottomans. Within two months, the Ottomans had effectively lost almost all of the empire's remaining possessions in the Balkans (with the exception of Eastern Thrace, including Edirne, the Straits, Istanbul, and its environs).[9]

This led the CUP to increasingly suppress the minorities and try to rally their core supporters by appealing to Ottoman Muslim sentiments. Fresh streams of Muslim refugees from the Balkans and other newly foreign-occupied provinces to Istanbul and the western coastal regions of Anatolia were receptive to such a message. They believed that inaction in places, such as Eastern Anatolia, might lead to a repeat of what had occurred in their previous home.[10] The majority of the CUP in 1908 were also sensitive to these concerns, as they tended to be Ottoman Muslims from the southern Balkans, the Aegean and Marmara coast, as well as the Caucasus, all areas they perceived to be under threat of foreign partition.[11]

CUP Politics

As a result, CUP politics were often highly conflicted between the fight against religious reaction, on the one hand, and suppressing rival liberals and non-Muslim nationalists on the other. This translated into a variety of seemingly contradictory political discussions, leading many historians until recently to conclude that one could divide the CUP in general into separate ideological camps. Following Yusuf Akçura's famous essay "The Three Types of Politics" (*Üç Tarz-ı Siyaset*),[12] they categorized the CUP into three core "identity groups": "Ottomanists" who (supported "Ottomanism" and) believed that granting equal rights to all the empire's Muslims and non-Muslims would lead to internal peace and external recognition; (pan-) Islamists who advocated the unity of all Muslims regardless of ethnic background[13]; and (pan-) Turkists who sought to unify only the Turks and give up on earlier political projects.[14]

This categorization fed into the teleological argument that Ottomanism died out after the Ottomans lost most of their remaining non-Muslim population after the Balkan Wars. Similarly, the argument ran that the Islamists lost steam after the loss of the Arab provinces during the First World War, leaving only Turkism as the only ideological option, even if it could only succeed in unifying the Turks of Anatolia.[15]

Niyazi Berkes, in his seminal work *The Development of Secularism in Turkey* (1964), uses the label of Westernist instead of Ottomanist, even though this terminology confuses advocates of a positivistic social secular reform program with an identity group. This interpretation is contradictory since, as we have seen under Mustafa Kemal (Atatürk)'s Turkey, a homogeneous Muslim nation shorn of all non-Muslim minorities could of course undergo secularization.[16]

M. Şükrü Hanioğlu contends instead that the CUP had opted for (pan-) Turkism before the 1908 revolt in order to counter rival nationalist movements among the Greeks and Armenians.[17]

Most convincingly, however, is Erik J. Zürcher, who sees that the CUP was instead a highly reactive type of eclectic Ottoman Muslim nationalist movement. While he admits that positivists heavily influenced CUP social reforms, he points out that Unionists as a whole worked systematically against non-Muslim minority rights after the 1909 uprising and that their predilection for Turkish nationalism, as a romantic Pan-Turkist tie to either the Turkish minorities of Russia or the more recent Turkist idealization of the Anatolian Turkish peasants after 1913, is easily overstated. Likewise, pan-Islamic rhetoric, despite the declaration of jihad at the behest of Germany in 1914, was far more defensive in nature focusing on Ottoman Muslims rather than actively seeking to unify all Muslims in one political entity.[18]

Still, the fundamental CUP effort after the 1909 uprising was to bridge the gap between the CUP and the more conservative Muslim masses through Ottoman Muslim identity politics. The CUP also echoed the Islamists of the Hamidian era, when it emphasized Muslims as the empire's dominant confessional community and the Ottoman sultan/caliph as head of state. In addition, the CUP won further credibility among conservative Muslims for its hardline stance against non-Muslim minorities and the foreign powers that often backed them.

Nonetheless, the CUP, in time, would embark on a series of controversial religious, social, and language reforms. These included the re-training of religious officials according to "scientific," non-dogmatic methods, seeking the eventual elimination of the Islamic legal court system, legislation promoting Western-style women's rights, and trying to modify the Ottoman Turkish alphabet.

Celal Nuri: The Contributions of a Unionist Journalist

Undoubtedly, one of the most outspoken CUP advocates of these seemingly contradictory policies of Ottoman Muslim identity politics and "scientific" social reform was Celal Nuri (İleri) (1881–1938).[19] Born in Gelibolu to Mustafa Nuri, a high Ottoman official who was the scion of the prestigious Helvacızade family of Crete, and Nefise Hanım, daughter of the Ottoman statesman and poet Abidin Pasha, Celal Nuri, like many of his fellow CUP members, came from the ranks of the Ottoman Muslim elite.[20] The permanent Ottoman loss of both parents' native lands certainly caused Celal Nuri a great deal of grief. Hawrutian Sharighian, an Ottoman Armenian *Dashnak* opponent of Celal Nuri, had sarcastically commented in 1913 that Celal Nuri's inventiveness and sense of the history of civilization stemmed from his father's Cretan origin. Celal Nuri responded: "I was not born in Crete. Only my father was born in Crete. If your exalted goal about the history of civilization and others is being Greek, you can be sure that I do not have a drop of Greek blood."[21]

Mustafa Nuri and his brother Sırrı Giridi Pasha, a prominent Hamidian theologian and statesman, passed on to Celal Nuri their sense of Sunni Muslim identity. Sırrı Giridi wrote extensively on Islamic "heresies" after serving as the lieutenant governor of Diyarbakir in 1885–6.[22] Mustafa Nuri authored a controversial tract on the Yezidis as a result of his impressions while governor of Mosul from 1902 to 1905.[23] Celal Nuri often referred to his uncle's description of heretics in his works and translated his father's tract into French along with his own commentary in 1909.[24]

Celal Nuri's education began under his family supervision. He was largely tutored at home since he and his family traveled from province to province where his father was assigned his post. It is no surprise that Celal Nuri would look up to his relatives as role models for his future career in politics and state affairs. Giridi Ahmed Saki wrote in 1919 that Celal Nuri was in the habit of writing at least two pages a day from five-years-old onward. He allegedly went so far as to scold a new tutor that "you should give me more challenging work instead of making me practice my handwriting. I am not a child any longer!" Celal Nuri also kept all the pens and books he used and read in his childhood in his personal library. Giridi Ahmed attested to Celal Nuri's strong character: he was a dedicated student, respectful to his parents and polite toward his peers.[25]

As expected for a gifted son of an elite Ottoman bureaucratic family, Celal Nuri was sent to boarding school at the age of twelve in 1894, Galata Saray (*mekteb-i sultani*), the oldest and most prestigious high school in the empire. There he studied under Feyzi Efendi, Zihni Efendi, and Ata Bey. Feyzi Efendi was noted for his translation of several American works prejudicial against Islam and was a close associate of Tevfik Fikret, the famous late Ottoman secularist poet and writer.[26]

Celal Nuri then went on to study at Istanbul's law faculty (*mekteb-i hukuk*),[27] where he and his classmates similarly absorbed the materialistic classics of the day: "We enthusiastically read works by Spencer, Büchner and Darwin," although the faculty often differed. Celal Nuri mocked this disagreement later in a fictional exchange between a student and a professor at the University. After the student asks the professor what he thought about Charles Darwin's claim that humans descended from apes, the professor replies:

> Darwin is mistaken. Humans cannot come from apes because this comparison is not logical. A human baby cannot control itself. It cannot stand up straight and relies long on its parents to do anything. But the offspring of an ape stands

upright immediately at birth and does what it needs to. Hence humans are not born from apes and Darwin's claim is based on false reasoning.[28]

After graduating with his law degree in 1904–5, Celal Nuri had trouble at first in finding steady employment. Besides working as a lawyer, he claimed to have been employed at various small government posts, including gigs at the scientific committee at the cultural ministry, and at the record offices at both the foreign and pious foundation ministries.[29] His disillusionment with his meager prospects for a bureaucratic career was obvious:

> I was employed as a clerk in the pious foundations ministry one year before the declaration of the Constitution. There were some 70 poor souls both young and old working in the hangar we called an office. Some wore turbans and Oriental clothes and others wore fezes and dressed in the European-style … Some of us sat down on chairs and others knelt down on the floor. Our boss worked separately behind a wooden curtain in the shape of a box.[30]

Celal Nuri's life would of course be forever changed by the Young Turk era.[31] He wrote at length about how he was dumbstruck on the morning of July 24, 1908, when he picked up a newspaper on his walk from the Istanbul's Şişli district to Galata quarter. Glancing at a column about some mysterious revolt in Macedonia, he, like the others around him, wanted further information.[32] He wrote once again about roaming the streets of Istanbul during the 1909 uprising:

> Emerging from hiding with a few friends that day we came across a few unruly commoners. They were half-tipsy with faces like those who had been administered with mercuric sulfide. 'All is well, we hope,' we said. One of them responded, 'Thank God it happened and finished. We obtained our goal … Islamic law (*şeriat*) is coming back.'[33]

Celal Nuri gathered that they were simply an ignorant reactionary crowd that had no idea of what the constitution meant.[34]

These experiences inspired Celal Nuri to embark on a new career as a journalist and active member of the CUP. He found his first press job with Ebüzziya Tevfik, CUP MP from Antalya, who owned the Istanbul-based French language paper *Le Courrier d'Orient* in the immediate aftermath of the 1909 uprising. He, along with several other CUP figures, including Ahmet Ağaoğlu, Moiz Cohen (Tekinalp), as well as the well-known foreign advisor Alexander Helphand-Parvus, worked with Zionists, such as Vladimir Jabotinsky, the future founder of Revisionist Zionism; David Wolffsohn, the second president of the World Zionist Organization (WZO); as well as Victor Jacobson, the official liaison between the WZO and the CUP. After a dispute with Ebüzziya Tevfik, who was critical of the Zionists, Celal Nuri worked with the WZO to found the newspaper *Le Jeune Turc*. According to the October 1909 contract, Celal Nuri served as editor in chief to this WZO-funded daily, which would advocate for peaceful relations between the Zionists and the CUP.[35] Popular among Unionists, business leaders, and European expatriates, the paper reached a weekly circulation of 11,000 in May 1910.[36]

Celal Nuri ended his relationship with the paper due to his own nationalist inclinations. The Ottoman government had suspended the paper in 1911 when he wrote an article critical of the Italians wish to occupy Libya. Celal Nuri then terminated his position in January 1912 about three months after the Italians had declared war. Celal Nuri, in line with other leading CUP figures, became skeptical that the Zionists too were plotting to establish a "separatist" state in Palestine.[37]

Celal Nuri then worked for Dr. Abdullah Cevdet (Karlıdağ)'s paper *İctihad*— whose controversial columns about materialism, social reform, and disregard for religious norms and traditions—was the leading voice of Westernism.[38] Embittered by the Ottoman defeat in the Balkan Wars, Celal Nuri left *İctihad* over a public feud he had with Abdullah Cevdet on who was to blame (as will be described later).

Celal Nuri would also work for a variety of different newspapers, including *Hak* (1913), *Hurriyet-i Fikriyye* (1914–15), *Serbest Fikir* (1915), *Uhuvvet-i Fikriyye* (1915), *Edebiyyat-Umumiye* (1916–17), and *İkdam* (1916–17). The most notable papers were *Ati* (1918–19) and *İleri* (1919–24), which he founded alongside Suphi Nuri, his brother. He was so proud of the last newspaper that he would eventually adopt *İleri* (or "progress") as his own surname.[39]

Between 1909 and 1932, Celal Nuri would write over 1500 newspaper articles and 33 books or pamphlets in Ottoman Turkish or in French.[40] His numerous publications, which ranged topically from politics, minority issues, Islam, social reform, and women to language, were largely nonfiction. Included among the books and pamphlets are seven novels, five of which were composed between 1915 and 1919, a time of war and press suppression. His writings no doubt are his greatest legacy as they reflect much on the political, social and cultural debates of the time.[41]

Celal Nuri became an active politician in the aftermath of the First World War. Elected as an MP to the last Ottoman Parliament in November 1919, he voted to approve the National Pact (*Misak-i Milli*) that sanctioned Mustafa Kemal's Turkish nationalist revolt against the sultan and the Allied occupying forces. The British arrested him in March 1920 and sent him to Malta to join other Unionist and Turkish nationalist prisoners. Released in Fall 1921, Celal Nuri went to Ankara to join Mustafa Kemal and his supporters.[42] Thereafter he was consistently re-elected as an MP from 1923 until 1935. In 1924, he was appointed as the rapporteur for the constitutional parliamentary advisory committee (*teşkilat-ı kanun-i esası encümeni reisliği*). In later years he wrote extensively on language reform and parliamentary traditions in his ongoing attempt to influence public policy.[43]

Intellectual Influences and Polemics

Celal Nuri, like many Unionists, was deeply influenced by European thinkers.[44] Celal Nuri borrowed ideas heavily from four of these authors when elaborating his evolutionary vision—Gustave Le Bon, Hyppolyte Taine, Max Nordau, and Ludwig Büchner.

Le Bon's works on the mass psychology of peoples, crowds, and political movements were immensely popular among the CUP,[45] as they were written from the perspective of a right-wing secular nationalist who, critical of the French colonization of Algeria, occasionally commented on the CUP and Turkish nationalists. Celal Nuri took heart from Le Bon's statement about an embattled nation: "One can often only understand the true meaning of a people's collective beliefs during a time of crisis. For the realities that shape a people's fate are often highlighted in war."[46] To Celal Nuri, this translated into an endorsement of the CUP's use of Ottoman Muslim identity politics efforts to rally their "nation."

Unionists also appreciated Le Bon's suggestions of how military governments might defuse popular anger.[47] It was no accident that Celal Nuri mentioned the participants in the 1909 uprising as a dangerous crowd, a not-so-subtle allusion to Le Bon's most influential work on the potential dangers of mob rule.[48] But while Le Bon personally sympathized with the CUP, he frequently argued that a secular government was virtually impossible to establish in the Middle East given the intrinsically Islamic nature of the peoples there.[49]

Taine, similar to Le Bon, provided Celal Nuri with a general historical vision. Taine was a literary historian who argued that nations were conditioned by race, time, and environment.[50] Celal Nuri did not share Taine's ideal of racial purity, believing that a historical people naturally diversified biologically over the centuries. He did agree with Taine, however, that time played a critical role in the rise and fall of a nation. This anthropomorphic vision of cyclical development reminded Celal Nuri of Ibn Khaldun's *Mukaddime*, a fourteenth-century Maghrebian work that had come into vogue in the nineteenth century.[51] Geographical environment was also critical to Celal Nuri: "We must consider the surroundings in which a people exists. For man is not alone in the world; nature surrounds him, and his fellow men surround him ... Sometimes the climate has had its effect."[52] He, like Taine, praised the cool continental northern climate, and he argued that Turkish society had advanced because of its proximity to it.[53] Such arguments naturally appealed to the Balkan and Caucasian elites that dominated the Unionists.

Celal Nuri identified himself even more closely with Max Nordau, the famous Viennese journalist, social/cultural critic, and committed Zionist. Nordau personally praised Celal Nuri for his novel *The Nightmare* (*Cauchmar?*) (1911).[54] Nordau was a member of the WZO and may well have met Celal Nuri during his stint as editor-in-chief of *Le Jeune Turc*. Celal Nuri also could have been introduced to Nordau by Abdullah Cevdet. Abdullah Cevdet had been in touch with Nordau as early as 1903 and had written an article for Nordau on Zionism.[55]

Although Celal Nuri would turn totally around and become anti-Semitic after breaking from *Le Jeune Turc* in early 1912, he still valued Nordau's belief that emerging non-Protestant Christian nations needed to imbue themselves with a bourgeois work ethic. Celal Nuri would continuously harp on the need for Ottoman Muslim Turks to take Nordau's lesson to heart, for if they were successful, they could promote a vision of self-help that would erase the gap between the elites and the masses. Such changes would also go a great way toward transforming their own military-dominated state into a European-style civil society.[56]

Nordau also wrote in mordant, sarcastic terms about social life in late-nineteenth-century Europe and saw no value in the emerging rebellion against middle-class sensibility—a rebellion that favored new "decadent" lifestyles and celebrated the alienated, intellectually gifted individual. Celal Nuri generally approved of these views: "Yes! The social condition in Europe became intolerable."[57]

Büchner's *Kraft und Stoff* (1855) and other works were perennial bestsellers among the Unionists, as they had previously been among Russian enthusiasts in the mid-to-late nineteenth century.[58] Büchner's vulgar materialistic argument that all phenomena can be explained through the scientific understanding of the interaction of matter and force was undoubtedly controversial, given its dismissal of religion and any non-worldly understanding of the universe.[59] While Celal Nuri did not openly embrace Büchner's atheism, he hoped to reform Islam in a way that would be compatible with the scientific worldview.[60] This would entail eliminating religious dogma and traditional Islamic social and judicial practices.⁶¹ Celal Nuri was likewise encouraged by writers like Thomas Carlyle and Ernest Renan, who endeavored to examine great religious leaders, including Prophet Muhammad, in a historical light free of canonical belief.⁶²

Celal Nuri also admired several prominent Ottoman thinkers, past and present. One of these was Midhat Pasha, the reformer and statesman who played a pivotal role in the drafting of the 1876 Ottoman Constitution. The fact that Sultan Abdülhamid II had Midhat Pasha killed made him a martyr for the cause of constitutional government. Celal Nuri's novel *Cauchmar?* provided a fictional account of the terrors of Abdülhamid II's reign, and Midhat Pasha played one of the starring roles.⁶³

Abdülhak Hamid (Tarhan), in Celal Nuri's mind, was the greatest Ottoman Turkish poet of his own generation.⁶⁴ Like Celal Nuri, Abdülhak Hamid was a Unionist who decried Western imperialism. Abdülhak Hamid also warned his readers of the dangers of totally secularizing Turkish culture, and he stressed the need to maintain the Islamic spirit in both literature and philosophy.⁶⁵

Celal Nuri had complicated relationships with a number of his Ottoman contemporaries. First and foremost among these was, of course, his one-time mentor Abdullah Cevdet, the person most responsible for introducing him to European political thought. Celal Nuri, as Buzpınar and Hanioğlu have shown, had a falling out with Abdullah Cevdet because of Celal Nuri's anti-Western polemics from the Italian invasion of Libya until the declaration of the Republic of Turkey in October 1923.⁶⁶ Celal Nuri argued in 1914 with Abdullah Cevdet that the Ottomans should resent the West since the Europeans only had designs to dominate and tyrannize them like they did with their other colonial subjects. Abdullah Cevdet disagreed, saying that the Ottomans had to take responsibility for their own errors in governance and society. In his opinion the Ottomans should fully accept European superiority both in culture and in politics, and not waste time trying to resist them. Abdullah Cevdet praised Lord Byron's statements and actions in favor of the Greek revolt against the Ottomans in 1821–9 and said that his Ottoman countrymen could learn much from him about liberty and tyranny. Celal Nuri denounced him as a traitor for lauding Byron, especially since Abdullah Cevdet had made his statement in the wake of the Balkan Wars, when Greece had annexed much of Macedonia and Thrace.⁶⁷ It did not help that Celal Nuri's father was from Crete,⁶⁸ an Ottoman island lost again to the Greeks just six years before.

After breaking from Abdullah Cevdet, Celal Nuri only partially changed his paradigm by calling for all Muslims to unify in support of the Ottomans in order to forestall plans of Western encroachment. But he never endorsed an Islamist agenda of reinvigorating traditional Muslim religious and judicial practices. Even when Celal Nuri argued in 1913 that the Ottomans and the Islamic world in general should embrace the scientific and technical aspects of the Western civilization without giving up Islam's superior moral and cultural values, he made no statement to renounce his own positivistic program of social reform.[69]

Indeed, as Buzpınar points out, Celal Nuri's own radical vision of *ictihad*, or interpretation of Islamic principles, saw laws and social norms as having to change according to the time in which one lives. He disregarded the traditional sources of Islamic jurisprudence and nearly the entirety of established Islamic law:[70]

> Today Muslims are unfortunately backward and entirely primitive because they … [are] governed according to thousand-year-old outdated laws … [But] Islam is founded on progressive principles and reforms that … [assure] the evolution of people.[71]

Eventually after the First World and Turkish Independence Wars, Celal Nuri gave up any pretense of "using Islam as a political and social device to achieve progress."[72] His reconciliation with the Westernizers was evident in a statement from 1926:

> We are following a civilization … which suits us best thinking, social relations, culture and administrative systems. Our duty is to imitate. We do not have to invent new methods of progress. We have tried and known methods that brought Europe to its present level of development. We take and apply them in our country.[73]

Ironically, Celal Nuri himself had his patriotic credentials called into question in 1917 by Ziya Gökalp, arguably the single most influential CUP ideologue of Turkish nationalism. In an official complaint filed with Interior Minister Talât Pasha, Gökalp accused Celal Nuri of being a "Persian imitator" whose praise of "ancient lyrical and commemorative poems" stood in the way of Turkish language reform. Gökalp saw Celal Nuri as holding back his government's wartime efforts to modify the alphabet and form a committee to rid the Turkish vocabulary of much of its "unnecessary" Persian and Arabic borrowed words.[74] These reforms aimed at bridging the gap between the educated elite and the common people and thereby laid the educational foundations for Turkish nationhood.[75]

Celal Nuri was hardly a reactionary, given his own opinion that the Turkish language change from an Arabic- to a Latin-based script.[76] Nevertheless, he saw it as counterproductive to dismiss the great literary heritage of Fuluzi and of great

Ottoman poets of the court.[77] Moreover, Celal Nuri questioned the idea that any language change could simply be accomplished by committee or governmental fiat. In his eyes, the end result of the 1917 version of "populist" language reform would be a Turkicized "Esperanto" that no one could understand, not even "Hamza the woodchopper."[78]

For Celal Nuri, it was instead the literary elite who, acting as enlightened educators, should gradually introduce linguistic changes in their publications for the populace to learn from and emulate. At heart, he thought that language itself, like the spirit of a people, changed fundamentally in a gradual evolutionary way that had to emerge organically from high society.

Celal Nuri also had an open dispute with Ahmed Hilmi Şehbenderzade (1865–1914), a Sufi scholar who denounced Celal Nuri's infatuation with materialism in no uncertain terms.[79] Their exchanges over the nature of Islam were particularly bitter, given the fact that Şehbenderzade was also a prolific journalist who embraced established Islamic law. Moreover, Şehbenderzade was not a member of the CUP.

Celal Nuri also reacted strongly to Hawrutian Sharighian, the abovementioned Armenian nationalist and *Dashnak* party member who was active until his death in 1915. Sharighian accused Celal Nuri of whipping up anti-minority sentiments, particularly against Christian Greeks and Armenians. Celal Nuri warned him that the *Dashnak*s would have no future if they did not profess loyalty to the Ottoman government. Nevertheless, he likely respected Sharighian's fanatic loyalty, and he longed for more similarly committed nationalist intellectuals on his own side.[80]

Finally, of course, one needs to consider Celal Nuri's relationship with Mustafa Kemal, the founder of modern Turkey. They had probably known each other at least from 1909 onward, when both men supported the proposition at the CUP Congress in Salonika that the military not participate in politics.[81] After praising Mustafa Kemal's leadership of the Society for the Defense of National Rights of all Anatolia and Thrace at Sivas in September 1919, Celal Nuri went on to support the Turkish National Pact in the Ottoman Parliament in January 1920.[82]

In the Wake of the New Republic

Both men also arguably expressed the same Ottoman Muslim nationalist rhetoric until the declaration of the Republic of Turkey in 1923. As Zürcher points out, this is the key moment when Mustafa Kemal moved on to a secular Turkish nationalist position. Celal Nuri, unlike many well-established former Unionist Istanbul-based journalists who opposed the abrupt break with their city's imperial traditions by moving the capital to Ankara, largely followed Mustafa Kemal's lead.[83] This transition was undoubtedly made easier by Celal Nuri's reconciliation with the full Westernizers, a point convincingly made by Buzpınar.[84] Celal Nuri would thereafter work under Yunus Nadi (Abalıoğlu), Atatürk's chief publicist and one of his closest aides. Celal Nuri served under Yunus Nadi to oversee the drafting of the 1924 Constitution. He also immediately joined the ruling (Republican) People's Party and refused to defect to the Unionist Progressive People's Party, which opposed Mustafa Kemal's radical Turkist reforms.[85]

Nevertheless, Celal Nuri's occasional outbursts against minorities would strain his ties to the new regime. In July 1924, for example, Celal Nuri would help stir up public opinion against the government, when the interior minister and several other prominent politicians allowed a number of wealthy Armenians who had fled the country in 1915 to re-enter the country. Kılıç Ali, a close associate of Atatürk and head of the Revolutionary Tribunal, went to his office and literally beat him into submission. Celal Nuri's statements apparently angered Kılıç Ali because the controversy called the Kemalists' patriotism into question.[86] Celal Nuri would not publish for the next two years. Similarly, Celal Nuri endorsed the Nazi Party's plans to deport recent Jewish immigrants and to register older Jewish residents as foreigners if they came to power in his final major publication in 1932.[87] The Turkish authorities likely saw this endorsement as problematic within a year when Hitler became chancellor of Germany given that Atatürk himself was sympathetic to the plight of European Jews and, ultimately, would give refuge to a significant number of them.

Equally important was Celal Nuri's frequent evolutionary approach toward reform even after the declaration of the Republic of Turkey. Writing in 1926, just two years prior to the government-mandated change from the Arabic to the Latin script, Celal Nuri warned that rapidly changing the alphabet was wrong because it would cut off new generations from their own rich literature from the Ottoman past:

> [A state-imposed immediate "alphabet revolution"] would sever the link between the nation's past and future ... If Turkish was not a written language with the science, techniques and archaeology of previous generations, we would not have hesitated for a moment ... But we have a language, and it is ourselves. It lies within our entire social and spiritual history.[88]

Celal Nuri further argued in the same book that efforts to rid the language of Arabic and Persian borrowed words should not be pursued since "we gained a lot from the rich [Persian and Arabic] vocabulary and derivatives that entered our language … If we did not have this treasury in our hands our situation would be very bad indeed."[89] Mustafa Kemal and the linguistic revolutionaries ignored Celal Nuri's caution, mandated a Latin-based alphabet in 1928, and purged the Turkish vocabulary of Arabic- and Persian-origin words from 1932 onward.

Celal Nuri's Place in Historical Scholarship

It is not surprising, therefore, that most historians until recently have generally dismissed Celal Nuri's importance. Şevket Süreyya Aydemir, the prolific historian and founder of the left Kemalist *Kadro* movement, claimed that Celal Nuri only wrote "simple books … which [have] … no scientific value. One might even call [them] a fantasy."[90] Hilmi Ziya Ülken, a well-known Turkish historian of ideas, derided him for being a popularizer, verbose with superficial ideas.[91] Even the more liberal Yusuf Hikmet Bayur dedicated a mere seven citations to Celal Nuri in his encyclopedic-scale history of the Turkish reforms.[92] Niyazi Berkes's seminal work, *The Development of Secularism in Turkey* (1964), does not mention him at all.[93]

Interest in Celal Nuri has begun to pick up in recent decades, reflecting the rise of Islamist political movements in Turkey. Celal Nuri's materialistic reinterpretation of Prophet Muhammad in particular has sparked considerable debate. Cemal Kutay, who translated Celal Nuri's work *The Last Prophet* (*Son Peygamber*) in 1998, wrote an extensive commentary on the need for a similar reformed vision. In light of Erbakan's successes during the 1990s, Kutay believed that a religiously conservative party may well take power again and threaten the secular republic.[94] In contrast, Ahmet İshak Demir wrote a detailed conservative critique of Celal Nuri's move away from established Islamic authorities and practices. Demir argued that such established Islamic traditions were ultimately compatible with modern life, a line of argument vaguely reminiscent of Şehbenderzade.[95]

Much more important for this study, however, is M. Şükrü Hanioğlu's pioneering book on Abdullah Cevdet in 1981[96] and his article on the Westernizers in 1997.[97] Hanioğlu discussed the previously mentioned exchange between

Abdullah Cevdet and Celal Nuri on the nature of Westernization, leading to a number of follow-up studies on the subject by Necmi Uyanık and especially S. Tufan Buzpınar.[98]

Buzpınar's groundbreaking articles—the most important work on Celal Nuri's place in Turkish intellectual history—lay out the most accurate explanation to-date of Celal Nuri's ideological development over time. As Buzpınar shows, Celal Nuri should primarily be seen as a Westernizer, with the exception from roughly 1911 until the declaration of the Republic of Turkey, when, affected by the patriotic fervor of the wartime era, he frequently alluded to pan-Islamist rhetoric. This thesis provides a sound general framework for my own study.

Recep Duymaz, a literary historian, also played a significant role in popularizing Celal Nuri. Outside of his 1991 dissertation,[99] which provides an exhaustive description of many of Celal Nuri's writings, Duymaz also translated a series of his articles on language and literature in 1995, as well as transliterating his book *The Turkish Reforms* (*Türk İnkılâbı*) into Latin letters in 2000.[100] This work occurred alongside translations of *Our Women* (*Kadınlarımız*) (1993),[101] *Polar Conversations* (*Kutup Müsâhebeleri*) (1997),[102] *Northern Memories* (*Şimal Hâtıraları*) (1997),[103] *The Last Prophet* (*Hâtemül-Enbiya*) (1998), *The Turkish Reforms* (2002),[104] *The Decline of the Ottoman Empire and the Fate of History* (*Tarih-i Tedenniyat-ı Osmaniye ve Mukaderrat-ı Tarihiye*) (2004),[105] and *The Crown-Adorned Nation* (*Taç Giyen Millet*) (2008),[106] as well as transliterations and exhaustive summaries of four of his later novels by Mustafa Kurt in 2012.[107]

At the same time, there has been greater coverage of Celal Nuri on a variety of topics. This includes Christoph Herzog's 108-page discussion of Celal Nuri's views on the origins of Ottoman decline,[108] Cemal Aydın's analysis of his Islamist rhetoric,[109] Banu Turnaoğlu on his republicanism,[110] and a number of articles and books which touch on his contributions to Turkish language reform.[111] Yet, as Buzpınar mentions, there has been no published historical monograph on the overall nature of Celal Nuri's work.[112]

Intended Contribution to the Field and Methodological Approach

While not pretending to be a full-blown biography of his life,[113] this book aims to fill that gap by providing a comprehensive view of Celal Nuri's contributions to five key discussions, namely on the future of the country's political system, on the question of minorities, on the plans for reforming Islamic beliefs and institutions, on progressive reform for women, and on his hesitations regarding the Turkish language reform. This broad analysis of Celal Nuri's political, social, cultural, religious, and literary views will no doubt confirm his ongoing commitment to the Westernist reform movement, as Buzpınar and Hanioğlu have alluded to previously.[114]

But Celal Nuri's views on these topics also provide unique insights into the Ottoman Muslim identity politics[115] so prevalent from 1909 until October 1923. One also can consider the extent to which those views were actively suppressed in the years following the declaration of the republic. Arguably, Celal Nuri's pragmatic acceptance of a more Turkish secular nationalism was also emblematic of many Unionists who did not share Mustafa Kemal's revolutionary program in the first years of the new regime. Collaborating with the likes of Mustafa Kemal and Yunus Nadi in 1923–4 did not necessarily mean he endorsed the pace and revolutionary nature of Atatürk's program as evident in Celal Nuri's dissent on Turkish language reform in 1926. Celal Nuri was thereafter silent on the topic and was left in comfortable but relative obscurity. But when on rare occasion Celal Nuri challenged the Kemalists, such as in 1924 when he ranted against the illegal return of the rich Armenians, he was quickly silenced.[116]

This monograph is based on a broad array of primary sources, largely from the rich pamphlet and journalistic literature circulating in the Young Turk and early republican era, mainly in Ottoman Turkish. This includes Celal Nuri's own substantial publications, including all of his main pamphlets and books, and many of his articles. The book likewise draws upon works by earlier Ottoman Turkish reformers and thinkers, such as those by Namık Kemal, Ahmed Mithat, and Mithat and Cevdet Pashas. It also highlights Celal Nuri's public policy debates with reformers of his generation, including Abdullah Cevdet, Ziya Gökalp, Cenap Şahabettin, and Ahmet Hilmi Şehbenderzade. Much of this literature was gathered from library collections and archives in Turkey: The Prime Minister's Ottoman Archives, State Library, Atatürk Library, and Islamic Research Center in Istanbul, the Prime Minister Republican Archives, and National Library in Ankara.

Moreover, I utilize the Western intellectuals that inspired and were popularized by the Young Turks, as exemplified by Büchner, Le Bon, Charles Letourneau, Nordau, Max Müller, and Taine. I utilized many of these books and other materials from a variety of research libraries throughout the United States and Canada, including Binghamton University, The Library of Congress, New York Public Library, The Ohio State University, Princeton University, Stanford

University, the University at Buffalo, the University of California, Berkeley, the University of California, Los Angeles, the University of Chicago, and the University of Toronto.

Outline of Chapters

Chapter 2, entitled "on politics," deals with Celal Nuri's changing concerns from the fear of conservative Islamic counterrevolution to his country's impending defeat and division by foreign powers which supported local non-Muslim minorities against his own state. The chapter provides a basic overview of the three main periods in Celal Nuri's life as a journalist and political activist. Originally entering politics in the wake of the April 13, 1909 uprising, Celal Nuri focused initially on counteracting that threat through a combination of governmental reform, liberalization, and transforming the Islamic legal and theological education through the adaptation of "scientific" principles. The principal result, he hoped, would be the formation of a modernized entrepreneurial class of Ottoman Muslim farmers, merchants, and small businessman who would integrate one-time Muslim rebels against the Unionists into a core constituency and therefore eliminate the possibility of further reaction.[117]

The Italian invasion of the Ottoman province of Libya in November 1911 led Celal Nuri to rethink many of his programs through a more Ottoman Muslim nationalist lens. He criticized many leading liberals, foreign and domestic, for supporting the "grand international conspiracy" to partition the empire and colonize and exploit his own faith community. Yet he interestingly went back to the idea of promoting Muslim entrepreneurship as a key way of combating "the enemy from within," this time the rival non-Muslim merchant communities. Such ideas complemented the Unionists' wartime policies of implementing the "national economy" by displacing the Greeks and Armenian entrepreneurs of Istanbul and elsewhere in the Ottoman Empire. He was not able to publish from March 1920 to October 1921 since the British deported him to Malta for his support of the Turkish nationalists. When Celal Nuri returned, he was effectively sidelined until Mustafa Kemal's forces won the Turkish Independence War.

The declaration of the new Republic of Turkey on October 29, 1923, put Celal Nuri in a difficult position. Yet even before he understood that he could not prevent Mustafa Kemal from abandoning the constitutional monarchy that Celal Nuri and many "moderate" former Unionists had originally advocated. But he ultimately could not persuade Mustafa Kemal and his loyalists to permanently define their republic as ethnically Muslim even though their citizenry was almost entirely so.

Chapters 3–6 follow up on Chapter 2's basic periodization of Celal Nuri's political life by exploring specific topical debates to which Celal Nuri contributed.

Chapter 3, for example, explores Celal Nuri's attitude toward minorities. He was deeply impacted by his father and uncle, who wrote very prejudicially about the Yezidis and Shiites in the Ottoman Empire.[118] Celal Nuri had similarly negative views on these groups, implying that assimilating such "heretics" was the only path forward.[119] Celal Nuri had a relatively positive attitude toward the Arabs, given that most Arabs and Turks were Sunni Muslims. He also appreciated the fact that Islam's holiest cities were in the Arab provinces. The loss of those lands would therefore undermine his country's claim to be the leading Islamic power.[120]

He judged non-Muslims in a far harsher manner. The Greeks, Celal Nuri opined, were like a fifth column, promoting a nationalist movement that threatened to "recapture" Istanbul from the Turks.[121] The Armenians, he hoped, would learn that they could lose their hard-earned privileges as members of the commercial elite if they pursued their own plans for separatism. He remained silent in 1915 when the CUP violently suppressed this minority throughout Anatolia after the *Dashnak* Armenian nationalist revolt in Van in advance of an invading Russian army, leading to crimes against humanity and devastatingly massive loss of life.[122] Celal Nuri was even concerned that the Sephardic Jewish community of Istanbul was willing to sell itself out to foreign interests.[123]

His prejudices and fears about these groups were rooted in his own evolutionary worldview about the rise, development, and fall of nations and empires. He thus thought the Turks should collaborate with Sunni Arabs, assimilate "heretical" Yezidi and Shiite subjects into their culture, and repress the rival non-Muslim Greeks, Armenians, and Jews who actively collaborated with foreign powers to undermine his country's legitimacy by seeking either autonomy or a separate state.

Celal Nuri's progressive views on Islam, all of which he published before the declaration of the Republic of Turkey, are the subject of Chapter 4. Like Abdullah Cevdet, he saw Büchner's vulgar materialism as a template for religious renewal.[124] Celal Nuri's scientifically informed rational approach toward religion was in the mainstream of Unionist thinking on the issue.[125] The CUP leaders would have no problem with his ideas on eliminating Islamic law. They would also agree with his insistence with making Islam compatible with science. Celal Nuri reasoned that this was a way to effectively control the masses.[126] The Kemalists after October 1923 would ignore Celal Nuri's earlier assertion that Islam remain central to Turkish identity. As late as January 1923 Celal Nuri feared that a purely secular understanding of Turkish nationhood aggravated the social gap between elites and the Muslim masses.

Celal Nuri had much the same approach toward women's issues as seen in Chapter 5. He strongly believed that eliminating the traditional Islamic law family courts would pave the way to ending abuses toward women. Thus, he hoped the CUP and later the Kemalists would put in place new, scientifically based social laws that would forbid polygamy, enable women to voluntarily rid themselves of the veil and other traditional garments, promote female primary school education, and even give women the right to vote. He was likewise in full support of the government's campaign to mobilize women on behalf of the government, both in peace and in wartime.[127] As such, he was in agreement with Turkish nationalists like Ziya Gökalp, who often extolled such ideas as "feminism."[128] Moreover, Celal Nuri, like Gökalp, was ambivalent about the right of women to enter the workplace and compete on an equal footing with men. Nonetheless, Celal Nuri's views on women's issues largely fell into the mainstream of not only the CUP but also Kemalist political thought.[129]

Celal Nuri had far more difficulty with language reform, the subject of Chapter 6. He concurred with Gökalp and fellow innovators that the language needed to progress in order to educate the public, and he certainly considered the adoption of a Latin instead of an Arabic alphabet as a positive step toward joining the "family" of European nations. But Celal Nuri saw literary cultivation as the domain of an enlightened elite, and not something that could be legislated per se. He therefore actively opposed the CUP's efforts to alter the Arabic cursive script, and to put in place a language institute for implementing grammatical changes and purging the vocabulary of "foreign" Arabic and Persian borrowed words. He was particularly incensed that Ziya Gökalp chastised him and other writers for using the Persian *izafet*, a grammatical particle that was used in Ottoman Turkish to link two words together. To him, banning the *izafet* was unnecessary, since people would give up on the practice if they saw it as superfluous.[130]

By 1928, five years after Mustafa Kemal came to power, there was a much more determined effort to "revolutionize" the language. Celal Nuri would write as early as 1926 in hopes that the alphabetic change to Latin letters would be implemented gradually, and with consideration to preserving the unique sounds of Arabic and Persian words that had become a living part of the language. His suggestions were ignored, however, and he refrained from openly protesting the purge of the vocabulary.[131] Hüseyin Cahit (Yalçın), a contemporary and former CUP member who shared Celal Nuri's convictions, argued at the First Turkish Language Assembly (*Birinci Türk Dil Kurultayı*) that Turkish should be allowed to gradually evolve. The linguistic revolutionaries openly ridiculed Hüseyin Cahit and thereafter redoubled their efforts.[132] The result of their hard-line approach was to further the breach between the more-secular urban and educated elite which embraced the reforms, and the more rural conservative elements of society who remained sympathetic to their language's Islamic heritage.

Overall, as the final chapter will suggest, Celal Nuri died a bitter man. Certainly his intolerant approach toward minorities was mainly rejected by the republican government. Equally important, Celal Nuri failed to convince Mustafa Kemal and his followers to embark on a more gradual, evolutionary path on language reform, a topic he had hoped to have an impact on after the declaration of the republic. From October 1923 onward he—like many of the less radical former Unionists of his generation—began to lose influence in state affairs.

2

On Politics

Introduction

As mentioned in the previous chapter, the CUP as a whole was highly reactive in its political approach. Remembering the April 13, 1909 uprising, the Unionists often took a series of liberalizing or secular reforms in order to stave off the threat of a conservative Muslim takeover. But, at other times of international crisis, they mobilized Ottoman Muslim nationalist opinion, raising the specter of European great power intervention on behalf of the "treacherous" non-Muslims who sought to break away from their beloved empire.

Celal Nuri (İleri) was in many ways a barometer of these shifts from modernization to nationalism and back again. From the April 13 uprising until the Italian invasion of Libya in Fall 1911, Celal Nuri, like most Unionist activists, emphasized internal reforms, such as trying to weaken the hold of traditional patronage groups in the palace, military, judiciary, and religious orders, and worked to empower entrepreneurship in both the urban and rural economy. He likewise tried to redefine the sultan as a constitutional monarch and jealously preserve the Unionists' role as the guardians of the state.

Celal Nuri, again in line with mainstream CUP opinion, pivoted toward combating "foreign threats" throughout the series of international crises and military conflicts that began with the Italian invasion and ended with the declaration of the Republic of Turkey on October 29, 1923. Celal Nuri railed in a flourish of rhetoric around the time of the Balkan Wars and the outbreak of the First World War against European "imperialist" powers and their alleged plot to dismantle the empire in favor of a series of separatist successor states under their "colonial" control. These outbursts justified the Unionist push for Ottoman Muslims to create a new, entrepreneurial "national economy" and hype educational, literary, and cultural renewal as "patriotic acts."

After the Battle of Dumlupınar in August 1922 and the consequent Greek flight from Western Anatolia, Celal Nuri, like many Unionists, began to accommodate to the postwar era. Recognizing that Mustafa Kemal (Atatürk), the commander-in-chief of the Turkish nationalists, was bound to set the tone for both the peace talks at Lausanne and the political order at home, Celal Nuri sought to convince him not to so enthusiastically embrace the earlier modernization efforts that he would scuttle Ottoman Muslim identity in toto. Ever the pragmatist, Celal Nuri supported Mustafa Kemal's drive to end the Ottoman dynasty, to declare the Republic of Turkey, and to make Ankara the new capital. Mustafa Kemal presumably awarded Celal Nuri for his support by naming him as the secretary of the 1924 constitutional committee.

Yet Celal Nuri hoped to gain something from this devil's bargain. He strongly defended the 1924 Constitution's declaration that Islam was the official religion of the new state, and was of the opinion that a "truly loyal" Turkish citizen was defined in large part by being a Muslim of the Hanefi Sunni traditions of Western and Central Anatolia. His hopes were soon dashed. Celal Nuri was forced to sit in silence as Mustafa Kemal and the radical wing of the Turkish nationalist movement would crush much of the "moderate" Unionist opposition in pursuit of radical secularization and political dictatorship.

This chapter will examine each of these three basic periods in Celal Nuri's political life in order to provide a critical backdrop to his more detailed views on minorities, Islam, women, and language—the subjects of Chapters 3–6.

The Reforms

What concerned Celal Nuri the most when first engaged in political discourse was the grave social situation he saw within the Ottoman Empire's Muslim community. He, like many of his colleagues in the CUP, was wary of the Ottoman Muslim masses, especially in light of the April 13, 1909 uprising.[1] He saw the reactionaries' cry for the return of Islamic law and the autocracy of Abdülhamid II during the uprising as a prime example of atavism, the unquestioned passing on of institutions and characteristics from one generation to the next.[2]

He no doubt kept in mind the stinging criticism Le Bon had of this event:

> What in truth could they [the Unionists] have done to change a people whose traditions have been fixed so long, whose religious passions are so intense, and whose Mohameddans ... legitimately claim to govern the sacred city of their faith according to their code?[3]

Celal Nuri certainly agreed that to reconvene the Ottoman Parliament in hope of greater public support for the Unionists was simply not enough. Instead, the CUP should try to modernize all levels of government and religious institutions from the sultan down to the lowest official and local imam, and then move on to liberalize Ottoman Muslim society at large.

The question of social and political decay was clear even to the most casual observer of the empire's recent history, he claimed. Problems had set in ever since Sultan Mehmed II had conquered Constantinople, when the Ottoman army took on its ruling role. The military elite engaged in a parasitical lifestyle that relied on the agricultural, artisanal, and commercial production of others. Most symbolic of that lifestyle would of course be the palace, where the sultan and his familial household would become the ultimate symbol of a feudal, patronage-run order. Celal Nuri, like many orientalists, would focus on the "evils of the harem." Here, the black eunuch (*harem ağası*) endlessly plotted through "scandalous weddings," banishments, and murders to depose whomever he wished.[4]

The rare sultan who escaped the black eunuch's clutches, such as Abdülhamid II, acted tyrannically. Just as this sultan forced women against their will to serve his every whim as concubines or wives, so too he would be willing to murder those subjects who obstructed his path to absolute power. Such was the fate of Abdülhamid II's brother and longtime sultan, Abdulaziz, as well as Midhat Pasha, the famous mid-to-late nineteenth-century *Tanzimat* reformer who had authored the original 1876 Ottoman Constitution.[5] Celal Nuri concluded that "our sultanate ... is indispensable for our national existence," but he certainly did not wish to go back to absolutism: "The Ottoman dynasty needs reforms. Otherwise, the children of Osman Gazi will be in a difficult position in the contest of life."[6] This meant, above all, that the sultan not be above the law, and must therefore obey strictures put upon him. Lack of accountability could seriously threaten the sultan's position as when Abdülhamid II was forced to abdicate his throne after the suppression of the April 13 uprising.

Celal Nuri complained too that the sons of Ottoman princes were marrying commoners or even foreign or native-born non-Muslims, going to Christian schools and "opening up shops for commercial transactions on the stock exchange at Galata."[7]

Well-trained officials in the provinces were few and far between. The government was not able to dispatch efficient governors (*valiler*) and district heads (*kaymakamlar*), and without a good judiciary, they were unable to maintain adequate land registries. The main tax that Muslim farmers paid, the tithe (*öşür*), was charged at far higher than the 10 percent required by law. Those that gathered the tithe from the peasants were tax farmers that colluded with speculators who offered usurious loans to peasants who were forced to pay the tithe even in bad harvests.[8] This undoubtedly was a reason why many peasants were prone to revolt or leave their districts.

The cities were hardly better off. Guilds still dominated the urban economy through the numerous autonomous pious foundations, whose age-old charters were written according to outmoded Islamic laws that escaped governmental supervision. The original trustees and progeny of these foundations had rented their properties and rights to second and even third parties, resulting again in speculation, waste, and abuse.[9] It was no wonder, therefore, that the ignorant urban Muslim masses, who worked in such a miserable, feudalistic system, could easily be provoked again to rebel, as seen in the events of April 13.

Regulation and retraining, to Celal Nuri, should apply to all involved in public life. The sultan and his sons should be legally required to marry monogamously to Muslim women of their own class and country. Members of the royal family must refrain from entrepreneurial or speculative activities and not seek education from non-Muslim schools in Istanbul or abroad. Islamic law should be abandoned or curtailed as much as possible and judges should only be licensed after being trained in modern secular law schools. Religious officials down to the local imam must be taught a progressive version of Islam that broke away from the traditional Muslim seminary (*medrese*) system. Officials in general, from governors to land registrars and city inspectors, should also be retrained so that they could use only the most up-to-date bureaucratic methods. This retraining would give the public confidence that the rule of law applied to everyone and revitalize the bureaucracy so that it could for once be able to register all land and properties within the empire. Proper registration was a prerequisite to privatization—a plank of Unionist financial and economic policies from July 1908 until the Balkan Wars.[10]

The government should then foster entrepreneurship in the Ottoman Muslim community. The government could empower business in the countryside by vastly expanding the funds available to the Agricultural Bank (*Ziraat Bankası*). The bank was established in 1863 by Midhat Pasha but only could give loans of up to 50 liras to landholders, an inadequate amount. Landholders who wished to get modern farming equipment would be forced to go elsewhere for loans, most often non-Muslim speculators or foreign banks. The government might be able to get sufficient funds for the Agricultural Bank and similar financial institutions for urban development by selling off the state's rights to arable land and auctioning off the immovable assets of the pious foundations. The state would then assess the new owners of the arable and immovable assets an annual property tax instead of the tithe on cultivation and the outmoded customs and fees levied on the guilds.[11]

Such actions, in total, would lead to the formation of a wealthy class of Muslim financiers, and farm-owner businessmen, and clear the way potentially for Muslim-owned factories in the cities that would employ Muslim immigrants from the countryside. The empire would then develop a new vibrant, self-sufficient economy, where all would be more likely to support and benefit from the progressive government that the Unionists would provide.[12]

Moreover, Celal Nuri also advocated a fundamental redefinition of the sultanate as a constitutional monarchy. He wrote extensively about Sahip Bey, the minister of religious affairs (*şeyhülislam*) in the immediate aftermath of the April 13 uprising, who had written an extensive religious opinion (*fetva*) justifying the abdication of Abdülhamid II and the accession of Mehmed V, because the former ruler failed to live up to his popular responsibility as caliph. Sahip Bey claimed that the caliph was subject to the election of the Muslim community and was not autocratic in nature.[13] The origins of this opinion dated back to Abu Bakir, the beloved companion of Prophet Muhammad, the very first of the "successors of the messenger of God," or caliph. Selected by consensus in 632, Abu Bakir proclaimed:

> Oh mankind! I was appointed as your governor (*vali*) and commander (*emir*) yet I am hardly worthy of you. Support me if I do my task well and correct me when I am wrong ... The strongest among you is the weakest in my eyes because the strongest can abuse the rights of the weakest ... None of you have given up the principle to fight for justice ... All the time I have respected God, His Prophet, and His law. If I do not respect them, you are no longer required to listen to me.[14]

The principle of responsible governance was later taken up by Sultan Selim I (1512–20), who was selected after he became guardian of the holy places in 1517. Thereafter, the Ottoman sultan, or hereditary dynast, was bound to the "elected" office of the caliph. As Celal Nuri pointed out from Sahip Bey's opinion, this principle was highlighted in the 1876 Constitution, where it states in Article 3: "Ottoman sovereignty, which includes in the person of the Ottoman sovereign the supreme caliph, is subject to its rules from antiquity." This clause meant in effect that those who were no longer accountable to the Muslim community could be removed from office. In this way, a caliph's election, and possible impeachment "was like the President of the United States of America."[15]

Despite the flowery language, Celal Nuri remained skeptical about popular rule. The biggest mistake the CUP made in July 1908 was to accept that Abdülhamid II quickly reconvene the parliament. This entailed immediate elections and trusting the future to "citizens [who] had hardly any idea how to run public affairs."[16] In effect, the CUP would be repeating the error of Midhat Pasha, the late *Tanzimat* reformer, who first crafted the original 1876 Constitution entirely on Western models, in the forlorn belief that it could transform the people. Just as popular outrage at the empire's horrible defeat in the Russo-Turkish War led to Midhat's death and the proroguing of parliament, so too the April 13 uprising almost deposed the Young Turks.

The lesson to be learned, Celal Nuri contended, was for the CUP to embrace its role as "the educator (*mürebbi*) and guardian (*vasi*)" of the people.[17] He was profoundly impacted by the words of the German General Helmuth Karl Bernhard Graf von Moltke: "The Turkish government is progressive … [but] the people are conservative. The government therefore must implement reforms top-down."[18] Celal Nuri would add that "this is the elite's job," meaning that successful governance depended on all branches of the CUP—the military, technocrats, statesman, and intellectuals—to introduce public policy regardless of their political opposition, even if the Unionists' liberal rivals were in control of the parliament. Celal Nuri's insistence on CUP control was a typical instance of the fear Unionists had of actual representative government.[19]

In sum, Celal Nuri spent much of his time calling for government measures that would consolidate Unionist control of the empire in the wake of the April 13 uprising. After denouncing abuse and corruption in the palace, the countryside, and the cities, Celal Nuri pushed for massive overhaul of the empire's civilian elite, from the provinces and palace to the courts and even the Islamic schools, as well as an elaborate redefinition of the sultan as a constitution-bound caliph. The reformed government could in turn transform the Muslim population from unruly, traditional atavists into a core constituency that would support the CUP and their modernized, progressive version of empire.

Yet, the reformist nature of Celal Nuri's policy prescriptions was also clear. Rather than calling for the abolition of local imams or judges, for example, he wanted them to be retrained instead in modernized seminaries and law schools. The sultan was to take an oath of fealty to the people's will but it would be justified according to Rightful Caliph Abu Bakir's promise to work according to the consensus of the Muslim community—a defining precept of Sunni Muslim governing principles.

This was in line with the thought of his longtime mentor Abdullah Cevdet (Karlıdağ) who "stitched" scientific modernizing reform in "an Islamic jacket" in order to "make their ideas more palatable to the Muslim masses."[20] As mentioned in Chapter 1, Celal Nuri worked intensely with Abdullah Cevdet in publishing *İctihad*, a controversial journal that sought to introduce vulgar materialist and other Westernist ideas among Unionist intellectual circles.

Celal Nuri and Abdullah Cevdet likewise shared the belief in the first years of the Young Turk era that the European liberals appreciated these reform efforts and sought to broadly support them. This appreciation, they hoped, would pressure the French and British governments into providing diplomatic cover and financial aid at times of grave international crisis.

Although a number of territorial losses occurred in short order after the reconvening of parliament in 1908, such as the Bulgarian declaration of independence, the Austro-Hungarian annexation of Bosnia-Herzegovina, and the Greek taking of Crete, this Unionist belief continued in large part until the Italian invasion of Libya. The indifference of the European public to this attack convinced the bulk of CUP members—including Celal Nuri—that Great Britain and France, and Western liberals in general, were hostile to their state.

Celal Nuri began to take a far more nationalistic line and thereafter denounced the foreign threat of European-backed aggression far more than he did prior to that event. The Italian annexation with minimal European complaint convinced him: "This international law is European and Christian ... [and thus] we do not have much authority to benefit from it."[21] In his opinion, "international law" was simply an excuse used to justify forceful and exploitative action of the strong over the weak. This "Machiavellian spirit" was invoked numerous times throughout the nineteenth and early-twentieth centuries.[22] European intellectuals, even outspoken advocates of international solidarism, like Leon Bourgeois, Charles Richet, and Anatole France, had remained silent in 1911.[23] One, Paul Adam, had even gone to the extreme of cheering the Italian invasion.[24]

Westernizers, War and the Threat of Pending Colonization

Abdullah Cevdet disagreed with Celal Nuri. He instead argued the Ottomans had to accept such territorial losses without slighting the European great powers: "Our role is to become an industrious and thankful follower of Europe. If we do not become its friend voluntarily, they [the Europeans] will force us to be one."[25] To him, the only "civilization was European civilization."[26]

Abdullah Cevdet used Lord Byron's trip to Greece in 1823 to support the Greeks and their rebellion as a historical example. Lord Byron did so, Abdullah Cevdet claimed, out of a sincere belief to fight tyranny, and not the Turks who still obeyed their sultan out of ignorance and religious superstition. Byron thus, he alleged, acted out of liberal humanitarian principles, the same that the Europeans had when they supported the Young Turks' successful revolt against Abdülhamid II's authoritarian regime. Those who resented European support for liberty had only themselves to blame. In Byron's own words: "You should excuse the fight of the nation that did not see reality. Then they knocked on the door of legend."[27]

Celal Nuri was appalled at such words, for he saw Byron and European support for Greek independence as just one in a long series of struggles that ultimately aimed at ending the Turkish presence in the Balkans and the Middle East, and subjugating all Ottoman Muslims to foreign imperialism. He wondered, for instance, how the Ottoman Muslims were to blame for the Italian invasion of Libya in 1911. The Ottomans thereafter waged a successful guerrilla campaign in Libya under the skillful leadership of Enver Pasha. The campaign only ended with the breakout of the Balkan Wars a year later, in which Greece took much of Macedonia and its beloved port of Salonika.[28] Did the Italians occupy Libya in order to liberate the Muslims from themselves, and were the hundreds of thousands of Balkan Muslims killed and expelled from their homes deserving of such punishment?

The key, Celal Nuri contended, was for his people to find the power in themselves to rejuvenate their national community and take revenge:

> We are in need of Envers in the world of commerce, farming, etiquette and culture. Enver is not the only Turk and Muslim who has the skill and logic [to do so]. The hero of Benghazi is not the only one of his kind. The country that was his womb gave birth to others. We should open a highway in front of them to make their way ... We would recover our ravaged countries. We would conquer our enemies. We would remove the cross on top of Kasimiye Mosque [in Selaniki]. We would transfer to the Military Museum the flags which fly like a mark of evil fortune above the sacred countries pulled from our hands.[29]

The first task to achieve this goal was building up popular will "to remove lethargy and indifference ... It is your economic prosperity and financial freedom," he wrote, "which will rescue you from political slavery ... You should not think that Muslims and Turks are in the last days of their lives. Never!"[30]

He shamed Abdullah Cevdet for forgetting the words of Le Bon that "European civilization was not suitable for Muslims."[31] The Ottoman Muslims, Celal Nuri concluded, would have to find their own way.

Celal Nuri also paid a great deal of attention to two of the leading authorities on international law: Friedrich Fromhold von Martens (1845–1909) and James

Lorimer (1818–90).³² Martens, a renowned Russian international legal scholar and diplomat, was an ardent defender of the capitulations, or special privileges, that Russia and the other great powers maintained in the Ottoman Empire, and other "Asian states" where they did not have direct colonial control.³³ The capitulations included the ability for their diplomats in the empire to employ expatriates, and affiliated local non-Muslims as consular agents on behalf of a foreign power without being subject to the Ottoman court system. The capitulations also granted the right to much reduced custom rates, and, often, the power to intervene in some of the most sensitive state matters ranging from tax collection and Muslim relations with non-Muslims to public health.

Martens argued that the great powers, themselves the most culturally advanced states, needed the capitulations to properly deal with the "uncivilized." This was because undeveloped states like the Ottoman Empire neither had proper legal safeguards nor did they separate their supposedly "fanatical" religious beliefs from temporal affairs. Moreover, the capitulations were the most effective way of "civilizing" the host state, as they would allow the more advanced powers to effectively mentor their "client" until they were ready to join the advanced countries as part of the "international community."³⁴

Lorimer, von Martens's British colleague, was even more outspoken in his opposition to the Ottoman Empire being counted as a "civilized" country. In his opinion, the Ottoman Empire was a "barbaric state" that, like other Asian countries, was deserving of only "partial political recognition." Lorimer detailed this argument in racist terms:

> In the case of the Turks we have had bitter experience of the consequences of extending the rights of civilization to barbarians who proved to be incapable of performing ... [their] duties and possibly do not even belong to the progressive races of mankind ... [There is] no instance of [such] a people that has been so long in contact with civilization without producing one single individual who has been distinguished in any intellectual pursuit. The art of war is the only art that they seem capable of acquiring, and even in it their success is the result of courage rather than skill. The subordinate position into which they are rapidly sinking, seems to be that for which nature has designed for them.³⁵

He also did not hesitate to denounce the Ottomans as a Muslim empire:

> The international character of Turkey ... [has not been] improved. The Quran would still have stood between it and the world without ... Whatever may be the absolute truth or falsehood of an exclusive religion, it is always false when seen from an international point of view; and a false theory, like a wrong road, only carries us farther from our destination the longer we follow it.³⁶

Lorimer was particularly irked that the Ottomans were granted great power status after the conclusion of the Crimean War in 1856, where it stated in Article 7 of the Treaty of Paris that "the Sublime Porte ... 'be admitted to participate in the advantages of public law and of the European concert.'"[37] To him, this was a "monument of folly" since it would only destabilize international relations.[38]

Celal Nuri, by way of contrast, criticized the great powers for not expanding on the privileges the Treaty of Paris gave the Ottomans. If the foreign powers really recognized his country as an equal, they then needed to abolish the capitulations, he posited. Their refusal to do so was in bad faith.[39]

But Russian and British military and diplomatic actions against the sultanate provided much more vivid examples. The Russians, fearful that the Ottomans would rebound after declaring their first constitution in 1876, invaded the Balkans a year later on the excuse that they must liberate the Bulgarians and other "oppressed Christians" who faced slaughter because of religious discrimination.[40] The British had similarly suppressed the Urabi revolt (1879–82) in the name of restoring public order, after the Egyptians demanded the end of European political and economic influence.[41]

The Russians and British, after getting their way by force, then insisted on using their rights under the capitulations regime to force the Porte to grant greater autonomy to selected local populations in the Ottoman Empire's remaining territories, as well as customs rates and monopolies which often favored foreign firms and their agents.[42]

The Ottoman authorities, contrary to von Marten's and Lorimer's far-fetched claims that they were a "warlike race" whose "fanatical" Islamic religion was evidence of their "barbaric" state, had sought to make peace with the powers who opposed it. The Ottomans had granted the exploitative capitulations only under duress, but nevertheless sought to build up diplomatic relations with the great powers. Indeed, the Ottomans had been at least partially inspired by the British and the French in their efforts to modernize their economy, and bring greater political representation to their people, as evident in the imperial rescripts of 1839 and 1856, as well as with the 1876 Constitution and Abdülhamid II's reconvening of parliament in 1908.[43]

Celal Nuri was, of course, increasingly pessimistic about the fate of the Ottoman reform movement. He would often compare his state to that of Poland-Lithuania in the late eighteenth century. Poland-Lithuania, whose constitutional monarchy contrasted greatly with absolutist Russia, suffered three partitions (1772, 1793, and 1795) that gradually erased it from the map. Russia, Austria, and Prussia—the powers that partitioned Poland—confirmed their conquest of that country in 1815, when they, Great Britain, and France formed the Concert of Europe.⁴⁴

Celal Nuri argued that the Ottomans faced three separate partitions of their own. The first was instigated by Russia in 1877–8, when, as noted before, the czar was nervous that the recently promulgated Ottoman constitution would revitalize the sultanate.⁴⁵ Bulgaria, Russia's client state, may have lost some territory to its Balkan neighbors after the ensuing Congress of Berlin, but the Ottomans nonetheless gave up a huge amount of its southeastern European territories. The second, in Celal Nuri's opinion, was the Balkan Wars of 1912–13, which resulted in the loss of all remaining southeastern European territories outside of Western Thrace and Istanbul. Russia, whom he blamed as the main instigator of the conflict, had predictably feared that the Young Turks might succeed with their reforms.⁴⁶

Celal Nuri prophesized in the wake of the Balkan Wars that a third and final partition of the Ottoman Empire was eminent. Russia now hoped to take over the Straits, Eastern Anatolia and the Turkish Black Sea and Aegean coastline. This time, Great Britain and France would join Russia. Just as England was interested in the Arabic territories of Yemen, Iraq, and the Hijaz, so too France desired to occupy Syria and Lebanon.⁴⁷

Celal Nuri concluded in the run-up to the First World War that the Entente powers posed a danger not only to the Ottoman Empire, but to the entire non-Western world:

> England and France are the greatest colonial powers, and many of their accomplishments have come at the cost of the material and spiritual well-being of humanity. It is possible to meet eminently knowledgeable French and English citizens in the schools and chemistry laboratories of Paris and London. The French write graceful literature, and are distinguished for their aesthetics. Their language is the most delicate and beautiful. The English are the most free to speak their minds, and their literature and arts do not fall far behind those of the French. Shakespeare, Milton, Newton, Carlyle and Stevens are English; Courney, Montesquieu, Lamartine, Lavoisier, and Pasteur are French. However, one wonders how they, along with their Russian allies, compare to our own Ottoman literature. England has 375 million prisoners of war; France, fifty million; Russia approximately 125 million. In total, this equals half the world's population. How much injustice has been wreaked upon these peoples, suppressing their humanity, extinguishing their talents and breaking down their self-respect and power? All of these victims have had brilliant pasts, noble goals and laws. Is it possible that a few works of art can erase the sin of this terrible crime? We should not be defeated by appearances ... The French are like wives, and the

English are preoccupied with holding onto their property. Consequently if the earth remains in their hands, civilization will decay, and mankind will vanish.[48]

Here he claimed that the very powers that sought to mercilessly exploit and plunder those weaker than them were bound to suffer the great moral consequence of civilizational decline. It was only the great Muslim civilizations, such as the Ottoman Turks, who bore in mind the eternal principle laid out in the Quran: "We gave and granted you a clear conquest. God should forgive your past and future sins."[49] Celal Nuri explained further: "He [the victor] should, in accordance with the knowledge of Islam, promote [of not only] the general welfare in politics and society, [but also] the pursuit of knowledge and literature."[50] In Celal Nuri's eyes, mercy was both a supreme command and the only way for a civilization to truly establish its power.[51]

Celal Nuri also drew inspiration from Le Bon, who, in an article on French Algeria, spoke pessimistically about the ability of the Europeans to sustain colonization and talked about the contrasting virtues of Muslim civilization. "The dangers that exist in wanting to impose on a people the institutions, ideas, and needs of different peoples," Le Bon opined, "are an absolutely impossible … [task] … and no European nation will ever succeed in realizing it."[52] Le Bon elaborated:

> Europeans may be skillful colonizers; but, since the Romans, one can say that the only peoples who can be called stabilizers have been Muslims. They are, in fact, the only ones who have succeeded in making other people adopt what constitutes the foundation of a civilization: religion, institutions, and the arts.[53]

After summarizing Le Bon's article nearly word-for-word,[54] Celal Nuri prophesied the victory of the Ottomans as the leading Islamic world power in the Great War:

> The recovery of Cairo, the rescue of the Caucasus, and the opening of Asia and Africa will once again inaugurate a Muslim to the rank of command. That day, others will write about our victory in the book of kings, new Aladdins will appear and work miracles in history, commerce, agriculture and art.[55]

Celal Nuri thus hoped that the Ottomans entry into the war would bring about a great shift from Western to Islamic civilization—views that characterized much Ottoman propaganda around that time.[56]

Nevertheless, Celal Nuri would be increasingly given to fits of despair as the Ottoman Empire faced warfare, and the need to mobilize the civilian population in support of it. He felt his first premonitions after the Balkan Wars, when he complained that urban elites failed their country during a time of great crisis. Young men, called to serve in the military, went AWOL:

> The universities are havens for draft dodgers ... [There the students lose their morals] ... and become internationalist and cosmopolitan. What does the state mean? What does the country mean?"[57]

Such people, he concluded, were the complete opposite of the Anglo-Saxon men, who, after boarding the Titanic, sacrificed their own lives for the women and children just as calmly as if they gave up their "seats ... in a railway car."[58]

In Celal Nuri's eyes, women too forgot to discipline themselves by remaining at home, supporting their husbands and sons and live virtuous, private Victorian lives. Instead of promoting education or ethics in the family, women would wander the streets of Beyoğlu shopping for clothes and perfume, inciting non-virtuous behavior among men. Celal Nuri despaired too of the clubs and bars that sprouted in the affluent quarters of Istanbul.[59]

The social situation continued to deteriorate during the First World War. In his novel, amply titled *The End Times* (*Ahir Zaman*), Celal Nuri described an endless series of affairs Ecmel Bey, a young student turned draft-dodger, has with the wealthy wives and daughters of Istanbul. One by one, these women are seduced in turn. Yet their fate is presented as unavoidable, given that most of their husbands and fathers were war profiteers and almost uniformly of non-Turkish, non-Sunni Muslim origin.[60]

Stories like these helped fuel popular sentiment in favor of the Unionist government's "national economic" policies. Such measures from 1914 to 1918 included the formation of a national consumer society, the passage of a law forcing non-Muslim shop owners to share their businesses with Muslim compatriots and display signs in Turkish, the foundation of an artisan and guildsmen association that represented the interests of over eighty government-sponsored Muslim nationalist urban companies, and a bank that offered affordable credit to sponsor them.[61]

Celal Nuri would witness political betrayal in 1918, just as he was presumably writing the novel. Faced with the surrender of the Ottoman forces to the Entente, and with a British fleet anchored in Istanbul's harbors, many of the CUP's liberal opponents decided to support the occupation. Committed Muslim nationalists like Celal Nuri were also desperate to seek alternatives. Celal Nuri briefly supported an American or Italian mandate in the belief that both of those foreign powers would grant his country a greater degree of home rule than London, whom he feared might award Istanbul and his country's Aegean provinces to the Greeks.[62] But his ultimate commitment to the Muslim nationalist cause was never seriously in question. Like many other former Unionists, Celal Nuri became an active member of the Association for the Defense of Rights (*Müdafaa-i Hukuk Cemiyetleri*) in 1919 after the Greek occupation of Izmir on May 15.[63]

Celal Nuri, elected as an MP to the last Ottoman Parliament, was actively involved in passing the National Pact (*Misak-ı Milli*) in February 1920, which rejected the pending partition of Anatolia. The Ottoman sultan and his grand vizier, virtual captives of the victorious Entente, were more amenable to its demands. Recognizing that the activities of his parliament were at an end, Celal Nuri further recommended on February 23, 1920, that the Ottoman constitution be amended to allow for a committee of MPs to be given emergency powers if parliament was disrupted, a bold attempt to legitimize the Turkish nationalist resistance within the rubric of Ottoman state tradition.[64] The passage of the amendment failed, and within a month the British arrested him and had him exiled to prison in Malta.[65]

The Turkish Revolution

Celal Nuri, upon being released from exile on November 1, 1921, faced a radically different situation. He was forced to suspend his literary activities in Istanbul, and flee to Ankara, to join Mustafa Kemal's forces since his paper closed on account of his support for the Turkish nationalist liberation struggle.[66] As a civilian, he could only play a supporting role in government, namely as an MP in the new Grand National Assembly (*Büyük Millet Meclisi*), and, in time, as the rapporteur of the 1924 constitutional committee. Mustafa Kemal gave him the post of rapporteur, probably in recognition of his support during the occupation as well as a detailed constitutional proposal Celal Nuri delivered on January 12, 1919, as part of a political party proposal, which directly supported the Turkish nationalist leader.[67] Celal Nuri also called Mustafa Kemal the "hero on horseback" and the savior of the Turkish nation in his letter to the Sivas Congress in September 1919.[68]

Celal Nuri's "conversion" to Kemalism was certainly not one of a sans culotte. In his 1923 pamphlet, written shortly before the Turkish Republic was proclaimed on October 29, he questioned the very nature of Turkey's transformation into a secular nation-state. He talked at length about the historical precedents his country could now follow under Mustafa Kemal's leadership. The country undoubtedly faced a crossroads, a phenomenon that could be seen in the very word then in vogue for the new style of rule, *inkılâp*, a term that means both reform and revolution.

Celal Nuri hoped that Mustafa Kemal would follow the example of George Washington, the American revolutionary, who, after leading the Continental Army, set up a liberal and constitutional government organized on Enlightenment principles.[69] Washington may have been the commanding general and first president but he also allowed for free debate among the founding fathers. Rather than establishing a military dictatorship, Washington presided over a "parliament" where both the ruling party and its opposition vied for control. Celal Nuri therefore implied that Mustafa Kemal play a similar role in Turkey by allowing for greater political dissent, culminating in a two-party system of "hardline" and "moderate" Turkish nationalists.[70] Although Celal Nuri does not name any opposition or dissenting party in Turkey at the time he wrote in 1923, one can surmise he was talking about the Second Group (*İkinci Grup*). An unknown number of the Second Group would coalesce with others in 1924 to found the short-lived Progressive Republican Party (*Terakkiperver Cumhuriyet Fırkası*).[71]

He feared, however, that Mustafa Kemal would try to emulate Napoleon and the Jacobins as his key historical examples:

> Even though Napoleon Bonaparte was the wisdom of the era, he reduced France at the end of his reign to a much weaker state than it used to be. The French understood after the these bitter experiences that calamity was certain if [such] a person was destined to administer their nation.[72]

Both Napoleon and the Jacobins ignored the principle that "every reform must be done gradually (*tekâmül-i tedrici*), or it will result in reaction (*irtica*)."[73] The Jacobins, Celal Nuri claimed, simply went too far when they came to power in 1793, as they successfully pushed for the execution of King Louis XVI for betraying the country when he tried to flee from France. To him, the Jacobins compounded their error by getting rid of not only the monarchy but also the Catholic Church, and by replacing it with a rationalist cult that rejected established religion. The reaction to such a movement was profound, including the Vendée Rebellion, and twenty years of war with the various states of Europe. Napoleon, who led France through almost all of its wars after the revolution, ultimately had himself crowned emperor by the pope in a desperate bid to consolidate his own power. This coronation, and the accompanying Concordat with the Catholic Church, reversed much of what the French revolutionaries had hoped to gain.[74]

The Turks, in Celal Nuri's opinion, certainly could relate in part to the French scenario. Abdülhamid II, like Louis XIV, monopolized power in his hands, which led to the flowering of absolutism and a decadent, secluded lifestyle behind the walls of his palace. An educated merit-based bureaucratic elite grew increasingly frustrated that they had no role in society, and they successfully rebelled years later, when the opportunity presented itself.[75] Thus, Celal Nuri insinuated that the original 1908 rebellion was the Turks true "Bastille Day," and that Mustafa Kemal, as the successor of the Young Turks, should not go too much farther than the CUP had done.

Celal Nuri also spoke about the 1791 French Constitution enacted shortly before the Jacobins came to power. That document promulgated a "national sultanate" (*saltanat-ı milliye*) that kept the monarch as an executive, but left legislative power in the hands of parliament.[76]

In a similar vein, Celal Nuri argued that Mustafa Kemal, the head of the National Forces (*Kuva-yı Milliye*) and guardian of the state, should grant legislative power to parliament and symbolic status to the caliphate, an office separated from the old sultanate but still occupied by a member of the old dynasty. Such plans were frustrated in quick order. Mustafa Kemal's abolition of the caliphate on March 3, 1924, roughly a month before the constitutional committee on which Celal Nuri sat presented their proposals to parliament, ended any hope of even a symbolic dynastic link with the Ottoman past.

Nevertheless, Celal Nuri insisted that Islam remain a key part of Turkey's governmental identity. This is apparent from the last section of his 1923 pamphlet, where he argued that "hostile secularism" (*lâ-dinilik*) had no meaning since "Islam is based on reason." The new government should be based on consultation (*meşveret*), a principle of constitutional government that was embraced ever since the days of Prophet Muhammad and the first four caliphs.[77] He arguably enshrined this idea in Article 2 of the 1924 Turkish Constitution: "The religion of the Turkish state is Islam."[78] This paralleled Article 11 of the old 1876 Ottoman Constitution, which declared that "Islam is the state religion."[79] Thus, Celal Nuri seemed to have achieved some sort of continuity between the old empire and the new state, a linkage that might allow for the evolutionary political development he so dearly wanted.[80]

This was a pyrrhic victory, however. Mustafa Kemal and the ruling People's Republican Party (*Cumhuriyet Halk Fırkası*) eliminated any reference in the constitution to Islam on April 10, 1928.[81] By 1938, a sentence describing Turkey's government as "republican, nationalist, populist, statist, secular and revolutionary" had replaced the original sentence in Article 2 that enumerated the "six arrows" of the Republican People's Party, the only official political organization allowed to exist at the time.[82]

Atatürk was now enshrined as the father of the Turkish revolution who ensured the birth of a secular republic. By using his prestige as the savior of the nation from Greek, British, French, and Italian foreign military occupation, and the political "betrayal" of Sultan Vahdettin, Damat Ferid Pasha, and the other members of the last Ottoman governments, he systematically put into place a new regime. The new nation-state, consciously modeled on the revolutionary French Republic, was unitary, secular, and dated its zero hour to Mustafa Kemal's landing at Samsun on May 19, 1919. Atatürk and İsmet İnönü, his successor, would sweep the earlier heritage, including that of Celal Nuri's CUP past, out of the political limelight for the foreseeable future.

Conclusion

In general, Celal Nuri, like most Unionists, was not consistent ideologically. From 1909 until 1911 Celal Nuri stressed reforming the political and bureaucratic system to put it in line with the "Western" model of political transparency, liberal property rights, and accountability before the law. He then sought to empower a new entrepreneurial class of Ottoman Muslims whose success would effectively silence the previous reactionary tendencies among that faith community.

Celal Nuri would then turn around and blame European and Ottoman liberals for his country's wartime travails from 1911 until 1923, accusing them of conspiring to destroy the empire through a series of territorial encroachments, supporting of various separatist projects among the minorities, and maintaining the capitulations which strangled the prospects of forming an Ottoman Muslim middle-class. While still obsessed with the Unionist goal of promoting Ottoman Muslim entrepreneurship, he reframed his support within a nationalist rather than a liberal rubric. This translated into the demonization of non-Muslim merchants and guildsmen as a threat to Ottoman sovereignty.

Once a combined British and French fleet sailed into the sea of Marmara after the Ottomans surrendered at the end of the First World War, Celal Nuri dedicated himself to supporting the largely Unionist Muslim nationalist resistance—an effort that ultimately led to his exile by the British to Malta in March 1920.

Within two years after his release in November 1921 Celal Nuri recognized that he could do very little to save these symbolic institutions of the Ottoman past—such as the Unionist vision of a nominal sultan/caliph like Mehmet V.

He similarly accepted Mustafa Kemal's abandonment of his beloved Ottoman capital of Istanbul in favor of the Anatolian provincial town of Ankara. He even was willing to give up on the political opposition of former Unionists to Mustafa Kemal's increasing stranglehold on power. Despite his arguments to the contrary in the months before the declaration of the Republic of Turkey, Celal Nuri refused to join dissidents within the Second Group in 1923 or the PRP in 1924–5.

The consolation Celal Nuri received in this Faustian bargain was his role in the 1924 constitutional committee—particularly his defense of Article 2 which proclaimed Islam as the state religion as well as his definition of the "true citizen" of the republic as a Turkish-speaking Hanefi Muslim. From the promulgation of the constitution onward, Celal Nuri would either acquiesce to the secular nationalism of the consolidating Kemalist regime or, on rare occasion, clash with Atatürk and his closest followers. Points of friction, such as Celal Nuri's protests in July 1924 that the interior minister and other government and police officials were accepting bribes and kickbacks from wealthy Armenians trying to reenter the country after the war, and his praise of Adolf Hitler's policies toward the German Jews, touch upon the most controversial part of his career: his troubled relationship with minority issues.

3

The Nationalities Problem

Introduction

In his novel *The End Times* (*Ahir Zaman*) (1919),[1] Celal Nuri (İleri) painted a dark picture of urban life in the Ottoman capital. While the army was struggling on the field, Istanbul's wealthy elites were leading a dissolute life, where material and sexual desires ran amok. It is no accident that this scene was dominated by war profiteers, often of non-Turkish and non-Sunni Muslim background. The immoral lifestyle along with cosmopolitan multiculturalism were just the first steps in "degeneration." Celal Nuri hinted also that such minorities, when in power, would be willing to sell their loyalties to the highest bidder and thus often work intentionally on behalf of an "alien" national cause.

Such "stab in the back" tropes were very popular in Turkish literature, particularly when they targeted the Entente's military presence in Istanbul from 1918 to 1922, since many of the city's residents were Greek, Armenian, or Jewish.[2] Yet, Celal Nuri often made such negative allusions throughout his intellectual career, and not just during the Turkish Independence War.

The reason for his hostility toward minorities had much to do with his own attraction to Social Darwinism, his belief that an empire in decay would become engulfed in a "contest of life" that would pit one ethnic group against the other to see which would ultimately survive. For him, such conflicts explained in part why the Ottoman Empire had become increasingly subject to dismemberment once Abdülhamid II agreed in July 1908 to reconvene parliament after the Unionists led a small-scale revolt in the hills of Macedonia. The "contest," in his mind, would continue even after the wars, when the Republic of Turkey was consolidating.

Celal Nuri would talk constantly about the need for the Turks to morally regenerate themselves before taking on such internal rivals, as discussed in Chapter 2. But he would work to no small degree in trying to "expose" how the Greeks, Armenians, and Jews were actually themselves immoral, and therefore deserved defeat even though they were supposedly more economically and educationally advanced. Such rhetoric exposed the hollowness of his supposed Islamic vision of governance, which in theory would have allowed for local non-Muslims to be citizens of the state, if they would respect the dominance of its ruling faith and remain loyal to its government.

Sometimes, Celal Nuri's chauvinism would be muted, as in certain statements on the Arabs and Armenians. He would laud the importance of the Arab language and people to the Ottomans as an Islamic empire.[3] He would also argue consistently until the outbreak of the First World War for the Young Turks to grant their country's Arabs regional autonomy.[4] Moreover, he would write a novel just after Abdülhamid II's reconvening of parliament in July 1908 that highlighted the heroic role the *Dashnaks*, or Armenian Revolutionary Federation, played in supporting the CUP plot against Sultan Abdülhamid II.[5] He would maintain that the Armenians should support the Ottoman Empire, and later Turkey, and forget whatever injustices had occurred to them in the past.[6]

This chapter will contend, however, that Celal Nuri often talked about the various minorities in the very Machiavellian tone and logic for which he condemned others. This can be seen not only in his views of Persians, Kurds, Alevis, Arabs, Greeks, Armenians, and Jews but also about the Yezidis, the very first non-Muslim group about which he spoke at length, a group his father Mustafa Nuri had also described negatively while a governor in the distant province of Mosul.[7]

The Yezidis

To Celal Nuri, the Yezidis were true infidels. This small religious community, largely scattered throughout the desolate deserts and mountains of what would become northern Iraq, "denied" Islam's validity. They not only rejected Muhammad as God's Prophet, but also refused the Quran, and even the unity of God. The Yezidis saw Şeyh Adi bin Misafir (1075–1162), the probable founder of the faith, in the likeness of a prophet.[8] His shrine at Lalesh, a former Nestorian monastery, was their most sacred temple. They revered two sacred texts (the *Djelve* and the *Mushafi Resch*)[9] but only a member of the priestly caste (*molla*) could read them, as the rest of the community was religiously bound to be illiterate.[10] They believed not only in the devil as a deity, but that there were seven gods who were involved in creation, not one.[11] They worshipped the Meleki Tavous, a god's fallen angel who was given the shape of a peacock, or rooster, and performed a pilgrimage to a bronze statue of it where they would make their donations.[12] While they acknowledged Adam as their ancestor, they dismissed Eve, believing that Adam's son Chehid came in part from a jar of the elements, much like the matter that the Meleki Tavous was turned into was when he was cast into hell. Saintly people also were reincarnated, as could be seen with Şeyh Adi, who transmigrated from Yezid ibn Muawiya (647–83), the Umayyad tyrant.[13] Even Jesus Christ was seen as undergoing metempsychosis.[14]

Celal Nuri then detailed the Yezidi belief in hierarchy as well as their ceremonials. The Yezidis were led by a princely caste (*mir*), which was led by the grand prince (*mir'ül-ümera*). The *mir'ül-ümera*'s spiritual counterpart, and the successor of Şeyh Adi, was the *şeyh*. A *şeyh* also referred to a member of the Yezidi religious hierarchy, including the priests, the spiritual guides (*pir*), bards (*kavval*), and attendants (*kiutchek*).[15]

Besides performing three daily ritual prayers, fasting three days every September, and an annual pilgrimage to the statue of the cock, the Yezidi took the sacraments of baptism and circumcision, and had prescribed marital and funereal ceremonies. Also noted were restrictions on diet, such as forbidding fish, gourds, lentils, okra, peas, cabbage and lettuce, as well as refusing to interact with Muslims.[16]

Celal Nuri mentioned that Şeyh Adi was a Muslim connected to Abdülkadir Ceylani, founder of the Kaderi Sufi order. While Şeyh Adi did establish himself in Lalesh, he failed to convert the monastery into a dervish lodge (*tekke*), and was ultimately forced out by his supposed converts. These converts would retain his name but pervert Şeyh Adi's faith entirely for their own ends.[17]

Celal Nuri refuted the argument that the Yezidis were in fact a Shiite sect. This is remarkable given that one of the chief advocates of this point of view, Selim Sırrı Giridi, was Celal Nuri's own uncle and a respected theologian under Abdülhamid II. Sırrı connected the Yezidis to Yezid bin Enise, a leader of the Abaziyyes, and a Shiite, who predicted that "God would send another prophet from Persia" and that they "would abandon the canonical law of Muhammad."[18] In the opinion of Celal Nuri and his father Mustafa Nuri, Sırrı had confused Yezid with Yezid ibn Muawiyya. Yezid ibn Muawiya's connection to the Yezidis was also false,[19] as it was an attempt to legitimize the community's privileges when under pressure from the Ottomans and other Muslim overlords. Mustafa Nuri also took issue with other Ottoman scholars, such as Muhammad Zahri Hayyatzade, a local Sunni Islamic religious authority from Mosul who dared to posit that the Yezidi's alleged devil worship[20] had at least a minimal basis in Prophet Muhammad's saying:

A satan disguised himself, entered the crowd and told them lies. When the people left, I heard a man whose face I remembered but did not know say the following 'there are satans in the sea, imprisoned by Solomon. One is close to appearing in the public and reading something to people.'[21]

In Celal Nuri's and his father's opinion, Hayyatzade had misinterpreted the satanic spirits (*djinn*) to mean satanic people. The Baqarah Sure made a similar reference to *djinn*: "When they meet those who believe, they say 'we believe'; but when there along with their evil ones, they say: 'We are really with you. We were (only) jesting.'"[22]

The Yezidis probably had a much closer connection to Christianity in Celal Nuri's eyes. This was clear from his theory that the Yezidis believed in multiple gods, akin to the Trinity. He also alleged that the Yezidis worshipped statues like those seen in the Catholic Church, acknowledged the priestly caste, drank wine as part of their ritual beliefs, underwent baptism, and were buried with a wake. Celal Nuri argued that these practices, along with the Nestorian heritage of their main shrine, showed that the Yezidis were, in a sense, continuing heretical Christian traditions.[23]

Regardless of which religion the Yezidis originated from, Celal Nuri depicted them as leading a life of moral decline. When the Yezidis embarked on their annual pilgrimage to Meleki Tavous, they would gather in the village in front of the bronze statue of the cock to the tune of the bard's trumpets, dance with the long-haired attendants, and pay their sacrifices to the cock for the bard's "services." Celal Nuri and his father hinted that the worshippers had group sex after drinking in excess during the ceremony. Adultery was permitted and the words for bard (*kaval*) and attendants (*kuitchek*) were synonyms in colloquial Arabic for male prostitutes.[24] Similarly, men and women bathed in a river in front of the statue after meeting annually at the mausoleum for Şeyh Adi to sacrifice and eat an ox without care for cleanliness. They would then gather around the statue along with the attendants, and once again have sex with one another. Also problematic from a sanitary point of view was the fact that they did not use toilets, bathrooms, toilet paper, or razors.[25] The mud from the river, he proclaimed, was their holy water, used to rid themselves of diseases and to accompany their funeral corpses to burial.[26]

Celal Nuri and his father also gave a shocking account of Yezidi marriage practices. The father would sell his daughter as a prostitute six times in order to pay for the dowry. The bride-to-be would then select her suitor at whim, and then have the mother negotiate with the groom's family on her behalf.[27] Thus, you had the almost mirror opposite of Islamic practices, where the fathers met to arrange the marriage of a virgin bride. In Islam if anyone initiated the marriage proposal besides the other members of the family, it would be the groom and not the bride. This practice confirmed that the woman was to be protected and that those who did not were breaking one of Islam's most sacred principles.

To Celal Nuri, the Yezidis' catastrophic loss of moral bearings was simple barbarity: "These are the Yezidis, people of Mesopotamia, who resist civilization, are hostile to all progress, and know greater sin than knowledge, reading and writing."[28] He even went to the extreme of quoting Adolphe D' Houdetot, a French writer: "The negro's devil is white. I love this retaliation."[29]

Although this statement implicated Celal Nuri and his father as racists, there were more ethnic than physical or racial references to the Yezidis. Once they mentioned them as "people of tall stature, sturdy, sharing many physical similarities with the Armenians of Van and Bitlis."[30] They asserted later that their leaders were of Arabic origin, but had now become assimilated Kurds.[31] Even *Resch*, one of the Yezidi's holy books, was the Kurdish word for black.[32]

Celal Nuri was concerned, however, that the government had yet to effectively deal with barbaric elements within their empire. Admittedly, the Ottoman government had tried to integrate the Yezidis on occasion. As Celal Nuri and Mustafa Nuri noted, Yezidi rebellions erupted periodically from 1784 onward, largely because of their young men's refusal to perform military service. This is confirmed in an 1872 petition whose first demand was: "It is impossible for Yezidis to serve in the Army." The petition also justified the military service exemption since the Yezidis were religiously bound not to interact with people of other faiths. They also could not go to a public bath, or eat or drink with a Muslim, and they had specific restrictions on diet, clothing, toiletries, and the carrying of holy mud and water. Moreover, a Yezidi must perform his annual fast at home or face automatic divorce from his wife.[33] The Yezidi insistence on the military exemption eventually resulted in Ömer Wahbi Pasha's 1890–1 campaign against Sincar and Sheykhan. Ömer Wahbi Pasha not only converted Şeyh Adi's mausoleum into a Muslim seminary (*medrese*), and established village schools to convert new generations, but also seized the Yezidis' holy relics and sent them back to Istanbul. Celal Nuri and his father said that up to two-thirds of the Yezidis' farms were destroyed during the course of the campaign.[34]

This account, originally penned by his father while acting as governor of Mosul, seemingly legitimized a plan to first militarily secure and then culturally develop the Yezidis to save them from their endless cycle of heresy, moral depravity, cultural backwardness, and rebellion against authority. The sultan's reluctance to aggravate ethnic and religious tensions in the area might have been the reason why Mustafa Nuri's pamphlet was published five years after his term had ended. The Ottomans also had increasing troubles with the Armenian minority, concentrated in Southern and Eastern Anatolia, an area not terribly far from the Yezidi homeland.[35]

But times had changed quite dramatically ever since the Young Turks took over and consolidated power in the wake of the April 13 uprising. The CUP had undertaken a series of measures to control hitherto marginal groups, such as the Twelver Shiites of southern Iraq, and the Bedouins of the Hijaz. They feared the British were agitating to gain control of these areas, given the strategic importance of the Basra in the Gulf and in the prominent role of the Hijaz as the site of the annual Islamic pilgrimage.[36] Both Celal Nuri and his father were concerned about similar foreign interests in the Yezidis, as many Orientalist and Christian missionary accounts of this people had been written since the nineteenth century.[37]

The solution to Celal Nuri was for his government to convert this population to Islam and effectively integrate them. For him, this civilizing mission was very much akin to Islam's expansion in Africa:

> People have come across tribes who have accepted Islam in the remotest parts of Africa, where no European explorer ever could go. Today, Muslims are helping African tribes to civilize themselves. This is far different than the Europeans, who simply conquer and exploit.[38]

While military force and the need to police such populations were no doubt part of the equation, the Quran required that the conquerors practice mercy: "We gave and granted you a clear conquest. God should forgive your past and future sins."[39] Celal Nuri added his own explanation:

> He [the victor] should command in accordance with the knowledge of Islam to promote [not only] the general welfare in politics and society, [but also] the pursuit of knowledge and literature.[40]

Thus, his government and people were duty-bound to spread "religious institutions, the arts, and other important cultural principles."[41] In his eyes, this was indeed the Ottoman Muslim man's "burden."

The Persians, Alevis, and Kurds

Celal Nuri thought almost as dismissively about the Persians as he did the Yezidis. Although the Persians started out as a great empire, rivalling the ancient

Greeks, with their military prowess and scientific and literary accomplishments, they had declined greatly by the birth of Prophet Muhammad. The Persians were riddled by corruption at that time, as seen in the seclusion of the rulers in a typical oriental-style harem. Even after the Arab armies conquered the Persians, these subjects refused to fully accept Islam and instead retained their ancient customs. The Persians' adoption of Shiism, and the Safavids' later adherence to the Twelver branch of that faith, only led to further degeneration.[42] This denominational difference promoted a distinct and separate sense of nationhood which led the Safavids to reject uniting with the Sunnis, the majority of orthodox Muslims under the leadership of the Ottoman state:

> If the Safavid Shah İsmail and his Alevis (*Kızılbaşlar*) did not confront Sultan Yavuz Selim there would have been an immense Islamic empire stretching from China and the Pacific Ocean and Moscow to the Cape of Good Hope that would last even today. No Christian empire could have stood against this united, [massive power].[43]

Celal Nuri unsurprisingly concluded that Safavid civilization declined both spiritually and politically because of the conflict. By the outbreak of the First World War, when Celal Nuri wrote, the Qajars, the Safavids successors, were engulfed in a power struggle between the shah and his pretenders who "disregarded their [brief] constitutional experience" between 1906 and 1908:

> Persia is in total anarchy. There is no administration, no reforms, no money and no soldiers. This country of ten million might seem like a state, but in reality is nothing but a tribal confederation, with the shah as its nominal chief.[44]

In his opinion, this decadence unfortunately had the potential to spill over into his own country. Celal Nuri was worried that the Kurds, who were brought by Sultan Selim to defend the empire against the heretical Safavids, themselves were in danger of "Persianization," perhaps because of social and linguistic similarities. It would be a grave mistake, he contended, if the Kurds were to separate, implying that they would remain culturally tribal and primitive:

> Our Kurdish supporters should know that as a secondary nationality, they need to unite with a primary one. They have a respected place in the Turkish family, just like the Circassians, Laz, and other minorities.[45]

In Celal Nuri's eyes, the Kurds fit in with the Turks in a similar way that the Basques did with the French, and the Scots did with English.[46]

The Ottoman Empire's Shiite minority was also a threat. "Shiism," he maintained, "is progressing in the Ottoman domains. Alevis and *Kızılbaş* are spreading into Anatolia, similar to the monstrous and disgusting [Twelver] Shiites near Baghdad."[47] While Celal Nuri admitted that freedom of religion should be allowed as long as it did not affect the public order, he warned that the government should not hesitate to get rid of them if they did rebel, particularly in Anatolia.[48] He went on to suggest that more peaceful methods might be employed, such as the spreading of Sunni Islam by means of the Sufis, the mystic orders who, through education, tolerance, and multicultural interaction, were the most effective in spreading the ruling faith.[49]

Celal Nuri's dim views on Shiites were likely inspired in part by his uncle Sırrı Giridi, the theologian. Sırrı highlighted several instances where Persians or Shiites capped off their active rebellion against mainstream Sunni Islam with assassinations. First was Lulu, a Persian Christian slave, who, after protesting Umar, one of the Righteous Caliphs (*Rashidun*), and a companion of the Prophet Muhammad, mortally wounded him in 644. Lulu struck him six times with a sword while Umar was performing his ritual prayers.[50] The next was Abdullah Bin Seba, a Jewish convert to Islam who perverted the faith by proclaiming that there would be a Messiah after the Prophet Muhammad. Mentioned as the first true Shiite, Abdullah Bin Seba would later be alleged as the mastermind behind the murder of Caliph Uthman, the successor of Umar, in 656.[51] Last but not least would be Hassan-i Sabah (d. 1124), the hashish-smoking founder of the Ismaili order of assassins, who, after setting up a secret mountain fortress in Almut, killed the famous Seljuk Grand Vizier Nizam ül-Mülk in 1092.[52]

All of these assassinations were carried out against Sunni Muslim authorities, suggesting that religious heresy and political disloyalty were synonymous. Celal Nuri's implication here, as in his writing on the Yezidis, was that the Shiite and Kurdish minorities had to at least recognize Turkish Sunni Muslim overlordship and peacefully assimilate. If they persisted in rebellion, they would face subjugation by force.

The Arabs

The Arabs were a different case, according to Celal Nuri. Beginning with Prophet Muhammad himself, the Arab empire that followed under the four Righteous Caliphs and the succeeding Umayyad dynasty had a grandiose history. Stretching from the borders of China and the Indian Ocean to North Africa and Spain, the Arabs were successful in establishing an Islamic civilization where knowledge, science, and medicine reached heights the world had never seen before. Indeed, the most lasting legacy of the Arabs was their language, the tongue of the Quran and of Muhammad and his companions. As such, Arabic remained absolutely central to maintaining all Muslim peoples' faith.[53]

These cultural accomplishments were so strong; they could be seen as far away as Spain. There, the fine arts had flourished, the wonderful palaces of Alhambra and Kasrüzzehra had been constructed, and men of knowledge had regularly gathered and founded libraries, inspiring Muslim explorers to pioneer the oceans: "In short, the Spanish Arabs were so advanced the West saw them the way we look at Europe today."[54]

Yet, according to Celal Nuri, the Arabs of Andalusia, the last great remnant of the Umayyads, would themselves begin to decline when they allowed local Christians to practice their faith without interruption. In time, the neighboring Christian kingdoms would provoke these elements to separate from their Muslim overlords and set up crusader-like states. Celal Nuri saw clear parallels here between the Andalusians' naïve tolerance of such minorities and what the Ottomans did with the Greeks under Muhammad the Conqueror.[55]

The colonial ambitions of the Europeans toward the Arabs had only grown over the centuries. Even in his day Celal Nuri complained that the Europeans were trying to separate Arabs from Turks religiously, linguistically, and politically. The French in particular had concentrated on the Levantine Marionites, who sought French protection by setting up a separate Arab country (Lebanon) on the Mediterranean coast.[56] In his opinion, the French established a state that would privilege "Christian debris" such as the Marionites, Chalcedonians, and Syriacs, a development with dire consequences for the entire region.[57]

Nonetheless, Celal Nuri took heart from Gustave Le Bon, who voiced skepticism about the French effort to colonize Algeria and elsewhere. Le Bon doubted the prospects of:

> imposing European instruction on indigenous inhabitants ... [since] this education, adapted by secular transformations to our own sentiments and needs, is not in accord with different sentiments and needs.[58]

Le Bon therefore insinuated that any effort to Christianize or secularize an Arab population in the Middle East would lead to France's failure, and its loss of blood and treasure.[59]

But Celal Nuri would regard British colonial designs of granting a form of "self-government" far more effective in the long run.[60] The British, after occupying Egypt in 1882, had designs on controlling Mecca and Medina.[61] The Ottomans held sway over the Islamic holy land of the Hijaz from Sultan Yavuz

Selim's conquest in 1517 until that time. Guarding the Hijaz was critical to the Ottomans' Islamic notion of the state, and it justified their rule over non-Turkish Muslims, most importantly the Arabs.[62]

Wilfrid Scrawen Blunt in his famous work *The Future of Islam* (1882) argued that the caliphate should be reserved for the Hashemites, the leading tribe in Mecca, in consultation with prominent Islamic scholars from Al-Ahzar, the most renowned Muslim Arab center of learning, housed in Cairo.[63] Al-Ahzar was also the home base of Muhammad Abduh (1849–1905), a believer in the compatibility of Islam with all aspects of modern life. The British appointed Muhammad Abduh as the chief Muslim religious authority in Egypt (Grand Mufti) in 1905. Rashid Rıda (1865–1935), Muhammad Abduh's close associate, would go on to echo Blunt's argument saying that the caliphate was only legitimate if it followed the democratic tradition of consultation, namely the holding of the grand council (*şura*).[64]

For an Ottoman patriot, however, Rashid Rıda's words justified British colonialism, albeit underhandedly. Such conspiracy was confirmed by Blunt's conclusion that the caliphate no longer should belong to the Ottoman Empire but "must be taken under British protection, and publicly guaranteed its political existence."[65] This meant, in effect, that the chief of the Hashemites would, after his formal selection, become a client of the British Crown.

The Young Turks answer to Blunt and Rashid Rıda's proposal was seen in the wake of the April 13, 1909 uprising, when Sahip Bey, the minister for religious affairs (*şeyhülislam*), blessed the selection of Sultan Mehmet V to the caliphate as he was approved by the Ottoman Parliament, their version of the *şura*. Celal Nuri enthusiastically approved of this "democratic tradition," which he saw as in line with the sayings of Prophet Muhammad and the decisions of the Rightful Caliphs and the Umayyads. While Mehmet V, like the other members of the Ottoman dynasty who held the post from the time of Sultan Yavuz Selim, was not of the Hashemite clan, he and his Ottoman predecessors had the advantages of long-standing political legitimacy and independence from the Christian colonial powers.

Celal Nuri remained optimistic up until the outbreak of war in 1914 that his government could sway Muslim Arab popular opinion in their favor. He personally translated a public letter that Blunt wrote in September 1910, four years after the Denshawai Incident, where two British soldiers died, four Egyptians were executed, and Mustafa Kamil's National Party was banned. Convinced that the British had no intention of granting their Egyptian subjects self-rule, Blunt urged that the Egyptians should rise up in protest and push to join "the Turks who are your fellow countrymen."⁶⁶ He had changed his mind about Ottoman overlordship after Abdülhamid II reconvened the parliament in 1908.⁶⁷

Celal Nuri also predicted that the Egyptians would overthrow British rule. In a pamphlet written just after the Ottomans declared war on the Entente, he said: "Egypt and Sudan would loosen the chains of slavery and use them instead on the necks of their former tyrants."⁶⁸

In support:

> The victorious Muslim [Ottoman] armies will pass through the desert, like the Prophet Moses did when he found the Holy Land on the eastern side of the Suez. Like Moses, we ... will find the Promised Land, but this time on the west side. We will block the canal, and in this way stop England and make it prisoner. In the process we will break up its colonial order, and knock the crown off of King George's head.⁶⁹

The Egyptians, along with the other Arabs of the Ottoman Empire, would, in the future, constitute "the second realm of the Islamic sultanate ... [where] they would have complete autonomy, much like Hungary has in the Habsburg Empire."⁷⁰ The Arabs in Egypt could largely run their own local affairs, including language and education—a kind of "home rule" with the added benefit of being subject to a Muslim dynasty rather than a foreign one.⁷¹ Such an arrangement by the Ottoman Turks would not alienate the Arab population, and it would avoid repeating the mistake of denying the Albanians' similar autonomy in the run-up to the Balkan Wars.⁷²

Needless to say, Celal Nuri would soon be disappointed. Sharif Husayn, the most powerful local leader in Mecca, resented the centralizing measures of the CUP, particularly the ongoing construction of the Hijaz Railroad. Husayn would conspire with the British and lead the Arab revolt of 1916–18. While most of the Ottoman Arab population remained loyal, Cemal Pasha, the head of the Ottoman military forces in the Levant during the war, had jailed or executed a number of notables because of alleged disloyalty.⁷³ Celal Nuri remained silent about the issue during this time, presumably out of embarrassment for he and his government's previous liberal position.

The Greeks

Celal Nuri saw the Greeks, like the Arabs, as comparable civilizationally to the Ottoman Turks. The Greeks, he explained, had a long imperial history that paralleled his own country's experience. The Byzantine Empire, the successor to Rome, had rapidly expanded its territory under the Justinian the Great (527–65) to Italy, North Africa, and even the shores of the Atlantic. Parallel with these conquests, however, was the decision to exploit his own people. It was no coincidence that Justinian favored the elite and ridiculed the urban masses: "The cruelty of the government increased, as the Emperor delighted in committing a variety of injustices."[74]

This argument followed Celal Nuri's familiar recipe for civilizational decay. The Byzantine Empire was a place for decrepit, feudal elites who lived a life of debauchery at the expense of their subjects. The Byzantines, in fact, established the harems in the oriental manner, let the slaves which they took as booty from the surrounding Balkan and Caucasian barbarians do their manual work, and had the commercially minded Italians of Genoa and Venice handle their trade.[75] The ancient schools of Athens and Rome were closed, and the Orthodox Church, subject to the whim of the Emperor, writhed in corruption.[76] During the Crusades Western European Christendom tried to take Constantinople, seen most visibly with the sack of the city in 1204 by the Norman knights and Venetian navy. These events helped weaken the Byzantines to the point to where a Turkish conquest was almost an afterthought.[77]

Mehmet II (1451–81), the conqueror of Constantinople, basically repeated what Justinian had done nearly a millennium before him. Although his forces penetrated the city walls, he too reveled in his conquest, destroying much of the town in a flurry of pillaging, enslavement, and general mayhem that lasted for three whole days. The conquering Ottoman army, revealing their "barbaric" roots, soon settled down for a life of leisure, leading once again to feudal decadence and the sultan's isolation in the harem. The Ottoman Turks, in their laziness, let the downtrodden Greek urban dwellers dominate trade and recognized the Greek Orthodox Patriarch as the Greek community's chief religious authority.[78] They also in time turned to the Europeans, especially the British, French, and Russians, who worked to subvert the empire. The new patrons awarded the Greeks, with a "homeland" in the Morea by 1829, which would periodically expand at the expense of the Ottoman Turks over roughly the next ninety years as an independent state.[79] Although the *Tanzimat* reformers tried to reverse this process, their attempts were halted by Abdülhamid II, who brought back the despotic, degenerate ways of the sultanate until 1908.[80]

The reactions by the Greek and Turkish people to these decadent empires were also important to take into consideration. The Greeks, for example, had been forced by their conquerors to take the cultural initiative. Although the

Patriarch of the Orthodox Church, an appendage of the Byzantine Emperor, had abandoned the people, their own priesthood had not. The priests catered to the needs of their own parishes, instilling in them a mystical bond between the church and the population.[81] The Greeks emerged as a disciplined, entrepreneurial people who brought their national culture again to life, this time under the Ottomans, where, as noted above, they helped establish a separate state.[82]

Celal Nuri emphasized that this process of cultural and political renewal transformed the Greeks. They no longer bore any real resemblance to the ancient Greeks, as they had intermixed with Slavic, Armenian, and other nationalities over time. There was no such thing as a racially pure Greek, a fact elucidated by Jakob Phillip Fallmerayer (1790–1861), the controversial German Romantic historian, and Le Bon, the famous French social psychologist.[83]

Celal Nuri therefore viewed the modern Orthodox Greek identity as oddly akin to the Ottoman Turks in that the centrality of the Orthodox Church, like Islam, led to an ethnically assimilationist model that took religion, as well as language, as its chief point of departure. Over the long run, the Ottoman Muslims should learn from the Greeks' spiritual and entrepreneurial attitude and morally reform themselves. This meant forming civic associations, led in part by "spiritual teachers," an elite of doctors, engineers, schoolmasters, and others who had been given a modern education.

They should recognize that their local imams had failed to match the efforts of the Greek priests due to their illiteracy and ignorance: "I am fully confident we can create a Muslim Turkish nation from nothing by implementing and extending national goals to the religious authorities and the Muslim theological students."[84] These local imams would make sure that "Turkish soldiers (*mehmetçik*) would not escape from his battalion."[85] Desertion was no small problem, as seen during the Balkan Wars, when many of the armies in the field were quickly depleted.

But Celal Nuri still feared that the Greek Patriarchate, which remained in Istanbul after the Young Turks took power, could potentially be used as the symbolic head of state, much in the way he argued the caliphate should have been used. The Greeks, unlike the Turks, who had the sultanate, no longer had to worry about dynastic oversight.[86]

Celal Nuri suspected that a plot had now ripened for the Greek Orthodox Patriarch to take his traditional autonomy to the next level and declare his office a new "republic." A French journalist who had visited Istanbul published a bombshell story for *Le Figaro* on October 2, 1912, just six days before Greece, Bulgaria, Serbia, and Montenegro launched the devastating First Balkan War, which led to the permanent loss of almost all of the Ottomans' remaining possessions in Southeastern Europe. Celal Nuri paraphrased the article entitled "Facing the Patriarchate in Constantinople" in which the French journalist interviewed Joachim III, the acting Greek Patriarch:

> Upon approaching his [the patriarch's] office after passing Istanbul's dirty and dilapidated streets, we arrived at the Phanariot, the old heart of Byzantium. Our car stopped, and we waited in front of a closed set of the Patriarchate's doors. The guide told us: "One time [during the Greek revolt] in 1821 [the Turks] entered through these doors and took Patriarch Grigoryos and strung him up on them. This entrance will be opened, God willing, when that murder has been avenged."[87]

Later, Joachim III would speak directly to the journalist. After asserting that he, a poor abused shepherd of his people, had suffered needless abuse, he stated:

> You are French, and therefore you have the honor of being part of that nation's goals. You and everyone else in the world understand that I too represent a thought and goal. This is what gives me a great and eternal power despite my material shortcomings. This thought sooner or later will overcome all obstacles. You cannot conquer this spiritual power. This thought cannot be stopped and will live. This is what has protected us for 400 years. If I am fortunate enough to see the first glimmers of our liberation before I die, I will count myself a happy man.[88]

Celal Nuri was shocked by the betrayal of someone from whom he had personally heard long reassurances of how he and his flock had been fairly treated ever since 1453. Celal Nuri reacted by calling for the permanent separation of the two people since the Greeks were "our natural enemies ... It is stupid to expect flattery let alone loyal sentiments from the Greeks ... A Greek is a Greek and a Turk is a Turk. There are no agreements possible between them."[89]

He concluded his statement with the Quranic injunction on infidels: "O ye that reject Faith! I worship not which ye worship, nor will ye worship that which I worship. And I will not worship that which ye have been wont to worship ... To you be your way, and to me mine."[90]

This harsh ending meant in effect that he saw no hope of including the Greek minority community within the Ottoman Turkish Muslim nation. That they constituted a grave threat to his country's sovereignty was clear. The Greeks had been entrusted with handling much of the empire's commerce, with overseeing the Ottoman navy and foreign service, and with large parts of the Balkans. These powers were wielded by a people that had shown disloyalty since their first major rebellion in 1821, and the Greeks might now use their influence to take over the capital itself. The threat of that, so acute in 1912–13 when Celal Nuri was at his most vitriolic, would not die down until Mustafa Kemal (Atatürk) came to power.[91]

Celal Nuri's fear was reinforced, no doubt, by the fact that his forefathers were Cretan Muslims. He would lament: "The Muslims of Crete were nearly half the population but they were killed off or kicked out because of the Greeks' national tenacity and perseverance."[92] When Hawrutian Sharighian, an Armenian *Dashnak*, responded to Celal Nuri's diatribe on the Greek Orthodox Patriarchate by sarcastically commenting that he was a Cretan Muslim whose creativity was probably due to his ethnic origin, Celal Nuri countered that he was not Greek and that only his father had been born in Crete.[93]

The Armenians

The *Dashnaks*, to which Sharighian belonged, was a nationalist revolutionary organization that in many ways worked in tandem with the CUP. The organization, founded in 1891, coordinated exiles abroad and promoted their cause among the European powers. The *Dashnaks* were dedicated to "liberating" Armenians in the Ottoman Empire and set up cells, which they used to agitate their community and commit numerous terrorist acts, such as the robbery and hijacking of the Ottoman Bank in Galata, Istanbul on August 24, 1896, and the attempted assassination of Abdülhamid II on July 21, 1905.[94] The group collaborated its efforts with the Unionists, as well as fellow Macedonian and Albanian nationalists, culminating in Abdülhamid II's decision to reconvene the Ottoman Parliament in July 1908 after a brief military insurgency near Bitola.[95] This cooperation continued even after the abortive April 13, 1909 uprising and the ensuing ethnic strife between Armenians and Ottoman Muslims in Adana the following month.

Both authors freely acknowledged this political partnership. Sharighian commented:

> One must never forget how the conquered nations (*milel-i metfuha*) supported constitutional Turkey unconditionally and enthusiastically both before and after the March 31 [April 13, 1909] Revolt. The entire [*Dashnak*] party and revolutionary society mobilized in support of the army of freedom's march on the capital.[96]

Celal Nuri celebrated the *Dashnaks*' efforts in his 1911 novel *The Nightmare? (Cauchmar?)*, when one of the heroes was the Armenian Vartran, who conspired with members of the CUP and even concubines of the Imperial harem to end Abdülhamid II's tyranny.[97] He also freely admitted that the previous sultan had unjustly massacred many of Sharighian's community after the *Dashnaks* had begun their activities.[98]

In addition, Celal Nuri went out of his way to express his admiration for this minority community's work ethic:

> The Armenians are very industrious, indefatigable, daring, and entrepreneurial. They are an indispensable element for the Ottoman nation, for the Turks can make up for their backwardness economically with the progress of Armenian commerce.[99]

He also must have recognized at least a bit of Sharighian in himself. Sharighian after all was trained like Celal Nuri as a lawyer in Istanbul. Sharighian then not only went on to become active in his party as a constant participant in political congresses and the Armenian National Committee, but also was a prolific journalist who was willing to take daring stands against authorities stronger than himself.[100] Here was the example of self-sacrifice Celal Nuri hoped other members of the Turkish elite might emulate, albeit for a different cause.

Nevertheless, over time, the two men came to differ profoundly on the nature of the Ottoman state and its relationship to the minorities. Sharighian clung to a series of statements Celal Nuri made in his *Memorandum (Muhtıra)* to the CUP Congress in Salonika in September 1909, where he proclaimed: "'Ottomanism' (*Osmanlılık*) is a force that preserves the legitimate aspirations, customs and traditions of the nationalities."[101] Celal Nuri argued that this concept was necessary "to make these people happy … with the administration in order to remove the notion of autonomy. They should not follow … [the nationalist movements] that led to Bulgaria and Greece, but instead be as comfortable as the Germans and French in Switzerland … Our nation is not a nation-state (*devlet-i milliye*) but a state of nationalities (*milletler devleti*)."[102] This type of union promised that being an "Ottoman" subject was a "public nationality" where one could also be "a Turk, a Greek or an Armenian in a private sense."[103]

But it is important to note, for instance, that he never used the slogan "union of minorities" (*ittihad-ı anasır*), the standard phrase used by the *Dashnaks* and Ottoman liberals for the overarching ideal of Ottomanism.[104] He preferred instead a declaration of Islamic unity (*ittihad-ı İslam*), where the government itself was ruled primarily by its Turkish Muslim community.[105] The promise of governing non-Muslims fairly and without coercion by following the Islamic principle of toleration was taken for granted. Loyalty to the Ottoman state, and the acknowledgment of the Armenians cultural rights, including those of the Armenian Orthodox Patriarchate, ultimately meant being subject to the will of the sultan, the Ottoman parliament, and the CUP elite.

In Celal Nuri's opinion, the European powers had continually disrupted this relationship since the Treaty of Berlin (1878) in order to create a separate, autonomous region in Eastern Anatolia in the six districts (*vilayet*) of Van, Erzurum, Mamuratülaziz, Bitlis, Diyarbekir, and Sivas—an area where the Armenians formed a substantial minority population until the events of 1915.[106] Though Celal Nuri favored greater local control after the Balkan Wars,[107] the great powers insisted that governors of their own choosing be dispatched to those provinces. This signaled the possibility of an independent Armenian state: "In the phraseology of the Eastern Question, a preliminary to amputation. The fiction of the maintenance of Turkish sovereign rights was, in every case, offered merely as an anesthetic."[108]

According to Celal Nuri, such interference was an excellent example of European power politics, which sought to conquer new territory at the expense of the vulnerable. International law really only applied to a club of Christian nations which excluded the Muslim Ottoman Turks. The Europeans, particularly the Russians, had offered the Armenians support for the plan to carve out an autonomous region and convert it to an independent state. Celal Nuri cautioned Sharighian and the *Dashnaks*: "The Armenians would be harmed if an autonomous administration is established in the eastern provinces since they are the minority."[109] There were simply not "enough Russians to [eliminate] the Muslim [majority]."[110]

Celal Nuri blamed *Dashnak* agitators like Sharighian for spreading the illusion that the Armenians could be independent from the Ottomans:

> It is regrettable that sometimes cunning ones who study in America and especially in Russia do not digest what they read, come back to our country and lead their people astray. I hope that the practical intelligence of the Armenians will understand this reality and will bring their community to reason.[111]

This certainly was true for the Istanbul Armenians, who, isolated from their compatriots in the east, were under increasing pressure by unsympathetic Muslim refugees from the Balkans and the Caucasus.[112]

Sharighian was upset in particular with Celal Nuri's condemnation of the Greek Orthodox Patriarchate, because he thought the Ottomans would harass the Armenian Orthodox Patriarchate next, particularly if the Armenians rebelled in Eastern Anatolia. Unionist attempts to use local Kurdish populations against the Armenians in the east or to provoke Muslim hatred of the Armenians in the capital were simply forms of "Islamic imperialism." The Islamic state Celal Nuri touted was doing to its subjects exactly the same thing that he claimed the Europeans were doing when they imposed colonial rule on others. Sharighian therefore depicted Celal Nuri's vision of progressive Islamic governance as a sham. In his opinion, Islam as a ruling religion was and would remain backward (*irtica*), obstinate, and oppressive. The only way out was for the Unionists to realize that each nation had a right to self-determination.[113]

Celal Nuri's response was that Sharighian himself was hypocritical. He and others like him publicly declared their allegiance to the Ottoman constitution, but privately they were disloyal. After the recent Balkan Wars, Celal Nuri alleged the Armenians would murmur among themselves: "The Turks who massacred the Armenians will disappear as the dominant nation. A Bulgarian is preferable to a Turk, and the Turks' defeat [by the Balkan Christians] was an act of divine punishment for … [murdering us]."[114]

It should be no surprise that Celal Nuri never interacted with Sharighian again. Within two years of their exchange, a world war would break out and push Sharighian into the very maelstrom both feared might occur. The *Dashnaks* fatefully chose in August 1914 not to commit to the Ottoman cause in the looming conflict.[115] The Ottoman defeat at Sarıkamış and the threat of Russia establishing an independent Armenian state led the Unionist authorities to enact the mass expulsion of the Armenians from almost all of Eastern Anatolia, and the hundreds of thousands of dead that ensued. The Ottomans quickly rounded up Sharighian and much of the *Dashnak* leadership in Istanbul in April 1915 after their group's takeover of Van. Sharighian was never heard from again.[116]

Celal Nuri commented later in July 1918 that the *Dashnaks* had irresponsibly whipped up the Armenians of Central and Eastern Anatolia into a "criminal crowd," a term Le Bon had elaborated in regards to the Jacobins provoking the masses who stormed the Bastille to "slaughter … the … enemies of the nation."[117] Celal Nuri thereby insinuated that the *Dashnaks* and the Armenians who supported them were ultimately responsible for their own fate, as they themselves had started a reign of terror against local Muslims. The remaining Armenian populace, he judged, was wise enough to learn from this painful lesson and would be able to survive.[118]

In January 1919, in the wake of the Ottoman surrender, Celal Nuri wrote his recommendations for a new Turkish national constitution, presumably at the behest of Mustafa Kemal, the future founder of the Republic of Turkey. Here Celal Nuri highlighted the "political and civil rights of the minorities" and even called for an inquiry and trial for the "Armenians, Turks and Kurds [who] were assassinated or deported."[119] This could be understood as an attempt to placate the Americans who are exploring the idea of establishing a mandate state in the name of protecting the Armenians.[120]

The Jews

Celal Nuri had an equally complicated relationship with Nordau, the famous Austro-Hungarian Jewish social/cultural critic and devoted Zionist. With the possible exception of Le Bon and Ludwig Büchner, Nordau was the most frequently cited single author throughout Celal Nuri's various works. Nordau's positivist arguments for a return to industriousness, Victorian-style morality, and for a social Darwinistic change in a bid to bring his community in line with the rigors of modern life truly inspired Celal Nuri.[121] Nordau's "collectivist" vision of bringing up a national middle-class mirrored Celal Nuri's campaign for empowering Ottoman Muslim entrepreneurship. Celal Nuri was also influenced by Nordau's frank statements that those nations that did not rejuvenate themselves were bound to be extinguished in the ongoing "contest of life."[122]

Nordau had proclaimed as early as 1903 that the Zionists would never harm the Ottomans: "The sovereign rights and the dignity of the Sultan shall never be infringed. The day in which we enter a Turkish province shall for all time be a great and happy day."[123] Yet right after the CUP had put down the 1909 uprising, Nordau complained:

> They [the CUP] tended to use their new freedom for themselves alone. They would not admit Jews to Palestine except on the condition of complete Turkish nationalization, and very few even on those conditions.[124]

Israel Cohen, a participant in the Ninth Zionist Congress where Nordau had made that statement, was angered by:

> Turkish Jews, mainly through the medium of certain local organs, have denounced their coreligionists as traitors. They have willfully distorted the ideals of Jewish nationalism, accused the Zionists of pursuing separatist aspirations, and even insinuated that the Zionist organization is working in the interests of some foreign power.[125]

Celal Nuri, who at the time of the controversy was the editor-in-chief of the World Zionist Organization-funded *Le Jeune Turc*, knew that the Turkish delegates that protested were angered by the 1909 publication of Jacobus Kann's *Erez Israel: das jüdische Land*. Kann's work pushed for "an autonomous Jewish colony in Palestine." Kann gave his cause no favors when he had passed on copies to leading CUP activists. Ebüzziya Tevfik, Celal Nuri's former partner, had publicly denounced the book in the Ottoman Parliament in March 1911.[126] David Fresco, writing in the Ottoman Ladino *Al Tiempo*, and Haim Naum, the chief rabbi, voiced similar sentiments.[127]

Celal Nuri soon soured on Zionism and became an outspoken anti-Semite after quitting *Le Jeune Turc* in January 1912 in the wake of the Italian invasion of Libya. He first agreed with Ebüzziya that the Ottoman government should closely monitor the Zionists, as they posed a potential threat to sovereignty by attracting foreign settlers and "naïve" Ottoman Jews to participate in their project.[128]

Beyond that, Celal Nuri made the preposterous claim that the Jews began as a religious community, but then "degenerated" into a "tribal" one after Prophet Moses led his people away from their captivity in Egypt.[129] The Jews, in his eyes, refused to give up their nation long after ancient Israel was destroyed:

> 4000 years ... have passed, but the winds have not touched [the Jew] as much as an atom ... How many nations have been born and died since ... [then]. ... Where are the old Egyptians, Assyrians, Babylonians, Huns, Vandals and Goths? ... But the children of Israel did not lose their identity, even though they mix with every nation.[130]

He also continuously questioned their moral character. To him, the Jews were greedy and dissolute, regardless of which national community they interacted with as nominal citizens. He continued with demonizing diatribes about Jews exploiting the poor Russian peasants through loansharking, and how up to two-thirds of the educated and financial elite of Western countries like France, Great Britain, and the United States were dominated by the "children of Israel" (*Beni Israel*).[131]

He also made sexual allegations. Elite Western Jewish women, such as the seductive "Madam S," he met while on a cruise to the North Cape, were typically libertine.[132] At another point he talked about how a Russian police official had intimated that the Jews smuggled young girls from his country to Istanbul to work as prostitutes.[133]

Generalizations about Jews as Zionists and moral deviants led him later to conclude that governments should try to exclude this minority as much as possible from citizenship. In 1932 he saw it as logical, for instance, that the Nazis would promise "to deport the Jews who have immigrated most recently there [while] the older Jews should be allowed only as foreign residents."[134] Celal Nuri therefore appears to have backhandedly rejected the pending application of Jewish intellectuals fleeing Adolf Hitler, who was about to take power in Germany. This lack of sympathy became even more striking when Celal Nuri refused to denounce the Nazis as anti-Semitic.[135] In his opinion, German Jews did not act in any way like the Catholics, a religious minority that nonetheless identified with being German first.[136]

Equally shocking was Celal Nuri's dismissiveness toward local Turkish Jews. This was clear even in late 1912, when, after the First Balkan War, he complained:

> The Jewish people of the city [Istanbul] are without virtue. These Sephardic Jews are not as well developed as the Ashkenazi of Europe. They do not even know [our] language. Whatever [Turkish] they speak is with a harsh Spanish accent. For this reason, a Jew who wants to advance seeks to westernize. But even if they become a foreign subject, they do not have any sense of patriotism ... [And] they can make any sort of mischief, intrigue, immorality and crime ... Like the French or Italians of today, they will take a fez off their heads for five to ten silver coins (*kuruş*)."[137]

Here Celal Nuri reacted much more severely than most devoted Turkish nationalists. For instance, Hamdullah Suphi (Tanrıöver), an ardent supporter of Turkish assimilation, called for Jews to learn Turkish.[138] In a debate that Celal Nuri led in the Turkish Parliament in 1924 when drafting Article 88 on the definition of citizenship in the constitution of that year, his response to Hamdullah Suphi was that the true citizens were "Hanefi Muslims who spoke Turkish."[139] This implied that for him the only way for Jews to prove their "loyalty" was to convert to the ruling faith. Otherwise, it would seem, they could only hold Turkish passports as second-class citizens, or, even more bleakly, as "guests ... without a nationality."[140]

Celal Nuri paid no heed to the efforts of two Turkish Jews, Avram Galanti (1873–1961) and Moiz Cohen (Tekinalp), who helped spearhead the campaign for their community to speak Turkish. Whereas Avram Galanti pointed out the republic's critical need to provide modern education for local Jews, Moiz Cohen believed that his community should do everything it could to adopt Turkish as their native language, including adopting Turkish names, giving up separate schools, learning only Turkish, and socializing with other Turks to the point where they no longer would recognize themselves as a separate minority. Yet, to both of these authors, full cultural integration into the Republic of Turkey did not mean giving up their religion.[141]

To be fair, Celal Nuri never defined the Jews as a biological category like the Nazis did. He also never questioned the loyalty of Jewish converts to Islam, many of whom were devoted members of the Young Turks and the Turkish national movement. This included Ahmet Emin (Yalman), a fellow journalist with whom Celal Nuri was sent to Malta in exile in 1920 by the British, or Mehmet Cavit, the influential finance minister under Enver and Talât Pashas, who was executed by the Turkish revolutionary tribunals in 1925, after he had allegedly plotted to take Atatürk's life. Still, Celal Nuri's silence about Moiz Cohen's tireless efforts to assimilate Turkish Jews as well as his refusal to recognize him or his fellow Ottoman and Turkish Jewish compatriots directly when they took a stand against Zionism tells us once again how deeply ingrained his anti-Semitism truly was.

Conclusion

Yet, Celal Nuri's tendency to alienate Ottoman and Turkish Jews was obviously no anomaly. All of the minorities discussed in this chapter, with the exception of the Arabs before the First World War, were vilified by him as disloyal "elements." He readily acknowledged that the Arabs, the first Muslim people, still played a vital cultural role. The Arabic language and literature still remained central to Ottoman Turkish religious identity, despite the inroads the French and British had made in promoting Arab separatists in Lebanon and the Hashemite caliphate project in the Hijaz.

Celal Nuri saw the Yezidis as a "primitive" group of "devil worshipers" who were hostile not only to the Ottoman authorities, but to the civilized Muslim lifestyle that they offered them. In his eyes, the Yezidis' refusal to interact with their Muslim neighbors, and perform their patriotic duties, was indicative of a totally corrupt, backward community that stubbornly held onto their ignorant, sexually perverse, and tribal ways. These views, developed from his father's account and Western orientalists, had unabashedly chauvinistic overtones.

Nearly as bad in his eyes were the Persians, whose Shiism denied them the civilizational benefits of Sunni Islam, leaving them in a pathetic tribal state. It was especially unfortunate that Anatolian Kurds and Alevis were in danger of following the same mistaken path, he reckoned.

Celal Nuri viewed the Greeks, in contrast, as politically and economically developed. Nevertheless, he saw them as unrepentant rivals to the Ottomans and later the Turkish nation-state.[142] The substantial number of Greeks that remained in Ottoman and Turkish lands until 1923 continuously planned for their "liberation" from the "trap" in which they lived. On October 14, 1918, Celal Nuri complained about local Greeks being "politically intoxicated" after the British, French, and Greek Navy had steamed into port once the armistice had been signed.[143] Thus, he saw the local Greeks has bent on stabbing the Turks in the back, just as Patriarch Joachim III had done some six years previously right before the Ottomans were about to be expelled from the Balkans.[144]

The effect of his writings on nationalities was to whip up public sentiment against them. While many of the Greeks under Entente occupation certainly toyed with the idea of "reuniting" with mainland Greece or living in a permanently internationalized city—somewhat akin to Jerusalem under the Palestinian mandate—the situation in fall of 1912 was fundamentally different. Railing against the alleged betrayal of the Greek Patriarchate came at a time when the hundreds of thousands of Muslim refugees who were about to flood into Istanbul and Anatolia could potentially start an urban riot, much in the style of what was later seen in 1955, when many Istanbul Greeks were dispossessed because of the ethnic strife in nearby Cyprus.

Similarly, Celal Nuri's anti-Semitic demagogy, which began so suddenly after his dramatic break with the WZO-funded *Le Jeune Turc*, continued non-stop until 1932, just before the Nazi takeover in Germany that would lead to Adolf Hitler and the Holocaust. Celal Nuri's inflammatory words helped to bolster resentment against both Jewish refugees and local Jews. His rhetoric, and those of a small but vocal minority in the Turkish press who agreed with him, led in time to the passage of the expropriatory "wealth tax" (*Varlık Vergisi*). Ultimately around 1400 unpaying victims who did not pay the tax were dispatched to the infamous Erzurum Aşkale concentration camp in 1943.[145]

But the question of Celal Nuri's rhetoric toward the Armenians still deserves further explanation. Celal Nuri had a remarkably subdued tone when talking about this nationality, even when in the midst of a heated debate with Sharighian in 1913. With the exception of his brief July 1918 denunciation of the *Dashnaks*, he was silent throughout the war. As noted above, he would change his mind again at the beginning of the Allied occupation of Istanbul, suggesting a tribunal. He would go on to claim that the Armenians had suffered a year of "czarist ... despotism" under the CUP.[146]

This "reconciliatory" attitude deserves scrutiny. Articles addressed to the Armenians just after the Entente forces had arrived could be seen as a way to appease the Americans when they were considering establishing a mandate over Anatolia in the name of protecting that minority.

It also was very convenient for him to disavow any connection to the CUP and the entire controversy over the Armenian deportations and the mass death that ensued.

Celal Nuri may have avoided such controversy immediately after the war, as he was only exiled to Malta, and not assassinated or executed. But he ultimately did change his tune one more time about the Armenians. Celal Nuri engaged in a heated debate in July 1924, when it was discovered that a number of "wealthy" Armenians who had earlier fled to different countries by using foreign passports had been let back into Turkey by the authorities there. Celal Nuri used his newspaper to denounce this "corruption," once again stoking up xenophobic sentiments among a population that had just gone through thirteen years of conflict.[147]

Two members of parliament, including Kılıç Ali (1890–1971), well-known as being one of Mustafa Kemal's enforcers, went to the offices of Celal Nuri and beat him badly, leading to his silence for the next four years.[148] Pressure on local Armenians continued, and the expropriation of property from the Armenians who went abroad resumed, yet the rhetorical heat went down.[149]

Atatürk, known for his famous slogan "peace at home, peace in the world" (*yurtta sulh, cihanda sulh*), was also increasingly concerned during the following fourteen years about the rise of fascism, and the repercussions it could have on domestic security. Pressure on the non-Muslim minorities that remained in Turkey, such as the Armenians and Greeks of Istanbul, could get out of hand, leading to the emergence of radical voices that might urge ethnic cleansing, or worse. Celal Nuri's rhetoric in the late 1920s and early 1930s demonstrated this danger, although his anti-Semitic commentaries were much more based on religious and perceived ethnic differences than racial ones.

Atatürk and Afet İnan's Turkish History Thesis, implied that there was no need to assimilate or expel minorities in their country since all civilizations in Anatolia, including Armenians, Greeks, and Jews, were in fact ancient Turkish peoples. The Turkish History Thesis thus provided the government with a type of political tranquilizer that stabilized new generations of Turks through educational curriculum. This, and the authoritarian controls on the press, effectively prevented the emergence of xenophobia taking the center stage.[150] Celal Nuri and others like him were thereby kept in check.

Celal Nuri's statements on nationalities are thus a cautionary tale about scapegoating minorities for military defeat and political gain. He had unfortunately ignored the warning Nordau gave in his *The Conventional Lies of Our Civilization*, a book known to most of the Young Turks:

> The journalist alone, whose power is practically equal to that of the legislature and government, wields the authority of a prime minister and a representative, need not be nominated by anyone or voted for by anyone. He is the sole authority in the state confirmed by no one but himself. He makes himself what he is, and can exercise his power as he chooses, without being in the least responsible for any misuse of it nor for his gravest errors ... A journalist can injure, even destroy, the honor and property of a citizen; he can deprive him of personal liberty by making his residence in a certain place impossible; but he exercises this judicial authority without proof of any previous study being required, without being appointed by anyone under the sun, and without giving any guarantee of his impartiality and conscientious seeking after truth.[151]

Thus Celal Nuri, the first to talk about morals and society, had failed to live up to the standards of his own profession. Perhaps Sharighian's talk about his hypocrisy had a point after all.

4

Vulgar Materialism and Islam

Introduction

When it came to Islam, Celal Nuri (İleri) was a wholehearted believer in his one-time partner Abdullah Cevdet (Karlıdağ)'s maxim that "religion is the science of the masses ... [and] science the religion of the elite."[1] Indeed, he expounded at length with Abdullah Cevdet in their journal *İctihad* about the need to fundamentally re-conceptualize Islam so that it would be fully compatible with a vulgar materialistic worldview. Vulgar materialism conceived that everything was subject to natural law and scientific inquiry. This meant, in effect, a zero-tolerance policy toward not only traditions, but also dogma and any belief in a divine spiritual presence or otherworldliness. Vulgar materialists even rejected metaphysical philosophy from Plato to present.[2]

This was undoubtedly a daunting task in the Ottoman Empire, where the vast majority of the Muslim population placed their trust in the traditional Islamic authorities from the Ottoman sultan/caliph to the local imam. Most of these "traditionalists" would never be able to read *İctihad* or any other related progressive publication, as roughly 90 percent of the population was still illiterate and many of those who did read the journal opposed it in no uncertain terms.[3]

Celal Nuri, Abdullah Cevdet, and other like-minded CUP members therefore tailored their message to a much more narrow audience, the literary elite.[4] They hoped to win over enough of this audience to form an intellectual vanguard that would, over the course of time, gradually reformat the ruling faith in scientific terms.

This task began with popularizing and translating key Western works on the topic, such as the virtual vulgar materialist "bible," Ludwig Büchner's *Force and Matter*,[5] in addition to well-known Orientalist studies on Prophet Muhammad and the foundation of Islam, including Reinhard Dozy's *Het Islamism*,[6] Thomas Carlyle's *On Heroes, Hero Worship and the Heroic in History*,[7] and Ernest Renan's essay "Muhammad and the Origins of Islam."[8]

The Ottoman vulgar materialists appreciated the efforts of Büchner, Dozy, Carlyle, Renan, and others to demystify Islamic conceptions by questioning the validity of the authoritative texts: the Quran, the sayings of Prophet Muhammad (*hadis*), comments by Muhammad's companions, and subsequent hagiographic literature.

Celal Nuri cited Renan, for instance, who pointed out that Bukhari, the compiler of the most definitive collection of sayings by Prophet Muhammad (7225 in all), had greatly reduced his collection from its original number. Renan remarked that "European criticism could assuredly proceed to an even more strict selection."[9] Celal Nuri then claimed that Bukhari did not examine the historical context of Prophet Muhammad's sayings, but merely verified the time and place of the person who claimed it.[10]

But to Celal Nuri, the greatest failings of Islamic authorities since the death of Caliph Umar had been to obfuscate or ignore Prophet Muhammad's contribution to statesmanship, religious reform, and the study of the physical and natural world.[11] The Islamic authorities instead allegedly misled themselves and others by engaging in such superstitions as seeking mystical union with God, practicing magic, or erroneously explaining the world in terms of corrupted dogmatic truths. These same authorities also denounced dissenting "voices of reason" whether it be Avveroes (Ibn Rushd) because of his belief that a person's soul dies with the body or contemporary vulgar materialists like himself and Abdullah Cevdet.[12]

This opened the way to Celal Nuri's own lengthy arguments about how his reinvigorated vulgar materialistic version of Islam led to a basic reframing of the evolutionary civilizational and political importance of Prophet Muhammad to contemporary Muslims and the world.[13]

Many of his readers profoundly disagreed. Ahmet Hilmi Şehbenderzade (1865–1914), a popular Young Turk author and Sufi mystic, actively denounced Celal Nuri's writings, seeing the vulgar materialists and Orientalists as active dangers to the faith. Celal Nuri often rebutted Şehbenderzade in his own writing. Postscripts to Celal Nuri's major works on the topic also complained that others went so far as to call him contemptible, a nonbeliever or an atheist.[14] Şehbenderzade had a similar commitment to preserving core Islamic beliefs and legal concepts as Ahmed Cevdet Pasha (1823–95), one of the most famous Ottoman statesmen and scholars of the late *Tanzimat* era and the person most responsible for compiling the Ottoman Civil Code (*Mecelle*) from 1868 to 1876.[15]

Yet, as this chapter will show, Celal Nuri and the Ottoman vulgar materialists did in the end gain the critical mass of elite support for which they were working.

Mustafa Kemal (Atatürk), then a member of the CUP, and an avid reader of vulgar materialist literature, seemingly endorsed Celal Nuri's efforts. He also clearly benefited during the Turkish Independence War from Celal Nuri extolling his country's leaders as warriors of the faith and worthy successors of Prophet Muhammad's struggle against the infidels. This can be seen not only in Atatürk's personal readings and statements, but also from his own revolutionary secularization program after Turkish independence, which brought religious authorities under state control and trained its entire bureaucracy—imams included—according to social scientific precepts. Nevertheless, Atatürk and his followers went further than Celal Nuri and the Ottoman vulgar materialists in their willingness to publicly abandon the few remaining symbols of Islamic nationhood in pursuit of a secular state after consolidating power in the wake of the Sheikh Said rebellion.

Popularizing Vulgar Materialism

Advocating what came to be known as vulgar materialism, Büchner argued that all philosophical and religious musings postulating a spirit independent from the material world were bogus and should be rejected out of hand. In his mind, matter was eternal. While it may have transformed, or evolved, over time, there simply was no proof that matter as such was created or destroyed by an independent force. Force was indeed bounded by matter and preordained to play an interactive role with it.[16] Therefore, people needed to embrace scientific research, which was continuously exploring what had hitherto been unknown in the natural world. As a result, disciplines once seen as philosophical or humanistic, such as logic, psychology, economics, sociology, political science, linguistics, philology, and even history, became measurable, quantifiable, and empirical social sciences. Technological and social advances were indications of such progress. Participation in this inevitable trend was a civic duty.[17]

Celal Nuri enthusiastically embraced most of Büchner's reasoning. He agreed fully with Büchner that philosophy was dying as a discipline, as exemplified by the likes of Arthur Schopenhauer or Nietzsche, whose ideas, he contended, were the nonsensical ravings of a decadent society.

But Celal Nuri qualified Büchner when he condemned religion. He asserted that Büchner only condemned Christianity and Judaism, since Islam accepted verified empirical knowledge without hesitation as true: "Islam, the religion delivered by Prophet Muhammad, does not include anything outside of material, demonstrated reality."[18] Islam thus accepted that while science must be given free rein in its rigorous pursuit of knowledge, religion was restricted to that which was still inconceivable and it spoke to its believers in "symbolic shapes" in order to promote social solidarity and scientific progress.[19]

Celal Nuri, however, had no tolerance for those Muslims who did not accept his version. "Spiritualist Sufis" who believed in mystical union with God, or traditional Muslims who viewed God as the actual creator or destroyer of matter, were reactionaries who hindered the faith. They, like the Islamic legalists of prior generations, prevented their civilization from continuously revitalizing itself with the most relevant scientific literature, regardless of whether it was foreign or not. According to Celal Nuri, one should unhesitatingly use people like Büchner and other vulgar materialist writers to revitalize the faith.[20] This recalled Muhammad's saying "to take knowledge even if it comes from China."[21]

Şehbenderzade, a professor of philosophy at Istanbul University (*Darülfünun*) and a "spiritualist Sufi guru," was highly critical of Celal Nuri.[22] Şehbenderzade indeed saw the various philosophical schools that had risen since the Renaissance as providing a diverse source of knowledge to the world. To dismiss them as Celal Nuri and Büchner had done was to ignore the many contributions that philosophers from Plato to Kant, Hegel, and beyond had made. Merely boiling down "metaphysical nonsense" to a series of quotes from Nietzsche was also a gross distortion.[23]

Beyond that, Şehbenderzade saw "vulgar materialism" as constituting a grave threat to Islam. On the one hand, Büchner's idea of rejecting revealed religion out of hand for its belief in divine creation and the world beyond led his readers to atheism. On the other hand, if Islam should rid itself of all spiritualist and mystical elements, as Celal Nuri advocated, it would essentially hollow out its core beliefs on the nature of God, creation, and the teachings of the holy Quran and other Scripture, all in the name of a new scientific cult.[24]

The results were catastrophic to Şehbenderzade. New generations of Ottoman intellectuals, trained in the top military, medical, and administrative schools in the country, were likely to absorb Büchner's vulgar materialism. This would prime them to either adopt westernizing liberalism, or embrace the more radical secular ideologies of anarchism or socialism. But if the Ottoman government actually started teaching Islam the way Celal Nuri wanted it, the masses would gravitate toward reaction, causing a great rift in society. Şehbenderzade counselled elites to turn away from vulgar materialism and search for their own spiritual identity.[25]

This tension is reflected in *Awakened Dreams* (1910), the famous novel where Şehbenderzade told the story of Raji, a privileged, educated young man, who, disillusioned with the philosophy, science, and religion he was taught, turns to the Islamic mystic Mirror Dede for guidance. Trained by Mirror Dede over time as a follower (*mürid*), Raji achieves spiritual gratification through mystic union with the divine (*vahdet-i vücud*) and then himself succeeds Miror Dede as a Sufi master. This book, therefore, justified a turn away from worldly affairs to a more traditional, nonmaterial-focused life that revolved more around personal spiritual relationships, individual autonomy, and self-fulfillment.[26]

Celal Nuri reacted by writing *Perviz*, a novel which again focused on a young man who is tempted by romance, the good life, as well as philosophical and spiritual self-absorption. The protagonist, also named Perviz, chose to look after the welfare of his people rather than to give in to these desires. And while he respected Muslim social customs and sensibilities, he believed in promoting science and modern medicine. Ambitious, he eventually became the head of government, but faced increasing opposition from differing political movements. United only in hatred of Perviz, these opponents eventually toppled him from power and dragged his body through the street. The novel generally highlights the need for young members of the Ottoman elite to not only adopt a vulgar materialistic worldview in order to better their own society, but also be willing to sacrifice themselves in the fight against the ignorant.[27]

In an odd way, Şehbenderzade and Celal Nuri's contrasting views are vaguely reminiscent of Ivan Turgenev's *Fathers and Sons* (1862), a story that highlighted the conflicts between two generations.[28] Şehbenderzade indeed seemed to embody the liberal spirit of the fathers, believing that one could read books about the West and reflect on the challenges it posed without giving up core elements of one's faith, national identity, and individual need. Celal Nuri instead appeared more like the "sons," the radical intelligentsia who sought an absolute break from tradition, a generation that would eventually form political movements stressing sacrifice to the community above all.

In a Turkish context, many today would clearly sympathize with the "fathers," people who, like Şehbenderzade, or even the original "Young Ottoman" reformers, believe that a modern Muslim nation can build upon and refine their religious identity without changing it beyond recognition. It is not mere coincidence that nearly all of Şehbenderzade's work has been carefully translated and published in modern Turkish within the past fifty years, a time when politics have shifted gradually away from secular standards.[29]

Yet, the trends were opposite when Celal Nuri wrote. The CUP government had become embittered with its liberal opposition ever since it came to power, and by 1913 ended any possibility of regime change through the ballot box. Worried about a repeat of the April 13, 1909 uprising, the political elite sought ways to suppress mass uprisings. Celal Nuri's formula for a scientifically conscious Islam appealed to this limited, but highly influential audience of policymakers as a way to gradually indoctrinate the masses.

Islam and the Evolution of Faith

Deeply influenced by Social Darwinistic ideas, Celal Nuri envisioned the history of religions, and the men who founded them, as following an evolutionary chain. Beginning with the non-monotheistic faiths and culminating in Islam, he saw a continuous line of progress that led him to conclude that his own faith was the most modern one. Islam had achieved its supremacy by offering the most coherent message—one that unified superior spiritual and moral values with the material world. Thus, Islam was the one faith most fit to survive.

Buddhism, in Celal Nuri's opinion the "most primitive of faiths," was founded by Buddha Sakyamoni in India eight centuries before Christ. Buddha, he explained, actually believed in three gods: Brahma the creator, Visno the protector, and Siva the destroyer. To Buddha, people were continuously seduced by the material world and their feelings for it. The solution, in Buddha's eyes, was to "seek their own annihilation," divorce themselves from this world, and gain spiritual serenity in Nirvana. Going through such a mystical process could gain them a higher form of being in the next life, when they would be reincarnated. Buddha utterly rejected earthly affairs and "would have been pleased if Haley's Comet destroyed the world." This goes to prove that Buddha would have never supported speculative philosophy in the twentieth century. Thus, Buddhism was flawed in terms of not only its misrepresentation, but also its fatalistic disengagement with the world. Nevertheless, he saw Buddhism in China and Japan as gradually abandoning their fatalism. This revealed the humble beginnings of religious evolution.[30]

Confucianism, founded by Hong Fu Tsu approximately 550 years before Christ, instead emphasized maintaining proper social ethics, such as focusing on the good of society and the family through hard work, respecting elders, and, above all, protecting the past. It was a communitarian faith that sought engagement with the world; yet, it did not have the ideal of progress. Confucianism also did not completely dominate its Chinese homeland, where it faced rivals in Taoism and Buddhism.[31]

In Persia the religion known as Mazdaism, Magism, or Zarathustra was rumored by the ancient Greeks to have arisen 5000 years before the siege of Troy, Celal Nuri related. This faith had a holy book, and it spoke of a universal struggle between Hurmuz, the God of goodness and light and Ehrimen, or Satan. Although Mazdaism more closely resembled monotheistic faiths, it still stressed spiritual purity and escape from material life, much like Buddhism did. Therefore, the followers of Zarathustra did not engage in the world, and, as such, were doomed to irrelevance.[32]

Next in the evolutionary chain were of course Judaism and Christianity, the first two great monotheistic religions. Moses's flight from Egypt to Canaan through the Sinai presaged Muhammad's Hijra, and in this act he elevated his people from their miserable status beforehand as slaves of the pharaoh. Yet, Moses, unlike Muhammad, had a much more difficult time in ridding his people of idol worship, as witnessed by his brother Aaron's casting of the Golden Calf. The idol worship continued even after ancient Israel was founded, leading to corruption and decay. This decay was reflected among the Jewish people as well. They had started out as a religious community (*ümmet*), but ultimately lost their faith. What remained after their exile, their punishment by God, was only a sense of tribal nationhood.[33]

Jesus, the next prophet, was, in Celal Nuri's eyes, "a perfect dervish."[34] Condemnatory of the corruption he saw around him in Israel, he instructed his followers to search within themselves for a new faith. But he failed to connect to his people, preaching passive resistance instead of leading his followers to freedom. In the end he was offhandedly executed by the Roman authorities. He was just one of the many heterodox persecuted by the Jewish authorities at the time. Celal Nuri cited a novel by Anatole France, where Pontius Pilate was asked if he remembered Jesus of Nazareth. He answered "which one?"[35]

Christianity, despite its flaws, was only truly completed by the likes of Apostle Paul and, later, Martin Luther. Apostle Paul would, after his conversion, do his best to resolve the contradictions within the Christian faith and build up the primitive church. His efforts to spread Christianity throughout the Roman Empire led to his martyrdom, but the process he unleashed could not be stopped. Yet, the corrupted empire would merely be replaced by the Papacy, another form of cultural decadence.

Luther's nailing of the ninety-nine theses on Wittenberg Castle signified not only the break of the Protestants from Roman Catholicism, but also the birth pangs of national culture. Luther's break with the Papacy heralded the beginning of the end for medieval aristocratic and monarchical order, since it relied heavily on divine right.

Celal Nuri further applauded Carlyle's argument that Luther was in fact repeating Prophet Muhammad's rampage against idol worship and tyranny:

> I find Luther to have been a breaker of idols, no less than any other prophets. The wooden gods of the Quraysh, made of timber and beeswax, were not more hateful to Muhammad than Tetzel's pardons of sin, made of sheepskin and ink, were to Luther. It is the property of every hero, and every time, in every place and situation that he come back to reality; that he stand upon things and not shows of things.[36]

Denouncing corrupt authorities and rebelling against despotism thus helped quenched a popular thirst for social and political justice.[37]

Yet, Islam, unlike Christianity, united the role of missionary and champion of the faith with that of the Prophet. Islam also had a coherent message of one God, who, as divine, was absolutely different from the men he created. There was no anthropomorphizing, or idol worship allowed, as seen in the Virgin Mary and the Papacy of Catholic Christianity, or with the ancient Israeli Golden Calf. Nor was it overly focused on its spiritual aspects, such as Buddhism or Zarathrustra.

In contrast to almost all of the other faiths, with the exception of Protestant Christianity, Islam was progressive in nature. Islam, the final religion, had freedom of interpretation as its foundational principle.[38] Accordingly: "Islam means civilization and progress, and never started with its final word, with nothing else to do."[39] Muhammad thus fully intended that scientists and thinkers, like politicians, have realistic and forward-thinking approaches. But Muhammad, unlike Luther and Calvin, did not want dogma to hold back such advances, according to Celal Nuri.[40]

The Protestants, however, had lost their spiritual compass and, in time, became completely focused on material pleasure and the exploitation of others. Islam alone, with its message of protecting human welfare, and maintaining communal solidarity, was the most balanced faith and therefore the most suitable for human society.[41]

Muhammad as a Rational Actor

Much of the Orientalist literature cited by Celal Nuri depicted Prophet Muhammad as a sincere, practical person. Renan, for example, posited:

> Muhammad did not want to be a miracle worker, he only wanted to be a prophet and one without miracles. He unceasingly repeats that he is a man like

any other, mortal like any other, subject to sin, and having need of God's mercy like any other.[42]

Carlyle likewise proclaimed that Muhammad "from an early age ... had been remarked as a thoughtful man. His companions named him "Al-Amin, The Faithful." A man of truth and fidelity; true in what he did, in what he spake and thought."[43]

His greatness, in their eyes, was in part due to his sincere humility in teaching that "Islam means in its way the denial of self, the annihilation of self."[44] He would openly appeal to his fellow Muslims to seek an apology from him if he had done wrong, as famously seen when he paid back a man who had publicly proclaimed that he owed him three dinars:

> "The Prophet said better to suffer shame in this world than in the one to come." And he paid him back instantly. This extreme moderation, this good taste, totally exquisite, with which Muhammad understood his role as Prophet, was imposed upon him by the genius of his nation.[45]

The key phrase here was not a man of faith, or a prophet of God, but the "genius of his nation." Carlyle noted Muhammad's command to his followers:

> "Your salutation shall be Peace." Salam, Have Peace!—The thing that all rational souls long for, and seek, vainly here below, as the one blessing. "Ye shall sit on your seats, facing one another: all grudges shall be taken away out of your hearts."[46]

This signified the Prophet's stress on the need for all believers to unite as one. Such unity no doubt was strengthened by the injunction to give alms to the poor and to be willing to sacrifice themselves for the sake of the Islamic community.

But one should never forget the Muslim call to faith, which proclaimed that not only Muhammad was the Prophet, but "there was no god but Allah." Carlyle commented:

> Out of all that rubbish of Arab idolatries, argumentative theologies, traditions, subtleties, rumors and hypotheses of Greeks and Jews, with their idle wiredrawings, this wild man of the desert, with his wild sincere heart, earnest as death and life, with his great flashing natural eyesight, had seen into the kernel of the matter. Idolatry is nothing: these wooden idols of yours, 'ye rub them with oil and wax, and the flies stick on them,'—These are wood I tell you! They can do nothing for you; they are an impotent blasphemous pretence; a horror an abomination, if ye knew them. God alone is; God alone has the power; he made us, he can kill us and keep us alive: Allahu Akbar, God is great.[47]

This call to rid people of idol worship had an unmistakable element of social justice. The Meccan establishment, those who stood to gain most from the annual pilgrimage to the Kabba, a rock originally carved into numerous idols, profited directly from the polytheistic beliefs of the Bedouins and the surrounding Arab communities. By uniting the Bedouins and local Arabs, as well as seizing Mecca and cleansing it of idols, a great historical transformation had occurred:

> To the Arab Nation it was as a birth from darkness into light; Arabia first became alive by means of it. A poor shepherd people, roaming unnoticed in its desert since the creation of the world: a Hero-Prophet was sent down to them with a word they could believe.[48]

From Prophet Muhammad's flight from Mecca to the conquest of all Arabia, he and his people resolved themselves to fight in the face of corruption, idolatry, and armed opposition. According to Carlyle, Muslims would not have "the sublime forgiveness of Christianity, turning of the other cheek when one has been smitten." Rather, the Muslims were to avenge themselves, "but it was to be in measure, not overmuch, or beyond justice."[49] Renan similarly concluded that Islam, rather than being a religion that preached love and suffering, was instead "a natural religion, serious, liberal, in short, a religion of men."[50]

Nevertheless, these descriptions failed to point out Muhammad's successes as ruler, lawgiver, and conqueror. That role would most often instead be given to Caliph Umar, the second of his successors and the conqueror of Egypt and the Persian Empire. Renan would go so far as to see Umar as:

> the sword which cuts and decides. The indecisive character of Muhammad would undoubtedly have jeopardized his mission, without the addition of this impetuous disciple, always ready to draw his sword against all those who did not immediately acknowledge the religion he had persecuted at first.[51]

Celal Nuri instead took his cue from Aloys Sprenger who contended that it was Prophet Muhammad "who awakened a sense of patriotism"[52] and not Caliph Umar.

Prophet Muhammad's political role was clear:

> In Islam the word "prophet" does not only mean someone who speaks in the name of religion. He is the head of state, a politician who defends his nation and is commander in chief ... Belief is not separated from politics. Alongside giving scripture, leading prayer and fasting, he was a decisive politician, a true diplomat and an unforgettable president.[53]

Celal Nuri pointed to the Treaty of Hudaybiyyah (628), when the Quraysh surrendered Mecca to Muhammad, and the Prophet became ruler of all of Arabia. He sent out delegates and drafted diplomatic correspondence with the Byzantine emperor, the Persian shah, the king of Ethiopia, the governor of Egypt, and others. Then, as in his earlier correspondence with notable Arab opponents, he made it apparent that he knew what would happen centuries henceforth. He would encourage fellow Muslims during times of tribulation, such as when the Sassanid shah sought to have the Prophet brought to his presence in chains. "'The Byzantine throne and crown of Persia will be yours,' Muhammad proclaimed. It happened."

This demonstrated that Muhammad:

> This great man was the master of judging the flow of history. He told the Muslim community victory that they need not to depart from the true path in order to achieve success one they had achieved victory.[54]

Yet for Celal Nuri, it was incumbent on the present-day Muslim community to contemplate the relevance of Muhammad's political mission. In his eyes, one should take into account Hippolyte Taine's hypothesis that you had to understand a historical people's epoch, their environment and race. Comprehending a historical epoch, or spirit of the time, meant in effect to look at the origin and development of a great civilization, namely that of Islam and placing it within world history. To Celal Nuri, Muhammad, as God's final Prophet, was ushering in Muslims to succeed the Jewish and Christian peoples as the standard-bearer of the great monotheistic religions. His readers, however, should be aware that this historical spirit, embodied in Prophet Muhammad, was still playing itself out.

In Celal Nuri's opinion, understanding the environment and the Arab people helped to clarify the political and social significance of Muhammad to a greater degree. The Arabs before Muhammad, Celal Nuri argued, were in a pitiful state. Thinking only in terms of tribal warfare and primitive idol worship, they often treated their wives horribly, letting their daughters die of exposure and aimlessly seeking their fortune as Bedouin mercenaries.[55] Agreeing with the likes of Carlyle, Renan, and Spengler, Celal Nuri saw the Arabs' transformation into the Muslim community, and the consequent overcoming of tribal superstition, backwardness, and social abuse as a great advance.

But he claimed that the Arabs soon lost their new religious spirit. Here he referenced Dozy who maintained that the Arabs as a whole never became perfect Muslims. For the Umayyad dynasty, the chauvinistic Arab nationalists that succeeded Muhammad and the four Righteous Caliphs soon became worldly and corrupt.

In Celal Nuri's view, the Abbasids, the next Muslim dynasty after the Umayyads, relied instead on Turkish soldiers and statesmen to help continue Islamic civilization for the next 500 years. He related that it was the Turks, not the Arabs, who understood the true religion that Prophet Muhammad brought. According to Celal Nuri, Jewish and Christian scholars have always subjected the Turks to abuse for this reason.[56] Voltaire, the author of a satirical play on Muhammad, wrote to the Prussian king in 1742 that if Muhammad was a modern-day Turk, he would continue to perpetrate injustices and tyranny, just as the historical Muhammad had done among the Arab tribesmen when he launched his violent and irrational faith.[57]

The next great Islamic leader in the historical past was Mehmet II, the fifteenth-century Ottoman sultan best known for his conquest of Constantinople in 1453. Yet he failed to consolidate his empire by peopling the city with Muslim artisans and merchants. Instead, the Greeks of Istanbul seduced Mehmet II and his followers with their riches and charms. Mehmet II let the non-Muslims in his empire dominate trade and industry. The issue here was that conquest alone would not make you a true hero.

Celal Nuri intimated what his country and Islamic civilization as a whole urgently needed was a new conquering hero to continue the "marching orders" of Prophet Muhammad. Celal Nuri's whole political platform of moral regeneration, cultural renewal, resistance to foreign control, and strengthening the Muslim "bourgeoisie" at the expense of the non-Muslims needed to go hand in hand. In his opinion, the one person who could tap into the moral strength of the people to unite and protect the Islamic community under the banner of Ottoman Turkish Islam was none other than Enver Pasha, fellow Unionist, the minister of defense, and undoubtedly the most powerful figure in the Ottoman government at the time.[58] His bold military exploits included helping lead the initial July 1908 rebellion against the tyrannical Sultan Abdülhamid II, commanding the Muslim guerrilla resistance against the Italians after they invaded Libya in 1911, and retaking Edirne from the Bulgarians in June 1913. After cementing his hold on power through a military coup in January 1913, Enver was set to lead his country into the First World War with pretensions no less than establishing hegemony over Islamic lands that stretched from Morocco to Central Asia.

Celal Nuri intimated that Enver should use Islam's rhetoric in order to achieve his goals and not push for a secular revolution. Celal Nuri directly cited Le Bon:

> One can often only understand the true meaning of a people's collective beliefs during a time of crisis. For the realities that shape a people's fate are often highlighted in war. [Those that live believe] in the hard unforgiving Yahova of the Torah in contrast to [those who perish praying to] the lovely tolerant Christian God of St. Teresa.[59]

The message here was to keep the faith in the austere, visionary teachings of Prophet Muhammad. For Celal Nuri the martial, political nature of Islam made it an invaluable asset in helping the Ottomans achieve mass mobilization. If Enver did not recognize this, he could possibly witness the end of the Turkish Islamic civilizational mission. As Le Bon stated:

> History shows us that peoples do not long survive the disappearance of their gods. The civilizations that are born with them also die with them. There is nothing so destructive as the dust of dead gods.[60]

Machiavelli similarly argued also that a princely ruler, or enlightened despot, who acted on behalf of a progressive, humanistic cultural elite could transform his government to a republic. The Prince, Machiavelli wrote, must master circumstance with martial *virtù*, while at the same time maintaining his spiritual tie to the people. Princes were the "armed prophets," the realistic leaders, who would take whatever actions were necessary to save their people. Those who sought only the otherworldly path, turning the other cheek when facing persecution, were doomed: "All unarmed prophets have been destroyed."[61]

Such words seem to vindicate Celal Nuri's depiction of Muhammad, the last great man of action against what he may well have seen as the corrupted cult of the Virgin Mary, a female idol who inspired her worshipers to resign themselves to fate. Here at last, he could use Machiavelli's analogies, like that of Le Bon, as a polemic weapon to retaliate against Orientalists who almost unceasingly accused Muhammad, and the Muslim community at large, of embracing fatalism.

Some of Celal Nuri's harshest critics seemed receptive to his methods and to certain arguments he made about Muhammad's political genius and martial prowess. Şehbenderzade also shared Celal Nuri's conviction that the Arab people had outgrown their limited historical potential and that it was now up to the Turks to carry on the task:

> Islam means Prophet Muhammad ... If he did not come, the Arabs would have no historical meaning. They would have remained stagnant and would never have been able to progress from a Bedouin life to a progressive society.[62]

At a later point he would chime in that:

history does not deny the Turks great service to the Islamic religion. Sunni Muslim historians have written that the Islamic world only survived Christian attack because the Turks accepted that religion.[63]

In other words, Turkish nationhood, while complementary of Islam, had a historical trajectory that predated that religion.

Celal Nuri's arguments also appealed to Mustafa Kemal. Indeed Atatürk had two copies of *The Last Prophet*, one of which was personally autographed by the author.[64] Atatürk would also be an avid reader of Carlyle, Dozy, and Le Bon and even highlight many of the passages Şehbenderzade wrote about Arabs and Turks.[65]

Atatürk, like Enver, seemingly lived up to Celal Nuri's model of a decisive general and politician who would frame his people's struggle in religious terms during the Turkish Independence War. Was he not known as the *Gazi*, the Islamic hero who would fight off the Christian invaders? Only after the war did he shed this appearance in the belief he could create a new secular Turkish culture that would break decisively from its Islamic past.

Conclusion

Nonetheless, Atatürk's attitudes toward Islam seem to have largely paralleled Celal Nuri's own designs. As we have seen, Atatürk was deeply immersed in the same literature as Celal Nuri and fellow members of the CUP, and he appears to have been deeply affected by them.

Renan, Dozy, and Carlyle's historical approach toward Muhammad no doubt inspired Celal Nuri to look not only at the Prophet, but also at Islamic scriptures—the Quran, Muhammad's sayings, and the writings of his companions and later religious authorities—in a critical light. Both Celal Nuri and Atatürk, following these Western scholars, rejected the doctrinal authority of Islamic scriptural sources and traditional accounts to the extent that they now only approached religion in terms of its political unity. This could be seen in both Celal Nuri's talk of Muhammad as a political leader and Mustafa Kemal's use of Islamic rhetoric to justify the Turkish nationalists during the Independence War. By taking the title *Gazi*, or "champion of Islam," Mustafa Kemal seemed to adopt exactly the role that Celal Nuri had preached just before the First World War had broken out.

Likewise, Mustafa Kemal seemed poised to gradually secularize his country. By abolishing the caliphate, held by a member of the now defunct Ottoman dynasty if not the sultan himself, the entire Islamic ecclesiastical apparatus was now directly under his control. Hanioğlu has argued that this action, along with the translation of the Quran into modern Turkish and the break with Islamic law, made Mustafa Kemal a reluctant type of "Luther," despite his own personal denial.[66]

There was no doubt that Mustafa Kemal, and the bulk of his followers among the republican political elite, hoped to eventually fully secularize the new state, and that the trappings of Islam, necessary during wartime to maintain cohesion, would eventually wither away as the masses slowly became incorporated into the new society. While mosques continued to function, the Sufi orders and Islamic headgear were abolished, as they were seen as spreading superstition. Ridding Arabic from the scriptures and even the call to prayer would also lead to the formation of a Turkish national "church." They imagined that a new more modernist, worldly ethic could take shape on the popular level.

Certainly, the Turkish republican elite fully imbibed the vulgar materialism of Celal Nuri and Atatürk's generation. This is apparent even in the Turkish Language, History, and Geography Faculty that Atatürk founded, where his saying was inscribed: "The most true spiritual guide is scientific knowledge" (*En hakiki mürşit ilimdir*), an endorsement that science, not spiritualism, was the only path that students should follow.

But the question of the pace of secularization remained deeply at issue. The abolition of the caliphate in 1924, the promulgation of the Swiss Civil Code instead of the *Mecelle* and Islamic family courts in 1926, the violent suppression of rebellions in Anatolia toward the secularization measures, and the elimination by 1928 of the clauses Celal Nuri had endorsed in the 1924 Constitution that the state was an officially Muslim nation and the parliament "executes the Holy Law" all may have created an impossible breach between the secular elite and the masses. Şehbenderzade's warning about this exact problem in 1914 was unheeded.

Rather than following Celal Nuri's instruction to retain the symbols of Islam, Atatürk, willing or not, planted the hope among many Kemalist hardliners that his own personality cult would lead to the creation of a "Turkish Lenin." The popular desire to resist such a new state religion would lead in the century ahead to continuing political resistance. This new popular Muslim push for political power, shying away from any vulgar materialistic model for development, seemed basically oblivious to Celal Nuri's message. Şehbenderzade, had he lived to see it, might have been gratified that his argument would eventually win the day.

5

Women, Family, and Society

Introduction

Leading historians have generally judged Celal Nuri (İleri)'s writings on women's issues—which pushed for the end of polygamy, veiling, and greater access to more equitable divorce, education, and employment—as that of a "westernizer" convinced that "the superiority of the West did not reside simply in its advanced technology but also in its rationalistic and positivistic outlook, which was free of the shackles of religious obscurantism and stifling superstitions."[1] His primary work on the topic *Our Women* (1912–13)[2] was an example of how "the Westernist outlook drew parallels between the rights of women and social progress."[3] These historians have not seen Celal Nuri as an Islamist on these issues, since he refused traditional prescriptions for polygamy and other women and family issues within the context of Islamic law.[4] Nor have they categorized Celal Nuri as a "Turkist" because he did not ascribe to Ziya Gökalp's contextualization of womanhood within a romantic return to "primordial Central Asian shamanistic values" that granted women and men a "separate but equal" place within the family, tribe, and nation.[5]

The problem is a familiar one: these scholars have accepted Niyazi Berkes's paradigm of dividing the Unionists into three distinct ideological camps, namely the Westernists, Islamists, and Turkists, when, in actuality, the debate on westernization cut across the ideological divide.[6] Celal Nuri, in equal part a modernist and a Muslim nationalist, was a prime example of this trend.

Celal Nuri, in contrast to the Turkists, had long contended that since Turks were bound to identify with Islam as central to their national spirit, women's rights activists should seek to change the nature of the religion itself. He thus sought to reform Islamic customs, ideas, and tenants of faith rather than imposing some sort of alternative revolutionary secular nationalism.[7] Thus Celal Nuri would argue that Prophet Muhammad and the Quran acknowledged Western scientific principles as the primary guide for social relations.[8]

Celal Nuri and other widely read publicists among Unionist circles, such as Ziya Gökalp,[9] Cenab Şahabettin, Salahaddin Asım, Baha Tevfik, and Halil Hamid,[10] would come to a common consensus that feminism strengthened the nation by seeking greater freedoms and rights for women. But women must not ignore the needs of the country. Indeed, women played a vital role during military conflicts as well as afterward when rebuilding Turkish society. Thus Turkish women could not remain passive in the face of wars that would culminate in the Ottoman surrender to the British and French in October 1918, resulting in the military occupation of Istanbul by those foreign powers, and the independence struggle that followed thereafter.

Patriotic consensus aside, there was serious debate among these Unionist "feminists." Celal Nuri focused on women's place within the family as emblematic of society as a whole.[11] According to his evolutionary line of thought, Ottoman Turkey's traditional family structure—primitive, patriarchal, and repressive—was slowly transforming into a more progressive, European-style one.[12] Key to this process, as mentioned before, was the reformation of his people's Islamic value system, under the gentle tutelage of the state and press culture. He drew primarily upon popular materialist and positivist writers, such as Ludwig Büchner, Charles Letourneau, and Max Nordau.[13] He also borrowed heavily from Qasim Amin, an Egyptian Islamic modernist who sparked considerable debate in 1898 and 1900 when he published two tracts that advocated liberal reform.[14]

Ziya Gökalp, his primary rival, looked at the women's question through the prism of Turkish nationalism.[15] While he agreed with Celal Nuri and most interested Turkish intellectuals of the time that the state of women was indicative of the country as a whole, he saw the Ottoman past in largely negative terms. This included even the recent past, given the widespread practice of polygamy and the seclusion of women that prevented them from becoming involved in the nationalist movement. His solution was to go back to the ancient Turkish traditions of Central Asia, where gender inequality was practiced in politics and in social life. He also posited that the nationalist elite could only accomplish this through top-down reforms, particularly by adopting changes to Ottoman family law and by inculcating values that promoted gender equality in the schools and the press.[16]

In contrast to Celal Nuri, Ziya Gökalp was close to the government—or at least to Interior Minister Talât Pasha—but did not substantially influence the Family Decree of 1917. He did submit a report to the commission in charge of the decree chaired by Muslim seminary- (*medrese-*) trained Mahmut Esat

Efendi and dominated by officials friendly to the office of the ministry of Islamic affairs (*Şeyhülislamlık*). Gökalp's recommendations were mostly tabled, and controversially, the parliament—much more amenable to reformist opinion—had no say in the matter. According to this decree, polygamy was restricted but not eliminated, all marriages were to be recorded by civil magistrate and the bride-to-be had to be at least seventeen years old, and a wife's right to divorce only slightly widened.[17] Celal Nuri and Gökalp's modest effect on this decree was reflected in their justification of their prescriptions with traditional Islamic principles. Thus, they both appealed to Islamic legal scholars (*ülema*) on the commission on the family law decree—like Mahmut Esat Efendi—whose authority they ideally did not want to recognize.

This chapter will compare Celal Nuri and Gökalp's visions regarding women's issues in work. After examining Celal Nuri's broad historical vision of the evolution of women's rights in the West, Islam, and the Ottoman Empire, the focus will turn to his idealization of the women Kazan Tatar Turks of Eurasia as a model of emulation for the Unionists' own social reform program. While Celal Nuri credited the successful parenting skills, education and modern outlook as a result of the Kazan Tatar Turkish women's adherence to scientific-based Islamic values, his choice of this Turkic minority was one that was bound to appeal to the likes of Gökalp and the Turkists at least to some degree. Thereafter the chapter will compare and contrast Gökalp's views on women and the family with those of Celal Nuri, showing the remarkable degree to which Celal Nuri and Gökalp justified their reforms on these issues in Islamic terms.

Celal Nuri on the Evolution of Women

Inspired by Charles Letourneau's sweeping anthropological study of the history and development of the family, Celal Nuri began his analysis of women's place in his own society with a panoramic view that spanned from the prehistoric era to the present and beyond. Borrowing from Letourneau and the Social Darwinists, he sought to study the mechanism by which a species, and later, a race or ethnicity was able to propagate and thrive. Thus, he saw humanity, races, and nations as adopting sexual mores and family structures that best fit their environment for the time being. Citing Le Bon and Letourneau, he pointed to examples of "primitive societies" as far as Polynesia, Africa, and South America. But most attention was given to the Middle East and Eurasia, particularly in India, China, Persia, and Egypt. Here, the development of agricultural societies led to large patriarchal harems, where women were kept in near-total seclusion, traded like cattle, and almost completely deprived of their humanity.[18]

Such oppression of women occurred, in large part, because of the corrupt nature of predatory empires, which after conquest and consolidation lacked the moral character and religious spirit to rule their subjects. As seen in the previous chapter, Celal Nuri saw the gods of ancient Egypt, the Zoroastrianism of Persia, and the Buddhism, Hinduism, and Confucianism of South and East Asia as ultimately insufficient in preventing such corruption.[19]

The only exception to this rule, however brief, was Rome in the very first days of the empire. Julius Caesar, in his law code, prohibited husbands from killing their wives. This was only a brief respite. The corruption that occurred after Nero led to the same sort of patriarchy and abuse of women that characterized other imperial societies.[20]

This pattern changed in Christian Europe, as polygamy was abolished, and yet women were still seen in a negative light. Eve, the temptress of Adam, was inferior to her husband, a dogma no doubt justified by the Genesis account where God creates Eve from Adam's rib. Christians therefore saw women, like Eve, as dirty and deceptive. Marriage was sanctioned as a necessary evil to produce children with at least a modicum of respectability. For Celal Nuri, the nuclear family was the moral anchor of society, an anchor that contrasted starkly with other aspects of Catholic tradition, such as the priests who took a vow of celibacy and lived an unnatural life.[21]

Women's place in Christian Europe continued to improve in the Middle Ages, when the rise of "courtly love" elevated them as a noble ideal from which the knights of the realm could take inspiration. Ultimately, this custom led to the romantic notion that one should in fact marry whom he or she loves, rather than following the dictates of the family.[22] More humane laws began to be implemented and, as a result, women, who up until that time where veiled, began to reveal themselves and become more openly a part of society.[23] The most obvious example of this was Joan of Arc (1412–30), the French maiden knight who, after valiantly fighting the English at the Siege of Orleans, was burned at the stake after her capture.[24] Later, during the reign of Louis XIV (1643–1715), women would begin to participate actively in social reform, such as in the Rambouillet Salon, where "they had a full impact on the customs, ethics, and language in … [that] country."[25] Madam de Stahl, the famous woman of letters who witnessed the French Revolution, wrote that "if politics is cutting the heads of women in a country, they [women] have a right to intervene in politics there."[26]

To Celal Nuri, women's rights developed in France gradually, and they were not accomplished simply as a result of the revolution. Indeed, he saw revolutions as often counterproductive. *The Declaration of the Rights of Man and Citizen* (1789) was, in his opinion, restricted to men only.[27] This was followed in the years ahead by Napoleon, whose famous Code firmly made her subject to her husband or father.[28] Celal Nuri's argument certainly seems vindicated by Napoleon saying that "women are nothing but machines to create children."[29]

Once again, we see the same pattern of conquest and humiliation for women. Napoleon conquered vast territories, including, very importantly, the Ottoman province of Egypt. There, he started to oppress women and families in a web of social exploitation that would continue in the century to come both at home and abroad. Other European powers followed his lead in oppressing non-Western peoples in their colonies.

Celal Nuri took inspiration from Abdülhak Hamid (Tarhan)'s *The Hindu Daughter* (*Duhter-i Hindu*) (1876), a novel that revolved around the evil exploits of Captain Thompson, a womanizing British officer who was stationed in India.[30] Thompson, after shamelessly taking advantage of Surucuyi, a young Indian woman, by sleeping with her with the promise of marriage, abandoned her for Elizabeth, the wife of the British governor of Gujarat.[31] Elizabeth, while having an affair with Thompson, initially refused to marry him because it went against her "honor."[32] The situation dramatically changed toward the end of the play, when a native rebellion that killed the governor would also force Thompson to marry both Surucuyi and Elizabeth. This polygamous marriage, initially based on lust, exploitation, and corruption, was certain to lead to a bad end.[33] Surucuyi not only married outside of her faith but left the community of her people. She was bound to be subjected to Thompson's ruthlessness, and she faced the prospect that Elizabeth, the Caucasian wife, would have a higher position in the household. Indeed, the British characters in the play cursed that Surucuyi and the other Indian subjects as "bats," "monkeys" or "apes."[34] In the end, however, Elizabeth also suffered a tragic fate, as she was confined to a gilded cage.

The play was indeed a strong statement that European conquest and colonization led to women's social repression. The British, like Napoleon, or any conquering empire for that matter, were exploiting not only native subjects, but also their own citizens. This implied that imperial wealth could not hide the hypocrisy and decadence of the society they had created.

Celal Nuri spoke to the current plight of the "Elizabeths" of the Western world when he said:

> Presently the Europeans are depriving their women of many things, and talking about how their nature makes them unsuitable for certain professions. Yes! Once upon a time, the slave traders used to talk about how pretentiously slaves did not have the skills ... [to live in] freedom.[35]

But what was there to prevent more "Surucuyis" from facing such ruthless exploitation? The Turks should avoid this problem by extolling the virtues of their own great Islamic civilization. He remarked, for instance, about the coming of Prophet Muhammad as a great turning point for women. He noted that "great Muhammad foretold the future and established a religion according to it. The Prophet [emphasized] ... monogamous marriage."[36]

This could be seen, for instance, when Muhammad remained married alone to Khatijah until her death.[37] He had done so deliberately, in Celal Nuri's estimation, because he wished to end the abuses of the pre-Islamic period of ignorance (*cahiliyye*) in the Arabian Peninsula, where families were known to have an almost limitless number of wives and, as "primitive people," were sexually immoral.[38] Khatijah, a wealthy merchant, was also the breadwinner of the family. But even after her death, when Muhammad married other wives, including Aisha, the daughter of his loyal companion Abu Bakir, he did so to protect them from the dangers of war, solitary life, and exile. The wives also played a prominent political, religious, and even military role.[39] Aisha was indeed the person who recalled the bulk of Muhammad's sayings after his death, thus providing one of the three primary sources of Islamic law. She also became a major player during the ensuing succession crises. At one point Aisha even led an army into the Battle of the Camel (656) to fight Caliph Ali.

The Prophet also gave women the right to conduct business transactions, manufacture goods, and work in the countryside. A woman could make contracts on equal terms with men, deal with taxes, and defend her rights in court.[40]

Prophet Muhammad was no mere empire-builder, but instead the founder of a new, morally just civilization that the world had not seen up until that point. He had liberated people, not conquered them, and this formed the basis of a new society that would acculturate the barbarians around them. For, "Muslims are the only civilized ones after the Romans. They were able to endow various nations with their own principles of social education."[41]

The Arabs, the first people to benefit from Prophet Muhammad, were limited by their ability to progress, according to Celal Nuri. As seen in the previous chapter, Muhammad successfully transformed their primitive tribal society into a religious community, but the Arabs could not become a true national community due to their limited abilities.[42] Celal Nuri implied that, after waging continuing campaigns of conquest in the wake of the Prophet's death, the Arabs simply could not sufficiently resist the corrupting influence of the Persian and Byzantine harems.

Islam, however, also had a mission for the other peoples of the world, including the Turks who were in the process of migrating from their ancient Eurasian homeland to Asia Minor and Europe. The Turks, Celal Nuri maintained, were up until the ninth century a primitive people, subject to the same patriarchal polygamous system of degrading social relations that weakened empires: "Mongolian and Tartar habits and customs were no different from the other [primitive forms of patriarchy] that we have examined."[43] Elsewhere he would allude to the Mongolian Turkish Khagans as despots: "Upon their death they were buried with their horses, and forty slaughtered virgins in order to have a harem [in the afterlife]."[44]

Although Celal Nuri never spoke directly about how the Turks' conversion to Islam impacted women, he did state that the Turks were only able to undertake a civilizing mission after they accepted Islam as the core of their national spirit. Osman and Orhan, the first two sultans of the Ottoman Empire, began, like Muhammad, as Bedouin tribal chiefs that embarked on a holy mission.[45] This mission, in fact, was not only to begin the process of transforming their tribal community (*kavim*) to a religious one (*ümmet*), as the Arabs did, but also to evolve further into a true nation (*milliyet*).[46] This civilizational progress implied that Islamic principles would have played a positive role in governance and all aspects of life, including the place of women.

Nonetheless, the Ottomans were severely tested after Sultan Mehmed II conquered Constantinople in 1453. His sacking of the city, and the lackadaisical attitude of him and his soldiers in managing it after the conquest, meant that the Ottomans were in jeopardy of following the legacy of earlier conquerors. Mehmed II and his successors indeed adopted the all-too-familiar practice of isolating themselves in a sumptuous palace with a great harem. The harem became a den of intrigue, where the mothers, wives, and the eunuch guards began to manipulate the sultans to do their will. Perhaps the greatest example of this was Roxelana (also known as Haseki Hürrem Sultana), who tricked the sultan into killing off Grand Vizier İbrahim and Mustafa, his most capable son and likely heir.[47] This was accomplished to ensure that her son, Selim II (1566–74), known derisively as "Selim the Sop," would take the throne. The sultan was thereafter virtually imprisoned in the harem, where the others made his decisions for him.[48]

The fact that the women of the harem played a decisive role thus did not strike Celal Nuri as a positive development at all. Roxelana, and other members of the harem, lived to pursue pleasure and ambition without any care at all about social progress.⁴⁹ They were, in an odd sense, much like Elizabeth when she cravenly accepted her polygamous marriage with Thompson after pursuing an immoral relationship with him. It was a sign that society, like a fish, began to rot from the top.

This dissent into social chaos, in Celal Nuri's opinion, continued more or less all the way down to the recent reign of Abdülhamid II (1875–1909).⁵⁰ Celal Nuri had vivid imaginings about this era in his novel *Nightmare? (Cauchmar?)* (1911).⁵¹ The book tells of Müghri İrem, a concubine of the late imperial harem who had originally entered the palace after being sold into slavery from her native Circassian homeland. Although she never forgot the plight of her native people, who waged a bitter struggle with the Russian czar's armies, she saw it as her duty to seek justice and a more progressive government in her newfound home. To that end, she becomes a concubine, and later a wife of Abdülhamid II, who, in the first years of his reign, flirted with the idea of constitutional reform. The sultan appeared to favor a change in the nature of the empire, from a purely authoritarian system to one in which parliament would play an ever greater role. But Abdülhamid II instead tried to force his wife to use her contacts with Midhat Pasha (1822–84), the famous Ottoman statesman and reformer, as a means to spy on the reformers so that he could instead get rid of them. Müghri İrem refused to act in such a manner and was quickly sent into exile. Abdülhamid II's paranoia about her was also encouraged by the other members of the harem, who were jealous of Müghri İrem and predisposed toward maintaining their decadent lifestyle.⁵²

Although Müghri İrem suffered a great deal at first in the Hijazi town of Taif, her morale picked up greatly after being united with Emir Ateş Ali, a Caucasian prince and son of the legendary Sheikh Shamil (1797–1871). Sheikh Shamil was the Dagestani Muslim who led a decades-long struggle against Russia, and who ultimately died in Medina. Miraculously enough, Abdülhamid II consented to Müghri İrem's monogamous marriage to Emir Ateş Ali. But, contrary to the sultan's wishes, the couple did not give up on their hopes to transform the empire.⁵³ While still in Taifa, Müghri İrem and her husband reconnected with Midhat Pasha, also a fellow exile. Through a variety of contacts, they set up a network that stretched from well-wishing British and American observers in Cairo and London to Armenians who, Celal Nuri alleged, suffered greatly at the hands of the "Red Sultan," and to such prominent Young Turks as the owner of a subversive newspaper *İleri*, an allusion to himself.⁵⁴

After Midhat Pasha was eventually assassinated, and Ateş Ali killed during a military revolt, Müghri İrem then returned to the palace at the bidding of Abdülhamid II, who thought he could bend her to her will.[55] Instead, she intrigued with others, including Razine, a Georgian member of the harem, to provoke massive protests against the regime.[56] When Abdülhamid II started to rally his forces to crush the revolt, she denounced him to his face in his private chamber as a tyrant, and he collapsed dead at her feet.[57]

Thus, though Müghri İrem had first humiliated herself by losing her "honor" in joining Abdülhamid II's harem, she refused to become just another victim of that corrupt court. Rather, she redeemed herself through marrying her true love. After seeing Emir Ateş Ali for the first time after many years on the streets of Istanbul, She uttered: "In my heart I am [still] a virgin."[58] Yet her honor was tied not simply to Emir Ateş Ali, but also to the nation. Her mission would not be complete until well after Emir Ateş Ali died, when she took vengeance on the sultan himself.[59] Through this story, Celal Nuri intimately linked monogamous marriage, as well as his heroine's own political role to her willingness to sacrifice everything for the country.

Müghri İrem's own background should not be forgotten, however. While Abdülhamid II might have tired of her constant talk about her mountainous Caucasian homeland, she continued to identify with the values of a Muslim people uncorrupted by a decadent cosmopolitan lifestyle. Rezine, the Georgian concubine, had similar sentiments, as shown in her brave long-distance correspondence from the palace with Müghri İrem while she was still trapped in exile in Taif.[60] The Muslim minorities of Russia thereby showed that common Islamic sentiment would save the country, rather than a purely Turkish nationalism. These people, although oppressed by the Russians, clearly were much more politically, and socially advanced than other victims of foreign colonization.[61]

The Kazan Tatar Turkish Women and the Need for Popular Reform

Celal Nuri also wrote extensively about the Kazan Tatar Turks, a Muslim minority in Russia very similar to the Circassians.[62] After visiting this small community on the Volga River, he found it amazing that Kazan Tatar Turkish women were well-educated and knew how to read and write. They too received training on how to run their households "in the European-style" and did not shy away from "public places, theaters, and gardens."⁶³ They were also frequently unveiled. Contrary to what conservative Turks might think, "Kazan Tatar Turkish women [remain] chaste and honorable."⁶⁴ Some were even so bold as to work in factories, a sign that industrialization was having a significant impact on social patterns there.⁶⁵

The ideal Kazan Tatar Turkish woman was striking because she was typically not a member of the elite. Celal Nuri's point was that this society was homogenously middle-class, and remarkably modern. Marriages were monogamous as a rule, and women could run their households and participate in professional life in a way that was good not only for their own individual interests, but for their community. Moreover, their Muslim identity became more modern and mature.⁶⁶

The Kazan Tatar Turkish woman contrasted sharply with her Russian counterpart. Education among the Russians was reserved for the elite, which, as a typical empire, was prone to corruption. Unsurprisingly, Celal Nuri depicted the Russian palace in decadent terms. Peter the Great had begun to target that decadence by enacting a series of modernizing reforms. Women broke free of the "harem" in the palace, and education became much more broadly available to not just the elite, but also a limited number of middle-class intellectuals. Nevertheless, the autocrat Peter's reforms failed to produce a more democratic government and ultimately alienated the educated, including women. This heralded a regression back to a more thoroughly atomized society, where the national good was forgotten. According to Celal Nuri's logic, Russian women would continue to suffer in society in a way much more like Western Europe.⁶⁷

The Young Turks, he hoped, would learn from the Russian and Kazan Tatar Turkish examples. They tried to promote social reform for women, not just among the elites, but at all levels of society. The first progressive measure he hoped to implement was the end of polygamous marriage.⁶⁸ In Celal Nuri's opinion, polygamy began to decline with the overthrow of Abdülhamid II and his autocratic overlordship. The imperial harem, while it still existed, could no longer control governments the way it once did, since power had passed to the parliament and army after the April 13 uprising. Legislation should be passed by the parliament and not take the Islamic legal courts into account.⁶⁹ The result likely would have been to end polygamy first at the palace, then among the urban population, and finally in the countryside.

Marriage laws also should be passed that would ensure women's rights to freely choose their husbands, and to divorce them when under duress. Turkish custom had allowed only men to divorce women on their own initiative, and this authority was often used by the husband to intimidate their wives. For instance, a husband could force his wife comply with his wishes by threatening to leave her and marry another. A divorced woman had the status of a widow, a social designation often scorned by the general populace.[70]

However, Islamic laws and practices did grant women many rights to hold property and they guaranteed that "bride money" granted by the groom at the beginning of the marriage would be retained after a divorce except in case of adultery. This differed significantly from the Western European tradition of a dowry given to the groom from the bride's family, a practice that impoverished women and limited their prospects for a future family. Select elements from such Islamic laws and practices could be incorporated into progressive legislation, also presumably passed by the parliament and implemented by the judiciary.[71]

The seclusion of women, according to Celal Nuri and most of the CUP elite, was also affected by veiling practices. Celal Nuri did not see an outright banning of the veil as wise. However, he did wish to end the practice.[72] Whereas women at one time covered nearly their entire body except for their eyes, women in his day generally used only a headscarf to cover the hair, eliminating the face-veil. Modest clothes were still worn, but women increasingly paid attention to changes in fashion, especially those from Europe. Simply giving women the freedom to abandon the veil and even the headscarf would likely end both practices over time.

Likewise Celal Nuri called for changes in the training of modernized Islamic religious authorities. Such authorities, beginning with the minister for religious affairs (*şeyhülislam*), presumably could reinforce the reforms by arguing their validity for the population at large.[73] It was critical too to instruct new cadres of local imams who could then be dispatched to urban neighborhoods, and the countryside, in order again to justify the new measures and the government's approach to women and family issues.[74]

Primary schools should teach girls as well as boys. Subjects to be taught would, of course, include reading and writing, presumably at the same level for both genders. Yet, special attention should also be given to home economics for girls, since that would make them aware of the most up-to-date scientific ways of child-bearing and rearing.[75] Schooling also would be a way to introduce both girls and boys to the state as a type of "alternative family," thereby ameliorating the atavistic tendencies of the nuclear family in favor of greater social collectivity. Moreover, the schools would be an ideal place to wean children away from traditional Islamic practices, and toward a much more progressive, materialistic lifestyle.

To what extent women should be included in the professions was an open question. That Celal Nuri had praised Kazan Tatar women for working in the factories apparently indicated that he favored opening the job market to women. But when he discussed Turkish women specifically, he put far greater emphasis on women doing their patriotic duty at home, and, when necessary, volunteering for the Red Crescent Society or becoming teachers in the schools. Be that as it may, he generally was skeptical about the extent to which women should play a direct role in social life. During the First World War, for example, he would write a series of articles critical of the push for women's rights under the assumed female pen name of "Afife Fikret." On January 1, 1918, he stated: "A woman can do any type of work if needed. She could for instance be an official or collect garbage from the street but this is not our goal. Some types of work naturally favor men and some women."[76] Afife Fikret elsewhere in the article posited that Turkish feminists should concentrate on "raising our nation ... We are going to train smarter and stronger children who will rescue our country in the future. This is our military service."[77]

"Afife Fikret" would go on to write the novel *The End Times* (*Ahir Zaman*) (1919), again sounding a cautionary note about women losing their sense of familial and patriotic duty. The novel focused on how a whole series of women tied to Istanbul's high society would completely lose sense of themselves in pursuing Ecmel Bey, the handsome draft-dodger. Each of the women, including the wife of a handicapped veteran, the spouse of a war profiteer, and even a mother and daughter, slept with him in turn. They not only committed adultery, but were hurting public morale at a time when the empire was in dire need of it. None of the women ever paid attention to their main task: to loyally look after their families.[78]

The purpose of writing such a novel was to remind his readers of their need to popularly mobilize on behalf of the country during wartime.[79] Celal Nuri was convinced that writers like himself were to play a critical part in that process. But just how far the government should go to implement his program of women's reform remained to be seen. Certainly government action in terms of legislation and training new educational and religious cadres was central to his vision. Still, there were limits to the pace of the reform, particularly regarding the headscarf— an issue which might trigger violent social reaction if banned outright—and hesitation regarding women entering the professions. Moreover, it is significant to note that he did not make any push whatsoever for the women's suffrage or their right to stand in elections.

Much of his hesitation may well have stemmed from his own masculine-centered vision of Western-style liberalism. This vision may have been influenced by Nordau, who argued that women had no chance to compete with men adequately in the professions and that they needed to be "protected" from harm.[80]

While Celal Nuri likely shared these sentiments at least in regards to women of modest standing, he seemingly had greater confidence in the benefits of educating elite women, and incorporating them into the power structure. This can be seen once again in the fictional character of Müghri İrem, who directly and positively affected state affairs. She was guided at one point by a certain Madam Werner, an American social scientist who, after traveling to Istanbul to study the harem and the place of elite women in that society, became actively involved in the plot to overthrow the sultan.[81]

Nevertheless, Celal Nuri, like Nordau, viewed the family as an evolving institution, critical to the success of his own society. If society did not adopt the family and women to the needs of modern life, the nation would likely suffer at the hands of those countries that did. This could be seen in terms of not only patriotic values, but also population growth. As Letourneau argued at the end of his book:

> In order to prosper and live, it is necessary that the ethnic or social unit should incessantly produce a sufficient number of individuals well-endowed in body, heart and mind. Before this primordial need all prejudices must yield, all egoistic interest must be bent.[82]

The logic of Celal Nuri's focus on the family and women's place within it leads to the same conclusion. Women and the family needed to modernize, or else the country seemed doomed to fail. Religious superstitions and outmoded customs should not get in the way of such progress.

Ziya Gökalp and the "New" Turkish Woman

Ziya Gökalp, the Turkish nationalist sociologist who wrote contemporaneously to Celal Nuri, likewise analyzed the question of women's place in family and society from a social scientific perspective. He no doubt shared Celal Nuri's concern about polygamy and the danger of focusing too much on individual women's rights. He too agreed that a woman's primary loyalty had to be anchored in the nation. The new woman, like the new family, was part of a modernization program that his society had to go through in order to thrive.

Ziya Gökalp fundamentally differed from Celal Nuri in terms of his overall historical paradigm, however. Instead of seeing the history of Turkish women as part of a gradual transformation from tribe to religious community to nation, he posited that the ideal for women was to restore the ancient Turkist ideal of a family hearth (*ocak*). From the time of the Göktürks up until they immigrated from Central Asia, marriage generally meant the creation of:

> a new family that unifies two people separated from their old families ... If a man is the chieftain of a household, similarly the woman was the lady of her home. In the hearth (*ocak*) the man and woman were on the same level in contrast to the patriarchal family.[83]

Here the father and mother were equals who united in monogamous marriage freely. Women at this time had full property and inheritance rights, wore no veils, and played a clear role in public life, often fighting side-by-side with men in battle. Women also played an equal role in the ancient Turkish dynasties, reigning as queen (*hatun*) alongside their king (*hakan*).[84] This was encapsulated for example in the *Orhun Kitabeleri* (732–35): "My father who is a khan (*hakan*) revived the state; my mother who is a lady (*hatun*) knows the state."[85]

Ziya Gökalp saw pre-Islamic shamanism as absolutely critical to cementing this relationship. The *hatun*, who sat to the left in her ceremonials, was recognized as one of two gods. She was the shaman who could channel her magical ties to nature through incantations, and she was recognized as "fire mother" ("*od ana*"). The *hakan*, known as the ruler of custom (*töre*), was likewise recognized as "fire father" ("*od ata*"). The *hatun*'s religious ideals, matched with her husband's judicial ideals, stemmed from a common origin, the hearth.[86] This symmetry was shown in the ancient Turkish tradition of the wife starting the fire in the morning and the husband extinguishing it at night.

Although recognized as equals, the *hatun* was emotionally and morally the teacher of her husband, while the *hakan* was superior in terms of his public and professional activities. To Ziya Gökalp, this division of labor recognized the natural differences between the two sexes, though in theory their roles were "separate but equal."

The Oğuz, or "western Turks," lost the "hearth" type of nuclear family when they immigrated into Anatolia and elsewhere in the Middle East. The Sufis, who converted the Oğuz Turks to Islam, initially recognized some of their shamanistic traditions. But Islamic religious elites set out over time to repress all aspects of the Oğuz Turks' previous belief system, leading to a degradation of women's status. This was revealed, Ziya Gökalp claimed, in Islamic law, where Muhammad said that "women are half the value of men."[87]

Although Ziya Gökalp admitted that Turkish women retained some basic inheritance and property rights in Islam, the tendency toward abuse and alienation would continue throughout the centuries. Ziya Gökalp, like Celal Nuri, pointed to polygamy and seclusion as growing practices. Originally intended by Muhammad to restrict the number of marriages to four, Abbasid dynasts abused the custom by building elaborate harems, as the earlier Persians and Byzantines had done. There the wives were cut off from the world outside them; and in their virtual imprisonment they began to manipulate each other.[88]

The Ottomans were no exception to this rule. Again agreeing with Celal Nuri, Ziya Gökalp pointed to the decadence of the harem in the imperial palace, although he identified it as beginning with Murat III (1574–95) rather than Mehmet II or Süleyman the Magnificent. The result for the Turks was a new familial type, the mansion (*konak*), where patriarchal rule by the husband over his wives and concubines fundamentally displaced the hearth.[89]

The *Tanzimat* reformers of the mid-nineteenth century tried to alter this reality by limiting the taking of concubines, abolishing most slavery, lessening taxes on brides, and aiming to get rid of the autocratic system. Such attempts largely failed, however, because they did not appreciate ancient Turkist traditions.[90] The reformers had been enamored, instead, with transitioning from the "mansion" model to a European-style "household."[91] Yet, according to Ziya Gökalp, the only way to truly eliminate the "mansion" was to engage in a Turkist nationalist movement that would teach the values of the past, and once again make women active participants alongside their husbands and children. While the Committee of Union and Progress could facilitate the movement by "reinstating" codes that would allow women to divorce, and have legal rights equal to men, they wanted women to participate in nationalist societies. Presumably this would include working in schools, although Ziya Gökalp does not make specific reference to it.

He, like Celal Nuri, was intent on preserving women's primary social role in the household. He argued that this was needed because men were physically stronger and more dynamic in social life than women. Yet, men could learn from women too because of her greater commitment to sexual and family ethics. In this sense, husband and wife should teach each other their strengths much in the way the ancient *hakan* and *hatun* did.[92] Therefore, Ziya Gökalp, like Celal Nuri, refused to acknowledge the full equality of women with men as an achievable goal.

Ziya Gökalp borrowed much from European social scientists in this regard. He saw established religion as reinforcing marital taboos that inhibited a society's progress, citing Durkheim's anthropological study on the nature and origin of incest. Changes in family patterns only occurred when the established religion itself was abandoned for a new faith.[93] For Turks, this was an argument for a secular nationalism that would idealize an imagined Turkist past. Romantic notions of an eternal, ideal family type and a liberated woman were part of the new myth he was creating. Turkist nationalism, like the shamanism of the ancient past, would empower women and give them a fundamentally new role in social and political life. The fact that he could rely on relatively recent findings by European historians of Central Asia, such as Leon Cahun, Vilhelm Thompsen, Vasili Radlof, and Gaston Richard, legitimized his theory.[94]

Ziya Gökalp's Turkish audience, overwhelmed by the horrors of war, devastating losses of men and territory, and the coming realization that the empire itself would be lost, were certainly receptive to a new national hope. The idea of the Turkish family as an ancient tradition that could revitalize and re-establish a nation and society hinged upon the complete, seemingly revolutionary rejection of the more recent Islamic imperial past.

Rather than looking to the French model of development, where, as Celal Nuri envisioned, women were gradually accepted from the late medieval period onward as thinkers, political agents, and even heroine-warriors, Ziya Gökalp pointed to the familial virtues of German and Anglo-Saxon barbarians before their assimilation by Rome. Going back to a state of nature, or primitive society for spiritual renewal, was indeed an argument that European revolutionaries, like Jean-Jacques Rousseau, would accept. For evolutionists like Letourneau, Nordau, and Celal Nuri, such dreams were a chimera. They would lead Celal Nuri to exclaim:

> Women will get their rights and place [in society]. This is inevitable. No Genghis Khan, no pharaoh was victorious during this era … [and achieved it]. For this reason, those who are preventing freedom are not different than those who are barking at the moon.[95]

In other words, imagining that women would be liberated by going back to their Turkist past was silly talk.

Islamic Explanations of Reform

Despite these profound differences in approach, Celal Nuri, Ziya Gökalp, and others who wrote on women's issues expended considerable energy in trying to convince the more religiously devout. Celal Nuri, for example, argued that the time was ripe to reinterpret the use of the face-veil in Islamic society. He highlighted Quranic verse 53 of *Al-Ahzab*:

> O ye who believe! And turn not the Prophet's houses—until leave is given you ... And when you ask (his ladies) for anything ye want ask them before a screen: that makes for greater purity for your hearts and for theirs.[96]

Celal Nuri also cited the Egyptian Qasim Amin's argument that seclusion only pertained to members of the Prophet's household, and not to women at large nor even to the wives of the succeeding caliphs. This coincided with Qasim Amin's further citation from the Quran that "O ye wives of the Prophet! You are not like any other women."[97]

Celal Nuri and Qasim Amin used an account about a conversation Caliph Umar had with his wife Umm Khultum. Umm Khultum, while in her house, asked her husband in the next room if he had a male guest with him. If he did, she would not enter without being properly attired with her face-veil. He responded that it was enough for her just to say her name. Umar then remarked to his companion that he should eat "for if she had agreed [to join us without the face-veil] your food would have been better than this."[98]

Celal Nuri then quoted Amin's statement:

> Allah did not divide the universe separately between men and women. He did not specify the advantages of women benefiting alone from one part of the earth. Similarly, he did not specify men's separate sphere from women. On the contrary, they shared their life together.[99]

Celal Nuri also seconded Qasim Amin's rejection of conservative Islamic authorities that uncovering a woman's face would attract strange men. Instead, Qasim Amin claimed that "it is possible that her total appearance might turn glances away from her."[100]

While Celal Nuri did not push for an immediate ban of the face-veil, he believed that in time women would be ready to liberate themselves: "We should raise the next generation [of women] in a free and honorable way."[101]

Qasim Amin even more bluntly concluded:

> If ... a person removes himself from those [traditional] factors that influenced the development of his feelings, if he disregards those garments inherited from his predecessors, if he explores the topic objectively from all its facets and is influenced primarily by empirical data, then he will be able to perceive that it is impossible for women to exist fully unless she can control her own life ... He will

also realize that the [face-]veil as we know it is a great hindrance to a woman's progress, and indeed to a country's progress.[102]

Celal Nuri likewise pointed out that the Quran can be read as preferring monogamous to polygamist marriage. Although verse 3 of *Al-Nisa* states that a man who is "unable to justly deal with orphans" may marry up to four women, on condition that he is able to "deal justly (with them)." If not, one wife would be "more suitable, to prevent you from doing injustice."[103] Verse 129 of *Al-Nisa* clarifies further that the husband cannot be fair and just between women "even if it ... [his] your ardent desire." He must, however, "not turn away (from a woman altogether), so as to leave her (as it were) hanging (in the air)."[104] This meant, according to Celal Nuri, that polygamy, an unnatural and inherently unfair arrangement for the wives, was only accepted out of duress.[105] In his view, Islam was an evolutionary faith that no longer sanctioned such an outdated, corrupt form of matrimony.

Banning polygamy in Islam, in line with the changing needs of modern times, would not be the first such reform. Celal Nuri noted that the Ottoman sultanate had issued laws accepting the taking of interest, a practice initially banned in Islam as an unjust activity. Circumstances changed with the modern banking and credit system, which necessitated loans with interest in order to develop the economy.[106]

Cenab Şahabettin (1870–1934), to whom Celal Nuri had dedicated his work *Our Women*, spoke in similar terms. Besides referencing the same Quranic verses, Cenab Şahabettin also alluded to a discussion between Prophet Muhammad and his daughter Fatimah. Fatimah had come to him complaining about her husband Ali taking a new wife, Jehl. The marriage did not occur after she had the conversation with her husband.[107]

It was an embarrassment, in Cenab Şahabettin's mind, that polygamy was still practiced. He allegedly saw this first hand when he went to the Hijaz to visit a "slave market" where concubines were being sold:

> There were wretched girls and women marshalled like an animal herd. Their bodies were naked, and their eyes full of tears and despair. Like sheep they were bereft of choice, robbed of their will. The cruel clients were forcing these unlucky creatures to stand one by one, showing all of their body and allowing them to inspect their most delicate organs.[108]

Here he conflated polygamy with slavery and concluded that this peculiar institution must stop.[109]

Celal Nuri had a more conservative stance regarding the issue of divorce in Islamic law. He again began his discussion with quotations from the Quran. Verse 19 of *Al-Nisa* granted men the right to divorce their wives on condition that they never touch the dowry, which is the wives' to keep regardless: "If ye take a dislike to them [your wives], it may be that ye dislike a thing, and Allah brings about through it a great deal of good."[110] A wife was also granted the right to divorce her husband if she "fears cruelty or desertion on her husband's part." An "amicable settlement," presumably regarding the woman's rights to the children and continuing support by her ex-husband, should be sought in such a case.[111]

But divorce, regardless, was seen as a measure of last resort. Celal Nuri noted Muhammad's saying that you should not divorce women except in cases of adultery. Allah disapproved of either spouse divorcing their husband or wife for a new one. Ali, Prophet Muhammad's cousin, son-in-law, and later caliph, stated that "you should marry but not divorce."[112] Ali went on to proclaim that the family is the foundation of both the state and the nation. To Celal Nuri, this meant that it was:

> necessary to ensure the family by many means. We should not delay a minute in making a law regarding divorce and marriage according to the commands and rules of religion. Because there is a lack of constraint and everything and lack of constraint in this too. Enough![113]

Ziya Gökalp, who was generally negative toward his country's Islamic heritage, made a surprising defense of the monogamous married family by using Islamic legal sources. He cited Prophet Muhammad's sayings such as "the woman is the ruler of her house and children," "heaven is under the foot of the mother's," and "the most blessed thing in the world is a woman with morality."[114] Absent in his discussion of Islamic sources, however, was any mention of divorce.[115]

When it came to women entering public life, Celal Nuri highlighted once again the example of Aisha, who played a critical role in not only recording the sayings of Prophet Muhammad, but also becoming an influential political and even military figure after his death. To him, she was the paragon of:

> behavior ... intelligence, and foresight in the affairs of the nation. Islam has shown great efforts in promoting women. No one can deny Aisha's place in Muslim society. [This is evidence] Islam knows the function of women in the evolution of humanity. It happened some 1300 years before feminism first began.[116]

Although he cited this as proof that women were capable of singular achievement in professions outside the home, he did not elaborate much further than saying women should have access to education, at least at the primary school level.[117]

Conclusion

Much of the discussion above shows that Celal Nuri and Gökalp followed women and family issues from the same basic approach. Both Celal Nuri and Gökalp were diehard Unionists committed to enacting reforms along westernizing lines regardless of their differing versions of Turkish and Muslim nationalism. As such, they were dedicated to eliminating polygamy and veiling practices in spite of the long-standing justifications for them by traditional Islamic sources: the Quran, the sayings of Prophet Muhammad, and the commentaries of the Prophet's followers.

Celal Nuri and Gökalp were likewise devoted to rallying the public to support the ongoing war effort at the time they wrote—the First Balkan War in Celal Nuri's case, and, in Gökalp's, just a year before the empire's ultimate defeat in the First World War. The critical task as they saw it was to boost morale on the home front by encouraging women to act as patriotic and upstanding mothers and wives who would protect and empower their families with progressive, nation-centered virtue.

They also wrote their articles and books on this topic to validate their party's ongoing efforts to employ women during labor shortages and as part of the "national economic" program, such as the opening of vocational courses to train Muslim bankers and presumably also include women among the new cadres of Muslim businesspeople, artisans, and laborers if the need arose.[118] This all goes to show that Celal Nuri and Gökalp—as Unionists—pursued women and familial reform like any other issue with an eye on "saving the state" be it from social stagnancy or the threat of foreign destruction.

Their actual achievements, however, were quite modest. The Unionists may have opened the doors of Istanbul University to women, improved the prospects for girls to attend primary and secondary schools, and made tentative steps to include women in the "national economy," but the family decree of 1917 did not ban polygamy and only somewhat expanded women's rights to divorce and inheritance.[119] It was left to the Kemalists to make far more dramatic changes, such as the implementation of the civil code of 1926 which allowed for purely secular civil monogamous marriages with full and equal legal rights for women as well as men to divorce upon demand. It was of course Atatürk who actively discouraged veiling practices and, with the help of Afet İnan, his adopted daughter, secured the right of all women to vote in local and national elections.[120] These were far more substantial steps of state-induced progressive, positive change in women's rights than that of their Unionist predecessors.

Nonetheless, the ideological difference between Celal Nuri's and Gökalp's competing identification politics is clear. On the one hand, Gökalp was a pioneer of what later would become the right-wing secular version of modern Turkish nationalism. On the other hand, Celal Nuri's views often resembled the eclectic westernized Muslim nationalism of the Unionist mainstream, and, arguably, of what was to become the Progressive Republican Party (even though he was not personally a member). This clash of political direction boiled over into other policy discussions between the two, most notably the question of language reform, the subject of the next chapter.

6

Turkish Language Reform

Celal Nuri's Arguments

In 1919, Celal Nuri (İleri) sarcastically wrote in his novel, *The End Times* (*Ahir Zaman*), about two Istanbul playboys who talked about the prospects for travel and women if they joined an academy being set up during the war to study Turkish languages, an apparent reference to the CUP attempts to reform Turkish from 1914 onward.[1] These reforms were intended not only to standardize the language's grammar and structure, but also to modify its alphabet and begin to purge Turkish from its Arabic- and Persian-rich vocabulary. Ziya Gökalp, one of the principal intellectual architects of the reform, wanted to bring Ottoman Turkish much more in line with Eurasian Turkish languages, such as Kazan Tatar, Crimean Tatar, Azeri, Uygur, and Uzbek. He thus hoped to rejuvenate his own national literary culture by re-establishing its linguistic ties to its original Central Asian "homeland."

In Celal Nuri's eyes, this effort was totally delusional. As seen in the novel, he saw it as a major distraction for the government and its leading intellectuals from conducting the war in its most critical stage. That the playboys were drawn to this opportunity smacked of the cultural and moral decadence of the time—allegedly a factor that ultimately led to the enemy occupation of Istanbul at the time Celal Nuri wrote. The satirical view that language reform was run by utter amateurs also spoke of his disdain for Ziya Gökalp and the other writers and academics committed to the reform. This raised the frightening prospect of what type of damage such an "academy" might do if it actually had the power to implement its ideas.

But Celal Nuri's concern with the Turkish language reform went far beyond this fictional vignette. He had, in fact, been obsessed with the issue ever since January 1912, when he wrote in response to the first edition of *Türk Yurdu*, the leading Turkist academic journal. He complained of the publication's "strange" idea to invent an artificial language by borrowing many:

New and unfamiliar words and compounds that do not exist in Ottoman Turkish, Tatar, and Azeri .... Trying to change language in this way would simply reinvent the Esperanto monstrosity.[2]

Celal Nuri would harp on this theme periodically for the next twenty-six years, reaching a crescendo in 1917, when he would have a serious polemical exchange about the issue with Ziya Gökalp. The subject would be publicly discussed periodically by Gökalp until his death in 1924, and by Mustafa Kemal Atatürk and his supporters beginning in 1920. Yet, the issue was increasingly brought up in the following years but the government only systematically pursued language reforms only after the consolidation of the Kemalist regime. Mustafa Kemal (Atatürk) formally embarked on his efforts in 1928, when, after forming a language advisory committee (*Dil Encümeni*), he announced a new Latin alphabet to be implemented within months.[3] The "Letter Revolution" (*Harf Devrimi*) was followed some four years later by the "Language Revolution" (*Dil Devrimi*), an effort to systematically purge "foreign elements" from Turkish grammar and vocabulary.

Turkish had been profoundly influenced by both Arabic and Persian ever since the Turkish people converted to Islam, and especially after 1071 when the Seljuks established their claim to Anatolia. The Turks came into contact with Islamic literary culture through the Persians, but were even more profoundly influenced by Arabic, the language of the Quran and the Sunni Islamic elite. This connection to Arabic deepened after 1517, when the Ottomans took over Mecca and arguably became the leading Muslim power. Celal Nuri thought that the effort to rid Turkish of its Arabic and Persian influence was just as nonsensical as eliminating all French and Latin borrowings from English, since such "purification" would destroy the cultural identity of the people.[4]

Much of the debate that Celal Nuri had with the likes of Ziya Gökalp and the Kemalists revolved around seemingly academic questions. Should the reformers eliminate the grammatical gender, plural forms, and word order they sometimes borrowed from Arabic and Persian grammatical conventions, or should they go so far as to get rid of the Persian character *i* (*izafet*), frequently used by poets of the New Literature Movement (*Edebiyat-ı Cedide*) to connect a noun to its qualifier?[5] Should the Arabic script be abandoned because it had only three letters to symbolize eight vowels, and because the letter "k" (*kef*) represented four separate constants (k, g, n, y)? If so, would it be more suitable to adapt Latin or even resort to the ancient Göktürk Orkhanic script?[6] Could a linguistic foundation accurately determine which Arabic and Persian words were truly superfluous, and could it succeed in inventing new "Turkish" terms to replace those that were not? Should new technical terms also be invented or should they be borrowed from the cultures that first coined them?

This certainly was not the first time such questions were asked. As early as 1851 the great *Tanzimat* reformer Ahmet Cevdet raised the issue of changing the Ottoman alphabet and reforming Turkish to make it more amenable to translating works from French and other Western foreign languages. Such modifications might also lead, in his opinion, to more effective participation in the rapidly emerging print culture. He was joined by a wide variety of Ottoman intellectuals from that time onward, ranging from Münif Efendi, Yenişehirli Avni, İbrahim Şinasi, Namık Kemal, and Ali Suavi—all active primarily during the 1860s and 1870s—to Hamidian figures like Şemsettin Sami and Ahmed Mithat. Those that survived into the Young Turk era would join associations like the *Türk Derneği* and *Genç Kalemler* to renew their calls for reform.[7]

Military and technological concerns were also raised. Military officers and high administrative officials since the 1860s were worried not only about having accurate translations, but also about properly utilizing telegraph technology, which only had Latin-alphabet characters. Mehmet Bey, an Ottoman foreign affairs official, had invented an ad hoc Latin alphabet in 1874 to transmit messages abroad. His alphabet was used for this purpose until the end of the empire. This development highlighted the concern that retaining the Arabic alphabet might hinder modern communications. No serious governmental push for language reform occurred, however, until political motivations came to the fore.[8]

Celal Nuri, and a good number of those intellectuals who questioned both the CUP and the Kemalist language reforms, agreed with their opponents that the language should be taught according to modern Western pedagogical methods. There was a nearly universal disdain amongst both the Unionists and Kemalists for what they deemed to be the traditional Islam education.[9] Celal Nuri once despaired, for instance, about the failure of elites to pass on their knowledge to students, mentioning the case of a daughter of a high-ranking religious official (*ulema*) who failed to learn Turkish from her teacher. She told Celal Nuri:

> The turbaned hodja made me read Naima's history along with Al-Kiba's *Am* but I could not understand their meaning .... [But] a Swiss teacher taught me a different way. I understood and enjoyed reading [French] and continued my education.[10]

The solution to the problem, in Celal Nuri's mind, was not to educate their children exclusively in French or other Western languages, but instead to teach Turkish in a way that approximated the West. This meant not only having secular, modern-trained teachers, but also spending considerable energy in translating and teaching classical European literature. There was no doubt that in time, Western terms and linguistic and literary influences would follow.

Celal Nuri's conflict would really boil down to the pace of the reform:

> Linguistics cannot change the words and compounds of a language when it nationalizes itself. On the contrary a language must develop and progress .... It is impossible to have a revolution as language is evolutionary. For this reason our reform must be limited to facilitating this development.[11]

The main participants in this evolutionary reform, in his mind, were members of the Turkish literary elite. Through continuous engagement in poetry, prose, and journalism, he and his like-minded countrymen and colleagues could lead the charge.

Celal Nuri's revolutionary opponents countered that only radical top-down reforms that aimed primarily at the uneducated masses could have any chance of success at all.[12] His opponents thought that the gap between demographically tiny circles of literate elites, primarily in Istanbul, and an illiterate population of at least 90 percent of the country could only be bridged by simplifying the language to a level that everyone could understand.[13]

Added to this problem were also the ideological ramifications of the Independence War and the growing desire to identify the new state as Turkish. The revolutionaries no doubt saw language reform as a practical way of reinforcing loyalty to the new republic. Authoritarian reform meant creating a new linguistic identity that would sever any remaining cultural links with the Ottoman, Islamic past. Mass education could accomplish this by molding and mobilizing new generations in the most basic, efficient manner possible.

Turkish linguistic revolutionaries from Ziya Gökalp to Atatürk also had their eyes firmly glued to Russia. Seeing an opportunity after the Russian Revolution to advance the Turkish borders from Azerbaijan to Central Asia, the language reform had the potential to culturally unify the Turkish peoples. As Sadri Maksudi (Arsal), an immigrant from Kazan who took refuge in Turkey after the revolution, would write as late as 1930:

> In recent years Turkish intellectuals who have examined Turkish dialects in Tashkent, Bukhara, Kazan, Baku, and Akmescit have shown a considerable capacity to determine Turkish orthography and invent technical terms. But these

attempts have been local and limited to smaller nations. They have remained far from beginning a new historical era in the civilizational and cultural development of the Turkish race. It is required that an independent Turkish government be at the head to carry out the sacred duty of correcting the Turkish language [and its literature] ... in order to successfully spread it to all Turkish countries.[14]

Such nationalistic ambitions also had to consider Soviet-led language reforms in Eurasia. The distant Yakuts were the first to adopt a Latin alphabet in 1917, and there was a push in Azerbaijan for a similar change under Soviet auspices to do the same. The Baku Turkology Congress, convened in 1926, indicated that Lenin and the Bolsheviks intended to use language reform as a means to draw their own Turkish Muslim minorities away from the Turkists' orbit. This undoubtedly was a consideration that Atatürk took into account when he began his own efforts.[15]

All told, it is not surprising that the Kemalists, like Ziya Gökalp and his Young Turk partisans beforehand, would look amiss at Celal Nuri and other Turkish intellectuals who contested the nature and pace of their linguistic revolution given the patriotic fervor and geopolitical tension in the air. Others like Hüseyin Cahit (Yalçın), a long-time supporter of the alphabet change, voiced caution in 1932 about too rapidly imposing the reforms, but he was tainted by being linked with the Unionist opposition to Atatürk.[16] By that time Celal Nuri had self-censored his opinions and meekly accepted defeat.

This chapter will begin by analyzing Celal Nuri's philosophical approach to language reform. It will then examine the political contours of the language reform debate in Turkey focusing on grammar and poetical structure, as well as the alphabet change and Language Revolution.

Evolution versus Revolution

Celal Nuri's thought was profoundly influenced by Max Müller, who wrote luminously about the development of Asian languages, and who devoted considerable time and effort to the study of Turkish languages. This could be seen in two of Müller's works: *Letter to Chevalier Bunsen on the Classification of Turanian Languages* (1854) and *Lectures on the Science of Language* (1861).[17] Celal Nuri summed up his theory as describing the truly evolutionary nature of all human languages from its most primitive stages onward. Evolution began with monosyllabic languages that slowly agglutinate, or unite syllables, and over the ages would become inflectional, meaning that they absorb words to such a degree that the original roots of the language lose their independence over time.[18] The "Turanian" languages were an example of this evolution. Members of this language family, such as Çağatay, Uyghur, and Uzbek, remained in their agglutinated form, but evolved into the higher inflectional stage when they came into contact with Aryan or Semite cultures. This could be seen when Hungarians migrated into Central Europe, adopting Aryan ways of life, or, most importantly, when the Anatolian Turks converted to Islam.

This argument is borne out in Müller, beginning with a statement on the initial stages of linguistic development in Eurasia:

> Turanian languages, particularly, are so pliant that they lend themselves to endless combinations and complexities, unless a national literature or a frequent intercourse with other tribes act as safeguards against dialectical schism. Tribes who have no literature and no sort of intellectual occupation, seem occasionally to take a delight in working their language to the uppermost limits of grammatical expansion.[19]

The branching out of originally Turanian languages, like Turkish, would come about as a result of evolution:

> The separation and divergence of the Turanian languages can be explained as the result of a gradual, natural, and simple process, which, out of many things that were possible in the mechanical combinations of roots, fixed a certain number of real forms which, under geographical and political influences, became consolidated into national idioms.[20]

Borrowing from this theory, Celal Nuri proposed that the Ottoman Turks, having absorbed Islamic culture from the Arabs and Persians to its fullest extent, were now set to advance even further by adopting Western European civilization:

> The Persians and Arabs used to have a great shining knowledge. While France was ignorant and vulgar, great philosophers in Granada, Córdoba and Seville used to explain and advance ancient Greek knowledge. When we Turks were connected with Arabic knowledge, that instruction did not remain in Arab cities. Yes! We finally obtained the beloved woman. However, soon after that that her beauty wore off, her teeth fell out, her hair turned gray, and she could no longer give birth ... Now we are giving up oriental culture since it does not correspond to any need.[21]

The implication here was that the Turks now needed a new "bride," namely Western European civilization and its literature. Nevertheless, Celal Nuri did not believe that adopting the new cultural identity was a total break from Turkey's culture, but instead was simply following its natural path of development: "no matter how much we imitate we cannot exactly copy [a different country's] literature. Literature will take on our own national color."[22]

Unsurprisingly, Celal Nuri's ideas paralleled his earlier vision of racial evolution, in which he posited that the Turks, in reacting to the Mediterranean environment of Anatolia, gradually changed their physiognomy from an Asian to a Caucasian people. Here, however, he borrowed from Hippolyte Taine, the famous French positivist, whom Unionist intellectuals favored for his postulation that nations emerged out of flexible circumstances.[23]

This contrasted sharply with the Turkist linguistic revolutionaries, who had their own interpretation of Müller. Sadri Maksudi, for instance, would highlight a passage from him in a huge font: "The grammar of the Turkish language is so uniform and perfect that we might imagine the language to be the result of the deliberations of some eminent body of learned men."[24]

This was a very problematic translation, given the fact that Müller actually said that no such academic society "could have devised what the mind of man produced, left itself in the steppes of Tartary and guided by its innate laws or by an instinctive power as wonderful as any within the realm of nature." The linguist instead should study the "inner workings" of such a language "as if watching the building of cells in a crystal beehive."[25]

Sadri Maksudi, writing to justify the Turkish language revolution, however, believed that cultural and linguistic engineering was the wave of the future. He cited the endorsement of Carl Brockelmann, another famous German enthusiast of Turkist Central Asian studies: "[The responsibility of the Turkish nation] is to create a culture suitable to its personality; this is a result of political salvation, and a manifestation of its independence."[26] Brockelmann also agreed that a Turkish language academy should immediately embark on such a project to purify the language by eliminating foreign words and finding or creating its equivalents.[27]

By "purifying" the language, Sadri Maksudi argued, you could go back to the original Turkish Müller allegedly alluded to, with the end goal of "liberating" the Turkish national spirit from Anatolia all the way back to its original Eurasian heartland. The radical ideological implications of this argument meant utterly gutting the Turkish language of its cultural Islamic heritage in the hope of creating a secular, and even perhaps pagan, Turkist identity.

Perhaps even Atatürk, who avidly read Sadri Maksudi and took his book as a cue to set up the first and second Turkish Language Conference (*Türk Dili Kurultayı*) in 1932 and 1934, ultimately had reservations—especially in the wake of a radical effort to replace as many originally Arabic and Persian borrowed words as possible. In 1936, he convened a third conference after having read an article entitled "La psychologie de quelques éléments des langues Turques" (1935) by Hermann Kvergić. Kvergić's argument, labeled the Sun Language Theory, claimed that all languages were ultimately of Turkish origin.[28] The logical consequence of this argument was that the purge of Turkish of foreign words was ultimately nonsensical as no vocabulary was ultimately foreign to it. This harkened back to Müller's original statement about Turanic languages being very fluid in their primitive nature, and that cultural and linguistic inter-mixtures were actually progress, not decline. Celal Nuri may well have been pleased to see his interpretation come back into vogue, however belatedly.

Ziya Gökalp and Poetry

Ziya Gökalp, one of those who spearheaded the initial push for reform, wrote a controversial article that castigated Celal Nuri as one of those who sought to "reinvigorate ancient lyrical and commemorative poems (*gazel* & *kaside*)."[29] This effort, he claimed, was symptomatic of those who "wanted to return to life before the *Tanzimat*."[30] He labeled such "reactionaries" as a "black danger" as they sought to numb the population by promoting a corrupt, foreign, and unnatural literary culture. In the end, such culprits aimed at "creating an artificial nobility." If allowed to succeed, such a "feudal class" might invite full-scale rebellion, given the desperate conditions at the end of the First World War. The Bolsheviks, whom he termed the "red danger," were on the prowl for exactly this type of opportunity to spread Communism to the Ottoman state.[31]

Celal Nuri protested greatly. He believed that Ziya Gökalp's denunciation of lyrical and commemorative poetry, which was characterized by the use of the Persian *izafet*, was horribly mistaken. He thought it was "error, unfounded accusation and calumny" to blame those "Persian imitators" for "not being patriotic." He pointed to the sixteenth-century Ottoman poet Fuluzi (1483–1556), who used the *izafet* unceasingly in his court literature (*divan edebiyatı*). Although he could have easily written in Persian, he sought to enrichen the language by incorporating new, high cultural forms.[32] Celal Nuri also believed that Turks should regard many other famous premodern poets, such as Nefi (1572–1635), Baki (1526–1600), Nedim (1681–1730), Şeyh Galip (1757–98), and İzzet Molla (b. 1785), in a similar manner.[33]

This debate reminded Celal Nuri of when he was just a high school student at *Galata Saray*. He took a class from a teacher, where he had to read Jacques-

Begnigne Bossuet's "Speech on the History of the Universe." Celal Nuri was shocked that his teacher had him read the assignment, given that he was instructed to write brief, clear sentences, and never to use rhetorical language with abstract ideas and assertions. But Bossuet wrote his sentences thirty-five lines long in continuous paragraphs. After asking his teacher why, the professor smilingly replied:

> My son! Bossuet is a literary man and orator who not only France but mankind as a whole should be proud of ... [If you examine the time before him], you would understand how revolutionary Bossuet was not only in French, but also in the world of ideas. It is necessary to read him and appreciate him, but not imitate him.[34]

Celal Nuri had learned a powerful lesson:

> I will not hesitate to give justice to the past. Thus I honor and sanctify poets like Nefi and Fuluzi whom many people now regard as non-national. [But] if those 'non-national poets' and 'Persian imitators' were not there, today none of us would have used this language of knowledge ... [Those poets] are people of invention who nurtured our nationality.[35]

He regarded the national past as sacred. It does not simply "wake up" from its slumber.[36]

Celal Nuri despaired at the number of contemporary poets who failed to live up to the greatness of Fuluzi and other classical Ottoman *divan* authors. In particular, he singled out Tevfik Fikret (1867–1915) and Cenab Şahabettin (1870–1934), members of the *Edebiyat-ı Cedide*, who believed that they should develop more intricate and complex forms of the *izafet* and Persian language in order to create a new, enlightened individual who would practice literary art for its own sake:

> Tevfik Fikret and Cenab Şahabettin ... used unnecessary and excessive Persian and Arabic ... They could not drink or digest the language and therefore others could not use ... [what they produced].[37]

He singled out Cenab Şahabettin for abuse:

> Cenab Şahabettin's prose and even his verse are a feast of dessert and candy ... Bonbons are followed by syrup, baklava, *revani, muhalebbi, kadayıf,* cookies, *keşgül,* etc. Each of his works are exquisite, but he is going to give us diabetes![38]

If this decadent fashion continued, Celal Nuri believed that the style would fade away quickly on its own: "If the *gazel, kıta,*[39] and other [classical Ottoman poetical forms] are diagnosed with malaria in the third degree, leave them alone and they will die a natural death."⁴⁰ Celal Nuri also believed it was not fair for Ziya Gökalp to label all those who used the *izafet* as practitioners of "*Yan Geldizm*," people who allegedly shrugged their shoulders at others' calamities during the wartime and simply sat around and enjoyed themselves.⁴¹

For Celal Nuri, the ideas and literary style of Abdülhak Hamid (Tarhan) best represented his own attitude. Celal Nuri lauded Abdülhak Hamid's poem "A Voice From Above" ("*Bala'dan Bir Ses*") in 1912.⁴² The poem, composed with heavy use of the *izafet*, urged the Ottoman intellectual to try to understand the trap that westernizing secularism posed to his own identity. Writing in an abstract but elegant language, Abdülhak Hamid called for new generations of scholars not to forget the fundamental Islamic principle that "human beings are the most sacred creatures," meaning that they should never fail to treat themselves and each other with the utmost respect.⁴³ By embracing secular humanism's false promise that they themselves were perfectible by breaking away from their fellow Turkish Muslims, they would ultimately wind up as fools, subject to ridicule from those who had tempted them:

> The fruit turns moldy and maggoty. The world similarly becomes old as its goods and creatures upon it. They are careless, incognizant of their shabbiness and say that 'if there was no mankind it was not possible to know the Creator.' The "satisfied" are worthy of sighs and tears, for each of them are both unlucky and fortunate. There is a distant hope in their natural constitution, a hope that is necessary for their lives. But it is not hope but wisdom. And while that wise human being is unhappy, humanity became happy. His actions, conceit and pride are worthy of ridicule. Laughing and laughing about this from morning till night.⁴⁴

Celal Nuri must have appreciated Abdülhak Hamid's patriotic vision as fundamentally rooted in an Islamic spirit that was fighting to maintain human dignity in the face of Western imperialism, and its liberal, secular extension. For both Celal Nuri and Abdülhak Hamid, pursuing a "spiritless" ideology, as reflected in any atheistic ideology, was a dead end.

This was proof indeed that the so-called "Persian imitators" could in fact provide spiritual guidance to their countrymen as long as they had the proper focus and dedication, according to Celal Nuri:

> I think that in order to respect and glorify the lofty reputation of Abdülhak Hamid, the writer of these lines [we must proclaim] … this famous poet and most glorious author … as having written poetry equal to the Iliad and the Odyssey … He is a genius of disseminating light. If the present century does not

appreciate Abdülhak Hamid's skills, the guilt does not fall upon the poet, but instead the time which is destitute of appreciating his degree of loftiness. Many magnificent people have only been appreciated many centuries later.[45]

Celal Nuri had almost the exact opposite reaction when he analyzed Ziya Gökalp's *New Life* (*Yeni Hayat*) (1916). Written in a simplified, pedantic style, the work was a collection of poems that intended to instill the values and ideology of Turkism to new generations of citizens. Celal Nuri poured ridicule on the work, making a vague reference to Voltaire, who after being forced to listen to a watchmaker who blurted out a poem to him every day eventually confronted him: "Voltaire: Master! What is your art? Poet: I am a watchmaker, my master. Voltaire: If that is the case, please repair the watch."[46]

Celal Nuri's main criticism was that Ziya Gökalp, a social scientist committed to rational, theoretical discussion, wrote his poems like academic or policy papers. One can see this, for instance, in Ziya Gökalp's poem on pious foundations:

> Two absolute treasuries of the state. One the pious foundation and the other the public treasury. Each constitutional year in parliament it is not possible to acquire two budgets ... The pious foundation does not serve in the provinces. Pious foundations can no longer stay as a ministry.[47]

Celal Nuri sardonically remarked: "When we read these lines of poetry we are satisfied with the destruction of registered and rich rhyme. I wish his meter, along with the treasury, could be enriched!"[48]

He then went on to make fun of yet another verse in a poem dedicated to Talât Pasha, then the interior minister and the most powerful person in government outside of Enver Pasha himself. Citing the line "all hearts covered with a personal tulle like Leibnitz's monad," Celal Nuri wondered:

> Is this type of poetry going to progress, stop or be utterly obliterated? Let us not allow ourselves to venture a guess. Who knows? A caravan of disciples start saying the ode, and, tomorrow we might see miracles occur.[49]

In any case, he could not see the harmony of such verses "ever capable of comparing with the metric (*uruz*)."[50]

Celal Nuri would not even make a substantive comment on Ziya Gökalp's poem "Language" ("*Lisan*") when he mentioned the phrase: "We don't speak words with *gayın*. We are a bosom, not a child."[51] His conclusion was simply that the author was a poetaster who failed to convey his message.[52]

Celal Nuri turned to ideology when he analyzed the central terms in Ziya Gökalp's Turkish nationalism. *Halkçılık*, or "going to the people," he found curious given the fact that the term itself was borrowed from the Russian populists. Why should Ziya Gökalp be so allergic to the adoption of the Persian *izafet*, when his own nationalist movement was not averse to borrowing from foreign countries? Nevertheless, he found it disturbing that Russian populism, itself an ideology of alienated, radically secular intellectuals who went abroad, was responsible in large part for the destruction of czarist Russia itself in the Bolshevik Revolution.[53] If Ziya Gökalp went as far as to secularize the Turkish language, thereby destroying the fundamentally Islamic spirit of the Turkish nation, might he not lay the groundwork for revolution, a counter to Ziya Gökalp's own charge that Celal Nuri and other "reactionaries" were doing the same.

That presumed, of course, that Ziya Gökalp would be able to effectively propagate his nationalist ideal (*mefkûre*) to the people. This was something that Celal Nuri publicly doubted Ziya Gökalp and his colleagues, after all, were forming his own "academy" at the university level; yet, he lacked the effective public educational structure to make his academy thrive. More importantly, he also lacked a true grasp of mass psychology.

Celal Nuri posited that social scientists could not engineer societies with simple calculations. Le Bon, in his work *The Evolution of Matter* (1905), maintained that reality was constantly subject to change, and, as such, social scientists, including sociologists, would have to acknowledge that their theories were relative.[54]

Celal Nuri then pointed to a Tolstoy parable about human nature. Tolstoy's "Where Does Evil Come from?" (1869–72) begins with a dervish who asks a crow, a pigeon, a snake, and a deer what they think evil is. The crow answers that it comes from starvation, since he struggles to feed. The pigeon says it comes from love, since all problems come from caring for others. The snake says that it is braveness, since you expose yourself to risk, and the deer says that it is fear, since that is the way you endanger yourself. But the dervish answers that evil is actually our nature and that we have to come to grips with it.[55]

The moral of the story for Celal Nuri is that people, no matter how much they believe in their own perfection, can only work for the goodness of society by realizing the individual has to respect the humanity of others. It is curious, nonetheless, that Celal Nuri agreed with Tolstoy that human nature was innately flawed, since this attitude fit much more with the Protestant view of man's sinful nature than it did with the Quran's teaching that everyone is born innocent of sin. This likely reflected Celal Nuri's own preference for reforming Islam in a way akin to sixteenth-century Lutherans or English Protestants.

Celal Nuri, in fact, idealized the open-ended nature of the English aristocracy, seeing that it was a model for Ottoman elites during his own time. Here was the ideal of an open-ended aristocracy that would welcome new elements when they merited it. Although there were established families in the Ottoman Empire (i.e., Köprülüzade, Karaosmanoğluları, Evrenos), there were many too who worked their way up through the ranks, particularly those involved in education. The Pirizades, originally sheikhs (*şeyh*s) who rose to high ranks because of their devotion to service, were just one example, but certainly there were others, like himself or Abdülhak Hamid, who distinguished themselves through their opinions. Such "democratic" values "were stronger among the Turks than other Muslim nations." Celal Nuri went on to reassure Ziya Gökalp, "a respected professor with noble and generous qualities, that the danger of aristocracy is less than that of what Don Quixote imagined with the windmill."[56]

In other words, Celal Nuri claimed that he along with the bulk of Ottoman intellectuals were performing a critical function in cultivating their own society: "For language expresses the thoughts, knowledge, sciences, and delicate feelings belonging in particular to high society ... We cannot find these words in the dialect of common people."[57] The only hope for true literary cultivation was for the lively exchanges among intellectual elites to filter down to the average Turk: "Language progresses through conservatism. You can be sure that excessive liberalism in language means decadence, decline and putrefaction."[58]

Aristocratic liberty was equally important, as it permitted the free function and progress of society. England was again a model in this regard, as it allowed people to speak their mind. This was especially critical for Muslim Turks to realize, since their own religion endorsed freedom of opinion. He remarked that this was the way that Muslim society preserved its original purity:

> Every opinion was considered in Baghdad, Córdoba, Damascus and Kufa. No one thought to dismiss them, to slander those who interpreted things differently and to prevent them [from expressing themselves].[59]

Woe to those who forgot Islam's basic command that "there was no compulsion in religion."[60]

Such principles were dramatically violated when, after Ziya Gökalp's protest, the government revenue apparently shut down Celal Nuri's newspaper.[61] Had Ziya Gökalp forgotten that the Ottoman intellectuals he now chastised as reactionaries were in fact the first to support the Young Turk Revolution against the autocratic regime of Abdülhamid II?[62]

Celal Nuri's words likely helped bring about his own troubles. Besides disparaging the reform effort, and ridiculing Ziya Gökalp personally at length, the claim of oppression and continuous talk about liberty as the British practiced it were no doubt jarring to many Turks, given that they were about to lose the war, Istanbul itself facing imminent occupation by the Royal Navy and allied forces.

The Alphabet Revolution

Yet Ziya Gökalp's push to get rid of excessive Persian and Arab influences, such as the *izafet*, was ultimately far more modest than the later Kemalist versions. Arabic and Persian words that were deemed part of the Turkish language spoken on the streets of Istanbul were not to be replaced by newly invented or archaic Turkish terms, and the Enver Pasha's 1914 alphabet reform, which substituted separately written Arabic capital letters instead of the connected cursive, was never made mandatory for the public.[63]

Any further reform was delayed from the Ottoman surrender in October 1918, until after the Independence War. An act with profound implications for nearly all aspects of cultural life, the decision to take up the cause where the CUP left off was made after Atatürk had fully consolidated power. It began in 1928, only after Atatürk abolished the sultanate and caliphate, created a one-party state, and enacted the Hat Reform despite numerous protests. The Kemalists now were able to begin the process of secularizing the Turkish language with the intent of broadening its appeal to other Turkish peoples, particularly those under Soviet and Chinese control.

Celal Nuri certainly understood there was no possibility to protest Atatürk and the language reformers the way he had done with Ziya Gökalp. It should be remembered that Celal Nuri's press was silenced in 1924 because of his articles on the return of non-Muslim expatriates. He wanted to continue to publish unhindered in the years ahead. He also must have been leery of being categorized yet again as a reactionary.

Kazım (Karabekir), the great military rival to Atatürk, dismissed a proposal to change the Arabic alphabet to Latin at the Izmir Economic Congress in 1923, saying it would lead their European enemies to "declare to the Islamic world that the Turks have accepted foreign writing and turned Christian."[64] After having helped found the Progressive Republican Party (*Terakkiperver Cumhuriyet Fırkası*) in 1924, Karabekir and many of his partners were banned for inciting the

Şeyh Sait Rebellion, and soon were jailed for the alleged Izmir plot to assassinate Atatürk himself.

In contrast to Karabekir, Celal Nuri was an early advocate of changing the alphabet from Arabic to Latin. This can be seen as early as 1912, when, in the wake of the First Balkan War, he wrote:

> Our letters are very bad. They are insufficient. It does not mean that their deficiencies make them useless, but we have to say that people cannot learn them easily. [Their artificiality] ... hinders our progress.[65]

His solution, however, was predictable: "I would be for boldly changing to Latin letters right away but [the Turks] would not accept it."[66]

Celal Nuri voiced even further caution against altering the alphabet in 1926:

> The basic prerequisite to changing the alphabet is evolution. [To ignore it would sever] the link between the nation's past and future ... This language is not only ours, but also is the property of our ancestors and progeny. For this reason, we, the present generation, cannot give it the shape we want. The pronunciation of those before us was different, and changes are only very slowly coming to the surface. Future generations will also have a different pronunciation. If there is no way of fixing the alphabet to prevent earthquakes in speaking and pronunciation, the relations between past and future generations will be cut. We will avoid this problem if we allow for evolution .... If Turkish was not a written language with the science, techniques, and archaeology of previous generations, we would not have hesitated for a moment ... But we have a language, and it is ourselves. It lies within our entire social and spiritual history. Language cannot be compounded but it forms. Those who want to change the alphabet should take such psychological linguistic and sociological factors into account.[67]

He then pointed to the Germans, who changed from a Gothic to Latin script but did so only gradually, and he even allowed for those hesitant to the shift to continue publishing their works in the Gothic alphabet.[68] Indeed, Enver Pasha's attempt at the alphabet change in 1914 was done in only a partial manner, as it was only required in military correspondence. Time had been allowed for the rest of the society to adjust to the reform but the war and the consequent surrender had disrupted these efforts.

Atatürk possessed an entirely different mindset. Enver Pasha had good intentions, in Atatürk's opinion, but was far too hesitant: "Be brave when you begin and do it completely," he remarked in 1918.[69] By 1928 just on the verge of announcing the alphabet change, Falih Rıfkı (Atay), his close associate, talked to him about the pace of the reform:

I told him there were two proposals, one long-term, of fifteen years, the other short-term, of five years. According to the proponents, in the first period of each of the two systems of writing would be taught side-by-side. The newspapers would begin with half a column in new letters, which would gradually be extended ... He looked me full in the face and said, 'Either this will happen in three months or it will not happen at all.' I was a highly radical revolutionary but I found myself staring at him, open-mouthed. 'My boy,' he said, 'even when the newspapers are down to only half a column in the old writing, everyone will read that bit in the old writing. If anything goes wrong in the meantime, a war, a domestic crisis, our alphabet will wind up like Enver's. It will be dropped immediately.'[70]

Celal Nuri, having aired his opinions on the subject publicly, and officially submitted proposals to both the language advisory board and Atatürk personally, only grudgingly accepted the rapid change in 1928. He consoled himself that the new alphabet would make Turkish much easier since the letters would correspond to the way that a word was actually pronounced, making it possible for a student to learn the language much quicker and be able to "acquire the axioms of reading and writing ... in a very short period. This much is enough for such persons."[71] Likewise, it would pose no major problem for the common illiterate Turk:

Imagine a person who does not know how to write nor what the Arabic letters stand for. All he would have to do in order to deal with his simple words would be to memorize twenty letters. Whatever noise comes out of his mouth could be arranged on a piece of paper.[72]

The real issue with the reform was how to salvage the country's rich literary and artistic heritage. His efforts emphasized the need to have alphabetic characters that could identify and pronounce words of Arabic and Persian origin. These letters included the Latin characters: a "q" for an Arabic-origin "*kef*," a "gh" for a Persian-origin "*kef*," a diacritic in front of a verb to designate what was a "*ayın*," or a "*hemze*," and a palatalized "a" or "u" in certain Arabic and Persian borrowed words. He hoped such special characters would salvage at least some tie to earlier pronunciation and intonation.[73] If they did not find a solution before the new alphabet was finally established, "there is no doubt that we will remain in great chaos."[74] His proposals, as before, met deaf ears.

He also feared, for instance, that the grand tradition of calligraphy (*hüsnühat*) in Ottoman Turkish would be lost after the new alphabet was adopted. Should they forget that world-renowned calligraphers like Yakut Mutasım and Hafız Osman ranked in quality alongside Rocco in Venice, Kirachi in Milan, Koryon in Rome, Augustino in Siena, and Kempis in Holland? The Ottoman writers were rooted in a great Islamic tradition that stretched back as far as Caliph Ali and should not be discarded. He suggested that the reformers be sure to teach Latin calligraphy, so that "the most aesthetic shape should enter into the natural disposition of a child, so that he or she would unconsciously write those letters legibly and beautifully." Such a seemingly trivial art was key to shaping the cultural subconscious of the people, as Le Bon had alluded.[75]

Although he sensed that his efforts at promoting some sort of continuity with the past were forlorn, Celal Nuri at least found comfort in the benefits the alphabet change might yield. The cultural reorientation toward the West that a new alphabet facilitated might provide a new beginning. Was it not possible that if the Turks worked hard in the years and decades ahead to absorb Western literature quicker through the new alphabet, a "literary evolution will follow this revolution?"[76]

The Language Revolution

Nonetheless, the linguistic revolutionaries saw the alphabet change as a prelude to a full-scale purge of borrowed Arabic and Persian words by a state-led language academy. As noted, Ziya Gökalp and like-minded Unionist language reformers had laid such plans earlier, but their reform was far more modest. According to Ziya Gökalp, Arabic and Persian words that truly had taken on a critical meaning of their own in spoken Turkish were not slated for elimination. Only words judged to be superfluous in meaning were to be erased. Ziya Gökalp's goal, however, was not to "revive ancient fossilized Turkish words as substitutes for those that are discarded." The reformers, in his opinion, should create new technical words, but this was to be done first and foremost by using "regular particles and methods of word formation and declension." If impossible to carry out, they should accept Arabic, Persian, and European language terms "that express specific events of certain errors, occupations, and names of technical implements."[77]

Sadri Maksudi, who led the charge for the renewed effort, blamed Ziya Gökalp for neglecting the so-called "archaic Turkish terms":

> Turkish vocabulary is an invaluable treasure of the Turkish race inherited directly from its distant forefathers. It is wrong for us to deprive the Turkish race of these holy jewels. We cannot accept this as it would deprive us of our national consciousness.[78]

According to this ultranationalist interpretation, the original Turkish vocabulary was eternal.[79] This original vocabulary, Sadri Maksudi postulated, was first developed by the Göktürks and other Turkish peoples of the Eurasian and Central Asian homeland. It was a shame, he exclaimed, that the Ottomans abandoned the vocabulary in the fourteenth through sixteenth centuries, just when they were becoming a great power.[80] This linguistic blow constituted a type of cosmopolitanism (*Türksüzlük*), a threat to the self-consciousness of the Turkish race.[81]

It was therefore left up to the Turkish nationalists to restore the original vocabulary, according to Sadri Maksudi. This effort had begun with figures like Buharalı Şeyh Süleyman Efendi, author of *Lugat-i Cağatay ve Türki ve Osmani* (1880–1); Doktor Bekir Çobanzade, author of *Türk-Tatar Lisaniyyatına Medhal* (1923); and Hüseyin Kazım (Kadri), author of *Türk Lugatı* (1927).[82] Sadri Maksudi's work sought to "restore" the true Turkish (*Öztürkçe*) to the greatest extent possible, so that it would be intelligible not just in Turkey, but elsewhere in the Turkish world. Sadri Maksudi rejected Arabic and Persian borrowed words entirely in favor of newly emerging *Öztürkçe* derivatives, although he tolerated a few European equivalents.[83]

Celal Nuri largely resisted the Kemalist movement's purge of Arabic and Persian vocabulary. He argued that going back to the most basic Turkish would reduce the vocabulary from 20,000 to roughly 350 words. Earlier he had sarcastically remarked:

> How is it possible to situate the nationalist ideal (*mefkure*) in an intellect whose entire knowledge totals 365 words? You know that fisherman, boatmen, carriers, fruit sellers, butlers, road workers, vegetable grocers, villagers, farmers, sailors, beggars, milkmen, drivers, distributors and shepherds constitute 90% of the existing population. They do not have more ideas than a child.[84]

If it was made that simple, he commented, "how are we going to express intellectual matters?"[85]

In 1928, he estimated Ottoman Turkish had almost 20,000 words, compared to English, which had 100,000. He admitted that 6000 of those Ottoman Turkish words might be eliminated because they were either outdated or used only by isolated literary circles. Other words too could be eliminated as they were redundant. Nonetheless, a minimum of 10,000 and a maximum of 60,000 were required for a people to adequately engage in intellectual activities,[86] even though the common people "could not digest them."[87] "We [Turks] gained a lot from the rich vocabulary and derivatives that entered our language." Indeed, there were up to thirty-five derivatives from each of the three-letter Arabic roots that were incorporated: "Yes, I say once again that the Arabic influence [benefitted Turkish] ... If we did not have this treasury in our hands, our situation would be very bad indeed."[88]

Clearly, in his opinion, Ottoman Turkish needed to be reformed. Vague, opaque writing permeated their literature, begging the question of what the ordinary reader could possibly gain.[89] He even gave an example, a fairy tale by Abdurrahman Sami Pasha (1794–1882), the first Ottoman minister of education. Celal Nuri himself admitted "that you almost completely forget the meaning of the passages above when you read it," the words seemingly being arranged at random.[90]

Despite such reluctance, Celal Nuri did believe that the current vocabulary was not sufficient to deal with new technical terms. They would have to be invented or incorporated from Western European languages. That process, along with the standardization of grammar and an etymological dictionary for words that were in the current vocabulary, would be the work of a Turkish language academy.

Beyond that, however, the academy should limit itself to collecting Turkish words, including Arabic and Persian borrowings, from all over the country. It was, after all, in the business of providing a framework for language development. In this regard the academy should work to balance the need to modernize the language with Turkish literature's own historical memory.[91]

Celal Nuri argued that Turkish in his day very much resembled France during the sixteenth century, when it tried to standardize the language, as it was spoken and practiced differently throughout its provinces. France at that time, like Turkey, was undergoing a transition from an illiterate to literate society. The French had many borrowed words from Latin, the language of the Catholic Church, and it was important for the country to make a gradual shift in a national direction. The success that the French had in making this transition led to the flowering of their language and culture in the centuries ahead, ultimately leading to the Enlightenment.[92]

Celal Nuri would soon face disappointment, as the Turkish Language Investigative Society (*Türk Dili Tetkik Cemiyeti*) moved ahead to enact the changes for which Sadri Maksudi had asked for. Celal Nuri's pen was silent about any language issue by the end of 1928, a full four years before the first Turkish Language Assembly (*Birinci Türk Dili Kurultayı*) was convened. Celal Nuri, unsurprisingly, was never invited to participate in the Society, or join the assembly organizers. That was reserved for a team of experts that Atatürk handpicked. Celal Nuri attended the first assembly, as reflected in the proceedings, but he never spoke.[93]

Nevertheless, Hüseyin Cahit, a prominent Unionist active in literary and political circles in both the Young Turk and early republican eras, dissented in much the same way Celal Nuri had done earlier. He posited, for example, at the 1932 Assembly that "language is a versifying and conservative force … a social institution that continues its path in a completely democratic manner that is tacitly accepted by the majority."[94]

Hüseyin Cahit warned that the Turkish Language Foundation, in beginning its activities, should limit itself to standardizing grammar and syntax, as well as creating a dictionary that would encompass the various dialects of Turkish.[95] But he thought that the foundation should not exaggerate its role by getting "rid of foreign words from the written language and replace them with purely Turkish ones."[96] This was a mistake, since they could not "pioneer novelties" through an impersonal approach that did not take into account what words the people were actually using.[97] He pointed to the word *tayyare*, or plane, which was likely to be eliminated because of its Arabic root of "*tayr.*" But, he noted, *tayyare* was understood by all Turks and was incomprehensible to Arabs, since it was written in a way that was unique to the Turkish language. Eliminating words like that would be like asking for a Turk to prove that his or her genealogy was racially pure, something that cut against the Turkish notion of citizenship.[98] Celal Nuri had devoted a similar effort, years before, in showing the evolutionary nature of the word for nation, *milliyet*. Although of Arabic origin, and once denoting the Islamic community (*ümmet*), it had developed into a more nuanced concept of a Turkish Republic united by its sense of Sunni Islamic identity.[99] Even Ziya Gökalp, had he lived, might have defended his own term for national ideal, *mefkure*, since he had constructed it from the Arabic root "*fikr.*" Once again, a Turkish word with Arabic origins had no equivalent in the Arabic language.

Hüseyin Cahit went even further when he defended the term *taksim-i âmâl*, meaning labor department, since it too had passed into the common language, making it a waste of effort to replace it with *iş bölümü*, the newly devised purely Turkish equivalent. It did not matter, therefore, that *âmâl* in its original Arabic meant "works" or that it used the Persian *izafet*, since the people assimilated the meaning, not the foreign grammar.[100]

Other scholars also opposed the purge in strong terms. When it came to the *izafet*, Abdülhak Hamid defended his prerogative "to write in this manner," proclaiming that it still was a living part of the language.[101]

Such views were loudly rejected by most of the participants in the assembly. They considered the assembly as both a scientific body and part of a nationalist political movement. The foundation's assembled team of experts believed they had the knowledge and foresight to determine a purely Turkish grammar and vocabulary, and had no time for their authority to be questioned. Were they not empowered by Atatürk, the great secular reformer and savior of the country, to take on this urgent task? They acted according to Sadri Maksudi's warning that "the pure Turkish which has found refuge until now in the villages is in imminent danger of losing its nature and spirit."[102]

It was therefore essential, in their view, that the "nationalization" process, which had picked up steam since the Independence War, now turn to language, something that Ziya Gökalp mentioned some eight years before: "Just as political capitulations are incompatible with political independence and sovereignty, so are linguistic capitulations incompatible with linguistic independence and sovereignty."[103]

But most participants were far more thoroughgoing than even Ziya Gökalp may have wanted. Hasan Ali (Yücel)—a supporter of the foundation, and later an extremely influential minister of education who translated many of the classical works of European literature—as well as Samih Rıfat, the head of the assembly and foundation, publicly ridiculed Ziya Gökalp's defense of "outdated" and "alien" Arabic terms. Hasan Ali disputed, for example, that the common people had any real notion what terms like *taksim-i âmâl* meant, as it would take someone twelve years of education at a traditional Islamic school (*medrese*) to learn them.[104] Samih Rıfat likewise said that keeping such terms would be like telling your children that "you will close your eyes and forget about the origins of your laws and principles."[105] In any case, it would be easy to invent terms from pure Turkish roots, since language itself was not fixed.[106] Hasan Ali noted that Hüseyin Cahit himself used the neologism *verim*,[107] showing that he had at least unconsciously begun to assimilate the new vocabulary.[108]

What Hüseyin Cahit and those who opposed the reform truly lacked, in their opinion, was the revolutionary nationalist will to succeed. This was ironic given that Hüseyin Cahit would later translate *Mein Kampf*, where Hitler preached exactly that message.[109] By defending Arabic borrowed terms, Hüseyin Cahit was allegedly on the deceptive path of sowing superstition. Should not he and his ilk heed the warning that someone "with baggy trousers and the *şeyhülislam*'s robe [cannot] … work in the laboratory?"—a thinly veiled threat that he was no better than those who had resisted the Hat Reform. Reactionaries of the previous generations were doomed, Samih Rifat predicted, since only the young "had no past to lose, and only the future to gain."[110] Hüseyin Cahit, Abdülhak Hamid, Celal Nuri, and anyone who opposed or had reservations about the foundation and their radical agenda, should either remain silent or be subject to punishment: they were old generation Unionists. The American General Douglas MacArthur, who conceivably watched the exchange as he attended the conference with Atatürk himself,[111] might have imagined, if he had known Turkish, that such people were bound to either "die" or "fade away."

Conclusion

Celal Nuri's aspirations for the Turkish language reached a bitter end. Fighting the label of "black reactionary" since 1917, all of his journalistic activities, and that of his like-minded colleagues, did no good. These individuals may have had a willing audience among literary elites, but their arguments had very little purchase in the nationalist movements and military-led governments of the time. Voices urging dictatorship and revolution carried the day, especially given the fact that an independent Turkey could no longer afford its ties with the political past. There seemed to be an unstoppable urge to make the decisive second step, a cultural revolution that would utterly destroy any lingering sentiment the people might have had with their historical memory of the Islamic, Ottoman past. Celal Nuri, who sought to modernize, and gradually transform the language to fit the needs of the moment, was not ready to endorse this radical position.

Within four years the Turkish Language Foundation eliminated at least 32,322 borrowed Arabic and Persian words,[112] and it standardized the grammar without the *izafet*. Yet, even Atatürk may have had regrets about how far the reform went. The 1936 Assembly, under Atatürk's direction, endorsed the Sun Language Theory, which had the practical effect of ending the language purge until the end of Atatürk's life. The damage, however, was done, "a catastrophic success" which cannot be denied.[113]

7

Conclusion

By the time Celal Nuri (İleri) died on November 2, 1938, his lifework was in question. Mustafa Kemal (Atatürk), Samih Rifat, Ragip Hulusi (Özdem), and Afet İnan, with the full force of the Turkish government, had acted swiftly to impose the change from Arabic to Latin letters and eliminate so much "foreign" vocabulary and grammar that new students would not be able to comprehend the rich Ottoman Turkish literature that had been written as recently as 1928. This alphabet and language revolution was precisely intended to cut the cultural and political links with the Ottoman, Islamic past.[1] Celal Nuri was one of the first to support the gradual adoption of Latin letters, but he saw it as a way to reform the language along Western lines, not as a way to completely eliminate the consciousness and symbolic connection to its past. The reform should be enacted by members of the literary elite, like himself, and not done simply by government committee or fiat.[2]

The Kemalists no doubt acknowledged Celal Nuri's early work on women and family reform during the Young Turk era. He, like Ziya Gökalp, was among the chief Unionists to call for an end to polygamy, the practice of veiling, and argue in favor of women having greater rights to divorce, educate, and employment. He and Gökalp saw these steps as critical to successfully liberating women and their families, paving the way for them to empower society, and their nation as a whole. They also wrote in large part to rally women to the patriotic cause by urging them to be moral examples to the public during wartime, and be ready to volunteer for service to the state as nurses, teachers, and, if necessary, even become trained as merchants, bankers, and artisans. And yet, Celal Nuri and Gökalp's program paled again in comparison to the later Kemalist reformers. They, like most other Unionist writers, did not call for women to have the right to vote, to stand as elected representatives, and to have full and unfettered access to the schools or the profession of their choice. The Kemalists too distinguished themselves from Celal Nuri and Gökalp in their utter contempt for justifying their reform efforts according to traditional Islamic legal sources, and their embrace of secularism.

This is curious, since Celal Nuri, along with Abdullah Cevdet (Karlıdağ) and other like-minded CUP members, had been attracted to the vulgar materialist philosophy of Ludwig Büchner, who had claimed that science itself was the only true faith, as the universe was restricted to the interaction of force and matter. Celal Nuri had argued that since Islam was of an evolutionary, scientific character, it could be redirected to promote this worldview. He focused on the great role Prophet Muhammad played in advancing Islamic civilization, and lending a political, moral, and even scientific example to later reformers.[3] Celal Nuri indeed hoped that the political leaders of his time, such as Enver Pasha and Atatürk, could complete this mission. He denied the fundamental spiritual aspect of the faith, such as the belief in an afterlife, judgment day, and mystical union with God. Ahmet Hilmi Şehbenderzade, a bitter critic of Celal Nuri, warned that this hollowed-out version of Islam would not be accepted by either the population, who would remain pious, or the secularizing elites that would embrace outright atheism. The events of the Kemalist era would confirm these fears.[4]

Celal Nuri was even more mistaken when it came to non-Muslim and non-Sunni Muslim minorities. Made during times of war, population exchange, ethnic strife, and mass death, Celal Nuri's statements dangerously incited his readers to persecute the Greek, Armenian, and Sephardic Jewish communities of Istanbul. One example of this was his warning about the treachery of the Greek Orthodox Patriarch Joachim III in 1912 just after the massive Ottoman defeat in the First Balkan War.[5] Celal Nuri later protested the return of "wealthy" Armenians and Greeks in the immediate aftermath of the Turkish Independence War,[6] and he spoke despairingly of the Jews in 1932, going so far as to claim that the fears of pending Nazi persecution in Germany were exaggerated.[7]

Celal Nuri's skepticism toward the minorities came in part from his own background. His father's side, Muslim Turks originally from Crete, must have resented that they had lost their homes, and they must have worried that their countrymen were doomed to replay that tragedy. His father and uncle, an experienced governor and a theologian respectively, expressed their prejudices in their own works about Yezidis and Shiites. This informed Celal Nuri's later vision of the empire, which he hoped would become a melting pot of ethnicities ("elements") coalescing around a unified identity of culturally Turkish Hanefi Sunni Muslims.[8]

Celal Nuri was certainly a committed Muslim nationalist, who is at his most venomous during times of international strife. Beginning with the Italian invasion of Libya in 1911, up until the decisive Turkish nationalist victory over the Greeks at Dumlupınar in 1922, Celal Nuri dedicated the bulk of his work through stoking up resentment against what he perceived to be foreign incursions and internal separatist threats. He ceaselessly sought to promote the emergence of a new Muslim entrepreneurial and artisan class that would displace their non-Muslim rivals, particularly the thriving Greek and Armenian merchants and artisans of Istanbul—the basic Unionist wartime program of developing the "national economy."

Celal Nuri had a hard time after Dumlupınar in toning down this rhetoric, as seen in the above-cited complaints about letting expatriate Armenian merchants back in 1924, and his praise of the Nazi program against the Jews in 1932. The state reaction—to shut down his press—was likely not just because of moral outrage but also because the Kemalists feared Muslim nationalists might use the press to stoke public opinion against them. Celal Nuri was forced to sit in silence, and, although he continued to serve as an MP until 1934, he only made brief public appearances, such as his terse defense of Mustafa Kemal and İnan's legislation to give women the national right to vote on April 4, 1933.[9] He also praised Mustafa Kemal's reforms in a book he wrote in 1926, but it should be remembered that much of that work cautioned the government not to engage in radical top-down language reform.

Celal Nuri was never to fully return to the reformist vigor he had in the immediate wake of the April 13, 1909 uprising. The core problem of course was that the Kemalists had utterly abandoned Celal Nuri and the mainstream Unionists' insistence on Islam as a political identifier, and that rejecting the faith entirely was far more on the cutting edge than reforming it from within. But even if Celal Nuri publicized his ideas, he was doomed to be silenced by a government that brooked no criticism of its policies, particularly after the Sheikh Sait revolt and the Law on the Maintenance of Order that followed.[10] He had thus joined the ranks of an older generation of Unionists whose ideas had become outmoded, or even deemed reactionary by the new government, that in many ways was just as autocratic as the sultan that they had originally rebelled against.[11]

If anything Celal Nuri was committed throughout his life as a politician and journalist to progressivism. This commitment was obvious of course not only in the name of his long-time newspaper *İleri*, or "progress" but also as it is the last name he took after the passage of the Surname Law in 1934. As noted above, being a progressive meant promoting modernizing reform, as seen in his prescriptions on politics, Islam, women, and language. His contributions in this regard, such as his call for a secular civil code, ending traditional Islamic education and thoroughly retraining religious officials from the highest governmental offices to the local imam, abolishing polygamy, discouraging veiling, and adopting the

Latin alphabet instead of the traditional Arabic, were all part of a long process of reform that the Kemalists built upon. But, like any progressive regardless of generation, Celal Nuri was obsessed by the fear of reaction, particularly by those who would manipulate still-lingering popular support for traditional Islam and an autocratic sultanate. That fear continued long after Sultan Abdülhamid II died, as witnessed in the early republican era, for example, in the Sheikh Sait revolt and the Menemen incident.[12]

Celal Nuri's gradualist approach toward reform contrasted sharply with his more revolutionary-minded counterparts, as seen in his advocacy of constitutional monarchy and not a revolutionary secular nation, his acceptance of a piecemeal approach toward women and familial reform in 1917, and his disapproval of a top-down government-imposed break from Ottoman Turkish in favor of a modern Turkish that "purified" its rich Arabic and Persian vocabulary. His fear was of course that pursuing uncompromising change once again might unintentionally provoke popular reaction against the state.

Celal Nuri's evolutionism was also deeply rooted in his own Social Darwinistic outlook. Having inculcated the popular works of Gustave Le Bon, Max Nordau, and Ludwig Büchner, Celal Nuri believed that promoting scientific reform was critical for his nation to survive the "contest of life."[13] It was thus a world of all against all where only the strongest nation would survive. He therefore tended to see his fellow Ottoman Muslims as in a death struggle with rival non-Muslim Greek and Armenian nationalist movements and continually pointed to the Western powers as plotting together with their enemies to seek his country's demise.

Such Social Darwinistic views reinforced his own intolerant attitude toward "dangerous" non-Muslim minorities and foreign powers in general. They comported well with that of a wartime propagandist who sought to justify and/or encourage hostility toward "enemies" on the part of his army, security forces, and the general population. Celal Nuri's bellicose writings—such as his declaration of the Greek Patriarch's treachery in 1912, his stern warning to Hawrutian Sharighian about the Dashnakiyun and the Armenians in 1913, or his rabble-rousing about the interior minister and the police chief of Istanbul's handlings with returning Armenian expatriates in 1924—resembled other reckless journalistic activities in later Turkish history, such as the false reports of the Greek burning of the Turkish Consulate in Thessaloniki in September 1955 that triggered citywide riots in Istanbul, resulting in much of the remaining Greek minority's immigration abroad.

Celal Nuri's intolerance toward rival political movements, particularly the liberal governments that opposed the Unionists, was also emblematic of political rivalries that have often gone awry in late Ottoman and Turkish history. The inability of governing parties to work with a loyal opposition was a continual issue. It must not have struck Celal Nuri as so strange that the Kemalists, once they came to power, would regard "moderate" Unionists like himself with suspicion. After all, the Unionists had done the same with the liberals and other non-Unionist Young Turks. Such ironies no doubt left him embittered when he reached the end of his days.

Notes

Chapter 1

1. Erik J. Zürcher, *The Young Turk Legacy and Nation Building* (London; New York: I.B. Tauris, 2010), 26–7, 33.
2. M. Şükrü Hanioğlu, *A Brief History of the Late Ottoman Empire* (Princeton; Oxford: Princeton University Press, 2008), 150. The CUP, originally founded in 1889, the centennial of the French Revolution, undoubtedly were inspired by that earlier historical example. Nevertheless, the addition of the Ottoman term "justice," a central concept in the Islamic justification for sultanic rule, to the slogan was telling. This catchword and the oft-chanted exclamation "long live the sultan" showed the CUP and their Young Turk supporters' commitment to transforming the empire into a constitutional monarchy, rather than a new revolutionary regime. Zürcher, *The Young Turk Legacy*, 213; Aykut Kansu, *The Revolution of 1908 in Turkey* (Leiden: Brill Academic Publishers, 1997), 73–113; Bedross Der Matossian, *Shattered Dreams of Revolution: From Liberty to Violence in the Late Ottoman Empire* (Stanford: Stanford University Press, 2014), 43–4.
3. Der Matossian, *Shattered Dreams of Revolution*, 49–71; Kansu, *Revolution of 1908*, 99–104.
4. Zürcher, *The Young Turk Legacy*, 34.
5. Zürcher, *The Young Turk Legacy*, 99–102.
6. Erik J. Zürcher, *Turkey: A Modern History*, third edition (London; New York: I.B. Tauris, 2010), 95–9; Zürcher, *The Young Turk Legacy*, 76–83.
7. Zürcher, *Turkey*, 80–3.
8. Zürcher, *Turkey*, 99; Zürcher, *The Young Turk Legacy*, 81.
9. The Western Balkan towns of Üsküdar (Shkodër) and Yanina (Ioannina) were also technically in Ottoman hands in December 1912 but were hopelessly besieged by the Montenegrins and Greeks respectively. Zürcher, *Turkey*, 107; Barbara Jelavich, *History of the Balkans Volume 2: 20th Century* (New York; London: Cambridge University Press, 1983), 99.
10. The Ottomans admittedly had been worried about the loss of Anatolia since the Ottoman loss of the war with the Russians in 1877–8. The Ottomans were forced in the ensuing Treaty of Berlin (1878) to implement reforms to protect local Armenians from Circassians and Kurds under European supervision, a measure that they feared would incite separatist movements. Abdulhamid II created the

Hamidian light cavalry units to deal with this perceived threat in 1891. Robert Olson, *The Emergence of Kurdish Nationalism and the Shaikh Said Rebellion, 1880–1925* (Austin: University of Texas Press, 1989), 1–7.

11 Zürcher, *The Young Turk Legacy*, 99–100, 107–8.

12 For further information on Yusuf Akçura, see Umut Uzer, *An Intellectual History of Turkish Nationalism: Between Turkish Ethnicity and Islamic Identity* (Salt Lake City: The University of Utah Press, 2016), 56–60; François Georgeon, *Aux Origines du Nationalisme Turc: Yusuf Akçura (1876–1935)* (Paris: Institut d'Études Anatoliennes, 1989).

13 Here and throughout the book I use the term "pan-Islamist" to refer to those who ideally sought to politically unify all Muslims into a single state. I use the term "Islamist" for those who supported forming a government and society based on Islamic principles and law.

14 Zürcher, *The Young Turk Legacy*, 216–17. Here and throughout the rest of the book I use the term "pan-Turkist" to refer to those who dreamt of uniting all the various Turkish ethnic groups from Anatolia through the Caucasus to Central Asia. I use the term "Turkist" for those who focused on establishing a definitively Turkish state in Anatolia.

15 Zürcher, *The Young Turk Legacy*, 216.

16 Zürcher, *The Young Turk Legacy*, 216 referring to Niyazi Berkes, *The Development of Secularism in Modern Turkey* (Montreal: McGill University Press, 1964), 337–66. Moreover, more recent scholarship such as by Zürcher, Ş. Tufan Buzpınar, and Hanioğlu stress the enduring influence positivism from the foundation of the CUP well into the Kemalist era, despite a dip in popularity from 1913 to 1923, when the CUP and, thereafter, the Turkish nationalists were courting Muslim popular opinion during wartime. Leading CUP publicists Abdullah Cevdet and Celal Nuri were examples of this tendency. While Celal Nuri embraced the nationalistic and pan-Islamic fervor of the wartime period, his former mentor Abdullah Cevdet did not. Zürcher, *The Young Turk Legacy*, 147, 214, 232, 238–9, 276–7; Ş. Tufan Buzpınar, "Celal Nuri's Concepts of Westernization," *Middle Eastern Studies*, Vol. 43, No. 2 (March 2007), 247–9, 252–5; Ş. Tufan Buzpınar, "Öteki üzerinden hesaplaşma: Celal Nuri ve Abdullah Cevdet'in Avrupa tartışmaları hakkında bir değirlendirme," *Dîvân: İlmî Araştırmaları* 19 (2005/2): 254, 274–5; M. Şükrü Hanioğlu, *Bir Siyasi Düşünür Olarak: Doktor Abdullah Cevdet ve Dönemi* (İstanbul: Üçdal Nesriyat, 1981), 291–2, 325–95; M. Şükrü Hanioğlu, "Garbcılar: Their Attitudes toward Religion and Their Impact on the Official Ideology of the Turkish Republic," *Studia Islamica*, Vol. 86, No. 2 (August 1997): 153–8.

17 Zürcher, *The Young Turk Legacy*, 217 referring to M. Şükrü Hanioğlu, *The Young Turks in Opposition* (New York; London: Oxford University Press, 1995), 211. Also see *The Young Turk Legacy*, 195–6.

18 Zürcher, *The Young Turk Legacy*, 147–50, 229–32. Yiğit Akın points out that the Ottoman propagandists themselves framed the conflict as a jihad in defense of the empire. Yiğit Akın, *When the War Came Home: The Ottomans' Great War and the Devastation of an Empire* (Stanford: Stanford University Press, 2018), 78–80.

19 There is no scholarly agreement on the year of Celal Nuri's birth. Christoph Herzog argues that he was born in 1881, Alaettin Gövsa says he was born in 1878 and Recep Duymaz claims 1882. Christoph Herzog, *Geschichte und Ideologie: Mehmed Murad und Celal Nuri über die historischen Ursachen des osmanischen Niedergangs* (Berlin: Klaus Schwarz Verlag, 1996), 88; Alaettin Gövsa, *Türk Meşhurları Ansiklopedisi* (İstanbul: Yedigün Neşriyatı, 1946), 80; Recep Duymaz, "Celal Nuri İleri," in: *İslam Ansiklopedisi*, vol. 7 (İstanbul: Türkiye Diyanet Vakfı, 1993), 242. I give more credence to Christoph Herzog's listing of 1881 as Celal Nuri's year of birth on the basis of an interview Herzog had with Rasih Nuri İleri, his nephew. Haydar Kemal's account, written in 1912–13, largely substantiates Herzog's argument when it says Celal Nuri was born in Hicri year 1298, which ran from December 4, 1880 to November 25, 1881. Haydar Kemal. *Tarih-i İstikbal: Münasebetiyle Celâl Nuri Bey* (İstanbul: Yeni Osmanlı Matbaası ve Kütüphanesi, h.1331 [1913]), 9. "Haydar Kemal" was likely a pseudo-name of Celal Nuri himself. Herzog, *Geschichte und Ideologie*, 92, footnote 2.

20 Originally given the name Mehmed Celaleddin, his first name was shortened to Celal. He almost immediately adopted the last name Nuri in deference to his father. His brothers Suphi Nuri and Sedat Nuri also followed this trend. Herzog, *Geschichte und Ideologie*, 88–9; Buzpınar, "Celal Nuri's Concepts of Westernization," 247–8; Buzpınar, "Celal Nuri ve Abdullah Cevdet," 153; Duymaz, "Celal Nuri İleri," 242; Recep Duymaz, *Dil ve Edebiyat Yazıları I: Celal Nuri İleri* (İstanbul: Kitabevi, 1995), 15–20; Necmi Uyanık, "Batıcı Bir Aydın Olarak Celal Nuri İleri ve Yenileşme Sürecinde Fikir Hareketlerine Bakışı," in: *Selçuk Üniversitesi Türkiyat Araştırmaları Dergisi*, Sayı: 15 Güz 2004, 232–3, 235.

21 Adum; S. Sirenes, translator, *Osmanlı İmparatorluğu'nun Tarih-i Tedennisi Celal Nuri Bey'in Tarih-i Tedenniyat-ı Osmaniyyesi'ni Tenkiden Azad Emarid Gazetesinde Münderic Silsile-i Makalat* (Der Saadet: Bâb-ı Âli Sadaret Kapusı Karşısında "Edeb" Matbaası, 1331 [1913]), 96.

22 Sırrı Giridi, *Âra-i Milel* (İstanbul: Bab-ı Âli Caddesinde Numero 52, h.1303 [1885–6]).

23 Ayandan Nuri (Mustafa Nuri), *Abede-i İblis: Yezidi'nin Taifesinin İtikadı Adatı Evsafı* (İstanbul: Matbaa-i İctihad, h.1328 [1910–11]); Abdulhamit Kırmızı, *Abdülhamid'in VALİLERİ: Osmanlı Vilayet İdaresi, 1895–1908*, üçüncü baskı (İstanbul: Klasik Yayınları, 2008), 70.

24 Djelal Noury, *Le Diable promu Dieu* (Constantinople: Imprimerie du "Jeune-Turc," 1910); Adum, *Azad*, 80–1; I Celal Nuri, *İttihad-ı İslam: İslamın Mazisi, Hali,*

İstikbali (İstanbul: Yeni Osmanlı Matbaası, h.1331 [1912–13]), 160–5; Celal Nuri, *Havaic-i Kanuniyyemiz* (İstanbul: Matbaa-yı İctihad, h.1331 [1912–13]), 113; Celal Nuri, *Tarih-i İstikbal: Mesail-i Siyasi* (İstanbul: Yeni Osmanlı Matbaası, h.1331 [1913]), 183–5.

25 Giridi Ahmed Saki, *Celal Nuri Bey ve Cezri Fikirleri* (Istanbul: Hukuk Matbaası, 1335-1338 [1919–22]), 5.

26 Mehmed Zeki Pakalın, *Sicill-i Osmani Zeyli*, VI. Cilt (Ankara: Türk Tarihi Kurumu, 2008), 131–2. There is, however, no record that Celal Nuri ultimately graduated from Galata Saray. Recep Duymaz, "Celal Nuri İleri ve Ati Gazetesi" (Unpublished Ph.D. Dissertation: Marmara Üniversitesi, 1991), 5–6.

27 Duymaz, "Celal Nuri İleri ve Ati Gazetesi," 6; Ahmed Saki, *Celal Nuri Bey*, 5–6; Kemal, *Celâl Nuri Bey*, 10.

28 Celal Nuri, *İlel-i Ahlâkiyyemiz* (İstanbul: Yeni Osmanlı Matbaası ve Kütüphanesi, h.1332 [1913–14]), 112–13.

29 Duymaz, "Celal Nuri İleri ve Ati Gazetesi," 6–7; Ahmed Saki, *Celal Nuri Bey*, 5–6; Kemal. *Celal Nuri Bey*, 10–11; Herzog, *Geschichte und Ideologie*, 89–90.

30 Celal Nuri, *Ahlâkiyyemiz*, 70.

31 In my opinion the Young Turk era is synonymous with what is commonly referred to as the Second Constitutional Period (*2. Meşrutiyet Devri*). It began when Abdulhamid II reconvened the Ottoman parliament on July 24, 1908, and ended October 30, 1918, when the Ottoman military authorities signed an armistice with their British counterparts at Mudros harbor, effectively concluding the empire's participation in the First World War. The presence of British and French forces in Istanbul and elsewhere in the empire after that date led to a new epoch of occupation and nationalist resistance.

32 Djelal Noury, *Une Année de Liberté Istanbul* (Constantinople: Imprimerie du "Courier d'Orient," 1909), 5. I would like to thank Dr. Birsen Bulmuş for very generously translating this and the other French language texts I have used in this manuscript to English.

33 Celal Nuri, *Kara Tehlike* (Dersaadet: Cemiyyet Kütüphanesi, r.1334 [1918]), 37.

34 Celal Nuri, *Kara Tehlike*, 36.

35 Ozan Özavcı, "A Jewish 'liberal' in Istanbul: Vladimir Jabotinsky, the Young Turks and the Zionist Press Network, 1908–1911," in: Abigail Green, Simon Levis Sullam, editors, *Jews, Liberalism, Anti-Semitism: A Global History* (New York: Palgrave Macmillan, 2020), 290–7.

36 Herzog, *Geschichte und Ideologie*, 90; Orhan Koloğlu, "Celal Nuri'nin Jeune Turc Gazetesi ve Siyonist Bağı," *Tarih ve Toplum* (Aralık 1992), 47.

37 Özavcı, "Vladimir Jabotinsky," 308–10; Özgür Türesay, "Antisionism eet antisémitisme dans la presse ottoman d'Istanbul à l'époque jeune turque (1909–1912). L'exemple d'Ebüziyya Tevfik," *Turcica: Revue d'études turques*, Vol. 41 (2009), 147–78.

38 Ş. Tufan Buzpınar, "Celal Nuri's Concepts of Westernization," 248–52; Hanioğlu, "Garbcılar," 153–8. I would broadly define a "Westernist" (*garbçı*) in an Ottoman context to mean someone who not only advocated the adoption of Western European social/cultural mores, customs, and political and economic practices but also promoted a positivistic worldview that scorned traditional Islamic beliefs and observances.

39 Duymaz, "Celal Nuri İleri ve Ati Gazetesi," 195–233. Celal Nuri took İleri as his last name after the passage of the Turkish Surname Law in 1934.

40 Herzog, *Geschichte und Ideologie*, 91.

41 For the most comprehensive summary of his non-fiction books and pamphlets, see Duymaz, "Celal Nuri İleri ve Ati Gazetesi," 111–92.

42 Celal Nuri returned to Istanbul on November 1, 1921. Bilal Şimşir, *Malta Sürgünleri*, 2. baskı (Ankara: Bilgi Yayınları, 1985), 182, 188, 404.

43 Buzpınar, "Celal Nuri's Concepts of Westernization," 248; Duymaz, *Dil*, 26–36.

44 As Zürcher points out, the Unionist pamphleteers seemed to be in search of some sort of "philosopher's stone" that he hoped would help save the state from its troubles. Zürcher, *The Young Turk Legacy*, 114.

45 M. Şükrü Hanioğlu, *Atatürk: An Intellectual Biography* (Princeton: Princeton University Press, 2011), 44–5. Zürcher rightly comments that Arab and Balkan nationalists shared the CUP's enthusiasm for Le Bon. Zürcher, *The Young Turk Legacy*, 321, footnote 22.

46 Celal Nuri, *Hatemül-Enbiya* (İstanbul: Yeni Osmanlı Matbaası, h.1331 [1912–13]), 127.

47 The two most famous books by Le Bon about this topic are: Gustave Le Bon, *The Crowd: Study of the Popular Mind* (Lexington: Aristeus Books, 2012) and Gustave Le Bon, *The Psychology of Peoples: Its Influence on their Evolution* (New York: Macmillan, 1898). The French original for the first was written in 1895 and the second in 1894.

48 Celal Nuri, *Kara Tehlike*, 36.

49 Gustave Le Bon, *The Psychology of Revolution*, translated by Bernard Miall (London; Leipzig: T. Fisher Unwinn, 1913), 56–7. The original French edition was published in 1912.

50 See Hippolyte Taine, *History of English Literature*, vol. 1 (New York: Frederick Unger Publishing Company, republished 1965 from 1883 edition), 16–22. The original French edition was published in 1864.

51 Celal Nuri, *İttihad-i İslam ve Almanya: İttihad-i İslam'a Zeyl* (İstanbul: Yeni Osmanlı Matbaası ve Kütüphanesi, h.1333 [1914–15]), 11; *Tarih-i Osmani ve Keşfiyyat, Rönesans ve Reform Harekatı* (Cemiyet Kütüphanesi, 1917), 28–9. See Ibn Khaldun; Franz Rosenthal, translator, *The Muqadimmah: An Introduction to History*, 3 vols. (New York: Pantheon Books, 1958). The original was written

in 1377. Also see how Celal Nuri employs these concepts in his discussion on Muhammad. Celal Nuri, *Hatemül-Enbiya*, 40–84.

52 Celal Nuri, "Muhit ve Türkler (I)," *Edebiyat-ı Umumiye Mecmuası*, Vol. 2, No. 28, 12 Mayıs 1917 [May 12, 1917], 33. Here he cites from Taine directly. Taine, *History of English Literature*, vol. 1, 19. Also see Mehmet Kaan Çalen, "Celal Nuri'ye Göre Muhit, Irk, Zaman Teorisi Bağlamında Eski Türkler İle Osmanlı Türkleri Arasındaki Münasebetler-1" at http://www.turkyorum.com/celal-nuriye-gore-muhit-irk-zaman-teorisi-baglaminda-eski-turkler-ile-osmanli-turkleri-arasindaki-munasebetler-1/.

53 Celal Nuri, "Irk," *Edebiyat-ı Umumiye Mecmuası*, Vol. 2, No. 26, 28 Nisan 1917 [April 28, 1917], 7. It should be noted that Celal Nuri was the first Ottoman Turk to travel to the North Pole. He wrote his work *Polar Conversations* (*Kutup Müsahabeleri*) to describe his experiences. Duymaz, "Celal Nuri İleri," 243; Celal Nuri, *Kutup Müsahabeleri: Müşahedat, Muhakemat, Mukayesat, Hikayat, İstiğrakiyat, Nisaiyat* (İstanbul: Yeni Osmanlı Matbaa ve Kütüphanesi, h.1331 [1912–13]).

54 Djelal Noury, *Cauchmar? Roman de Temps Hamidiens* (Pera: Edition du "Jeune-Turc," 1911). *Cauchmar?*, it should be noted, was published by *Le Jeune Turc*. Archibald De Bear also made an English translation of the book under Djelal Noury, *The Sultan: A Romance of the Harem of Abdul Hamid* (London: Cassell, 1912).

55 Şükrü Hanioğlu, *Preparation for Revolution: The Young Turks, 1902–1908* (New York; London: Oxford University Press, 2001), 61; Haydar Kemal, *Celâl Nuri Bey*, 15.

56 Famous works by Nordau include: Max Nordau, *Degeneration* (translated from the second edition of the German Work) (Lincoln; London: University of Nebraska Press, 1993); Max Nordau, *Paradoxes*, English edition (Chicago: L. Schick, 1886); Max Nordau, *The Interpretation of History*, translated by M.A. Hamilton (London: Rebman Limited, 1910). The original editions of the above-mentioned titles are 1892, 1885, and 1909.

57 Celal Nuri, *Tarih-i İstikbal: Mesail-i İçtimai* (İstanbul: Yeni Osmanlı Matbaası, h.1332 [1913–14]), 91. He makes this comment shortly after translating much of Nordau's "The Economic Lie" in his well-known *The Conventional Lies of Our Civilization* (1883). Celal Nuri, *Tarih-i İstikbal: Mesail-i İçtimai*, 45–71.

58 Ludwig Büchner, *Force and Matter or Principles of the Natural Order of the Universe. With a System of Morality Based Thereon* (New York: Truth Seeker Company, 1950). Hanioğlu, *Atatürk*, 49–52.

59 For a classical summary of Büchner's ideas, see Friedrich Albert Lange, *The History of Materialism and Criticism of Its Present Importance* (London: Routledge & Kegan Paul LTD, 1950). Lange, a contemporary of Büchner, wrote the German original in 1865. For a recent discussion, see John Abromeit, *Max Horkheimer and*

the Foundations of the Frankfurt School (Cambridge, UK; New York: Cambridge University Press, 2011), 126–40.

60 See, for example, Celal Nuri's comments on Büchner in *Tarih-i İstikbal: Mesail-i Fikriye* (İstanbul: Yeni Osmanlı Matbaası, h.1331 [1912–13]), 25. He did not see Büchner as necessarily the final authority on materialism and certainly not reducible to the conclusions of the already outdated *Force and Matter*. Nevertheless, he saw Büchner's more recent work as illustrating that "the philosophy of materialism, if understood well, has an important principle which conforms to the spirit of Islam."

61 Celal Nuri, *Kendi Nokta-i Nazarımdan Hukuk-ı Düvel* (İstanbul: Osmanlı Şirketi Matbaası, h.1330 [1911–12]), 172–3, 178–91. As Buzpınar notes, this section of the work originally came from his first series of articles in Abdullah Cevdet's *İctihad*, entitled "İslam'da Vücûb-i Teceddüd" ("The Necessity of Renewal in Islam"). Buzpınar, "Celal Nuri's Concepts of Westernization," 248, 256 ft. 13.

62 Celal Nuri, *Hatemül-Enbiya* (İstanbul: Yeni Osmanlı Matbaası ve Kütüphanesi, h.1332 [1913–14]), 27–8, 31–2; 289–90. Here Celal Nuri refers, for example, to Thomas Carlyle's *On Heroes, Hero Worship and the Heroic in History* (New York: Thomas Y. Crowell & Co., 1891) as well as Ernest Renan's essay "Muhammad and the Origins of Islam," in: Ibn Warraq, editor and translator, *The Quest for the Historical Muhammad* (Amherst, NY: Prometheus Books, 2000), 127–66.

63 Djelal Noury, *Cauchmar? Roman de Temps Hamidiens* (Pera: Edition du "Jeune-Turc," 1911), 4, 7, 35, 40, 42–3, 53–8, 72, 91–7, 117, 120–35, 177–92.

64 Abdülhak Hamid Tarhan; İnce Enginün, editor, *Bütün Şiirleri*, vol. 2 (İstanbul: Dergah Yayınları, 1882), 25–6.

65 Celal Nuri highlighted two works in particular, the poem "Bâlâdan Bir Ses" and the play "Duhter-i Hindu." See Abdülhak Hamid Tarhan, "Baladan Bir Ses," *Bütün Şiirleri*, vol. 2, 179–90; Abdülhak Hamid Tarhan; İnce Enginün, editor, "Duhter-i Hindu," in: *Bütün Tiyatroları*, vol. 3 (İstanbul: Dergah Yayınları, 1882), 35–153. İnci Enginün, "Abdulhak Hamid Tarhan," in: *İslam Ansiklopedisi*, vol. 1 (İstanbul: Diyanet İşleri Bakanlığı, 1988), 207–10.

66 Buzpınar, "Celal Nuri's Concepts of Westernization," 248–9; Hanioğlu, "Garbcılar," 145.

67 Buzpınar, "Celal Nuri's Concepts of Westernization," 250–2.

68 Adum, *Azad*, 97; Giridi Ahmed Saki. *Celal Nuri Bey ve Cezri Fikirleri* (Dersaadet: Hukuk Matbaası, 1335–8 [1919]), 4.

69 Buzpınar, "Celal Nuri's Concepts of Westernization," 250, 252–4.

70 Buzpınar, "Celal Nuri's Concepts of Westernization," 253. Here Buzpınar quotes directly from Celal Nuri, *Türk İnkılabı* (İstanbul: Sühulet Kütüphanesi Semih Lütfi, 1926), 86.

71 Celal Nuri, *İttihad-ı İslam: İslamın Mazisi, Hali, İstikbali* (İstanbul: Yeni Osmanlı Matbaası, h.1331 [1912–13]), 43–4.

72 Buzpınar, "Celal Nuri's Concepts of Westernization," 252.
73 Buzpınar, "Celal Nuri's Concepts of Westernization," 252.
74 Celal Nuri, *Kara Tehlike* (Dersaadet: Cemiyyet Kütüphanesi, r.1334 [1918]), 5–8. Celal Nuri's *Türkçemiz* (Konstantiniye: Cemiyyet Kütüphanesi, 1917) was the volume that set likely off the controversy when it was published.
75 Agâh Sırrı Levend, *Türk Dilinde Gelişme ve Sadeleştirme Evreleri* (Ankara: Ankara Üniversitesi Basımevi, 1972), 371–6.
76 Celal Nuri, *Tarih-i Tedenniyat-ı Osmaniye; Mukadderat-ı Tarihiye. İki eser tevhid ve baz-ı fasl ve fıkralar ilave edilerek musahhah bir surette ikinci defa tab edilmiştir* (Yeni Osmanlı Matbaası ve Kütüphanesi, h.1331 [1912–13]), 33, 182–3.
77 Celal Nuri, *Türkçemiz* (Konstantiniye: Cemiyyet Kütüphanesi, 1917), 9–10, 52.
78 Celal Nuri, *Türkçemiz*, 28–34, 85, 92–3. Celal Nuri, *Kara Tehlike*, 23–6.
79 Ahmed Hilmi Şehbenderzade, *Huzur-ı Akl ü Fende Maddiyun Meslek-i Dalâleti* (Darulhilafe: Matbaa-ı İslamiyye, 1332 [1913–14]), 3–103 in Ahmed Hilmi Şehbenderzade, *Huzur-ı Akl ü Fende Maddiyun Meslek-i Dalâleti*, translated into Turkish by Erdoğan Erbay and Ali Utku (Konya: Çizgi Yayınları, 2012), 123–79; Ömer Ceran, *Şehbenderzade Filibeli Ahmed Hilmi'nin Dini ve Felsefi Görüşleri* (Bursa: Sır Yayıncılık, 2013), 35–7.
80 Celal Nuri, *Tarih-i İstikbal: Mesail-i Siyasi* (İstanbul: Yeni Osmanlı Matbaası, h.1331 [1912–13]), 178.
81 Celal Nuri, *1327 Senesinde Selanik'te Mün'akid İttihad ve Terakki Kongresine Celal Nuri Bey Tarafından Takdim Kılınan Muhtıradır* (İstanbul: Osmanlı Şirketi Matbaası, h.1327 [1909]), 45; Erik Jan Zürcher, *The Unionist Factor: The Role of the Committee of Union and Progress in the Turkish Nationalist Movement: 1905–1926* (Leiden: Brill Academic Publishers, 1984), 51.
82 Giridi Ahmed Saki. *Celal Nuri Bey ve Cezri Fikirleri*, 20, 26–8.
83 Zürcher, *Turkey*, 167.
84 Buzpınar, "Celal Nuri's Concepts of Westernization," 254–5.
85 Celal Nuri would go so far in 1926 to declare that "the Ottoman Empire was nothing else but a long, tortuous game for the Turkish nation" since Turks were trapped as a "minority within it." Celal Nuri, *Türk İnkılabı*, 27–8.
86 Herzog, *Geschichte und Ideologie*, 94.
87 Celal Nuri, *Devlet ve Meclis Hakkında Musahabeler* (Ankara: TBMM Matbaası, 1932), 82.
88 Celal Nuri, *Türk İnkılabı*, 302–3.
89 Celal Nuri, *Türk İnkılabı*, 152.
90 Erol Köroğlu, *Ottoman Propaganda and Turkish Identity: Literature in Turkey during World War I* (London; New York: I.B. Tauris, 2007), 68.
91 Hilmi Ziya Ülken, *Türkiye'de Çağdaş Düşünce Tarihi* (İstanbul: Ülken Yayınları, 1992), 399–408.

92 Yusuf Hikmet Bayur, *Türk İnkılâbı Tarihi*, third edition (Ankara: Türk Tarih Kurumu, 1991), vol. 2, part 4, 403, 440, 441, 444–7, 453; vol. 3, part 4, 429, 491–2.
93 Niyazi Berkes, *The Development of Secularism in Modern Turkey* (Montreal: McGill University Press, 1964).
94 Cemal Kutay, *Tarih Önünde İslam Peygamberi* (İstanbul: Aksoy Yayıncılık, 1998), 362–5.
95 Ahmet İshak Demir, *Cumhuriyet Dönemi Aydınlarının İslam'a Bakışı* (İstanbul: Ensar Neşriyatı, 2004), 343–68. A number of recent MA theses have been written on this debate within the past decade. Examples include Hatice Çöpel, "Celal Nuri İleri'nin Din Anlayışı" (Unpublished M.A. Thesis, Selçuk Üniversitesi, 2010); Habip Demir, "Celal Nuri [İleri] ve İslam Tarihçiliği" (Unpublished M.A. Thesis, Ankara Üniversitesi, 2006).
96 M. Şükrü Hanioğlu, *Bir Siyasi Düşünür Olarak: Doktor Abdullah Cevdet ve Dönemi* (İstanbul: Üçdal Neşriyat, 1981).
97 M. Şükrü Hanioğlu, "Garbcılar."
98 M. Şükrü Hanioğlu, *Abdullah Cevdet*, 363–6; Hanioğlu, "Garbcılar," 143–5; Ş. Tufan Buzpınar, "Celal Nuri's Concepts of Westernization," *Middle Eastern Studies*, Vol. 43, No. 2 (March 2007), 248–52; Ahmet İshak Demir, *Cumhuriyet Dönemi Aydınlarının İslam'a Bakışı* (İstanbul: Ensar Neşriyatı, 2004), 88–90; Uyanık, "Celal Nuri İleri," 252–4.
99 Recep Duymaz, "Celal Nuri İleri ve Ati Gazetesi" (Unpublished Ph.D. Dissertation: Marmara Üniversitesi, 1991).
100 Celal Nuri; Recep Duymaz, editor, *Dil ve Edebiyat Yazıları: Celal Nuri İleri* (İstanbul: Kitabevi, 1995); Celal Nûri İleri; Recep Duymaz, editor, *Türk İnkılabı* (Ankara: Atatürk Kültür Merkezi, 2000).
101 Celal Nuri, *Kadınlarımız. Umumiyeti İtibariyle Kadın Meselesi ve Tarihi. Müslüman ve Türk Kadınları* (İstanbul: Matbaa-i İctihad, h.1331 [1912–13]); Celal Nuri; Özer Ozankaya, translator, *Kadınlarımız* (Eskişehir, Anadolu Üniversitesi, 1993).
102 Celal Nuri, *Kutub Musahabeleri* (İstanbul: Yeni Osmanlı Matbaası, h.1331 [1912–13]); Celal Nûri; İbrahim Demirci, translator. *Kutub Musâhabeleri* (İstanbul: Mavi Yayıncılık, 1997).
103 Celal Nuri, *Şimâl Hatıraları* (İstanbul: Matbaa-i İctihad, 1330 [1911–12]); Celal Nûri; İbrahim Demirci, translator, *Şimâl Hâtıraları* (İstanbul: Mavi Yayıncılık, 1997).
104 Celal Nuri; Özer Ozankaya, translator. *Türk Devrimi: İnsanlık Tarihinde Türk Devriminin Yeri* (Kültür Bakanlığı, 2002).
105 Celal Nuri, *Tarih-i Tedenniyat-ı Osmaniye; Mukadderat-ı Tarihiye. İki eser tevhid ve baz-ı fasl ve fıkralar ilave edilerek musahhah bir surette ikinci defa tab edilmiştir* (Yeni Osmanlı Matbaası ve Kütüphanesi, 1915); Celal Nuri İleri; Mahir Aydın, translator, *Uygarlık Çatışmasında Türkiye* (İstanbul: Ulus Yayınları, 2004).

106 Celal Nuri, *Taç Giyen Millet* (İstanbul: Cihan Biraderler Matbaası, h.1339/r.1341 [1923]); Celal Nuri İleri; Şennur Şenel, translator, *Taç Giyen Millet* (İstanbul: Berikan Yayınları, 2008).

107 Mustafa Kurt, *Celal Nuri İleri'nin Romanları [Perviz-Ölmeyen-Merhume-Âhir Zaman]* (Ankara: Kurgan Edebiyat, 2012); Mustafa Kurt, *Celâl Nuri İleri'nin Romanları Bir İnceleme* (Ankara: Kurgan Edebiyat, 2012).

108 Herzog, *Geschichte und Ideologie*, 88–195.

109 Cemal Aydın, *The Politics of Anti-Westernism in Asia* (New York: Columbia University Press, 2007), 99–104, 231–2.

110 Turnaoğlu goes so far to suggest that Celal Nuri had a "Jacobin commitment" to Atatürk's radical nationalist agenda of "a unitary conception of the state to deliver political stability, maintain social cohesion, and protect the country from the politically subversive inclinations of counterrevolutionaries." Banu Turnaoğlu, *The Formation of the Turkish Republicanism* (Princeton; Oxford: Princeton University Press, 2017), 241–2. I find this view problematic when judging his politics, especially before the declaration of the Republic of Turkey. As late as January 1923, roughly nine months before the declaration, Celal Nuri warned Atatürk and his supporters in detail about the dangers of pursuing a radical revolutionary path, and that they should seek more gradual evolutionary political change. Celal Nuri, *Taç Giyen Millet* (İstanbul: Cihan Biraderler Matbaası, h.1339/r.1341 [1923]), 68–72.

111 Kılıç, "Türkiye'de Harfler Meselesi: 1908–1926," 551–4, 569–71; Nurettin Gülmez, *Tanzimat'tan Cumhuriyet'e Harfler Üzerine Tartışmalar* (Bursa: Alfa Aktüel, 2006), 3, 47–8, 132–7, 146, 150, 153, 161, 163–4, 168, 211, 230. It should be noted, however, that the recent works on language reform have not deviated from the standard Kemalist practice of citing only parts of Celal Nuri's work that endorsed the reform, namely his preference for the Latin over Arabic alphabet.

112 Buzpınar, "Celal Nuri's Concepts of Westernization," 256, footnote 7. There have been several unpublished dissertations in Turkey written on Celal Nuri, including: Recep Duymaz, "Celal Nuri İleri ve Âti Gazetesi"; Necati Uyanık, "Siyasi Düşünce Tarihimizde Batıcı Bir Aydın Olarak Celal Nuri [İleri]" (Unpublished Ph.D. Dissertation: Hacettepe Üniversitesi, 1993); Necati Aksaryan, "Çağdaşlaşmaya Giden Yolda Celal Nuri ve Fikir Alanında Etkinliği" (Unpublished Ph.D. Dissertation: Hacettepe Üniversitesi, 1993).

113 It should be noted that biographies of Turkish politicians and intellectuals active between 1908 and 1938 continue to be a rich source for students of late Ottoman and early Republican Turkish history. Outside of scholarship previously mentioned in this chapter, I have been personally inspired in particular by Hanioğlu and Mango's studies on Mustafa Kemal Atatürk and Shissler's monograph on Ahmet Ağaoğlu. M. Şükrü Hanioğlu, *Atatürk: An Intellectual*

Biography; Andrew Mango, *Atatürk: The Biography of the Founder of Modern Turkey* (New York: Overlook Press, 1999); A. Holly Shissler, *Between Two Empires: Ahmet Ağaoğlu and the New Turkey* (London: I.B. Tauris, 2002).

114 Buzpınar, "Celal Nuri's Concepts of Westernization," *Middle Eastern Studies*, Vol. 43, No. 2 (March 2007), 247–9, 252–5; Ş. Tufan Buzpınar, "Celal Nuri ve Abdullah Cevdet'in Avrupa tartışmaları," 254, 274–5; Hanioğlu, "Garbcılar," 153–8.

115 Again I have borrowed this concept from Zürcher, *The Young Turk Legacy*, 229–31.

116 The Kemalist authority's harsh response to Celal Nuri in this case markedly contrasted to the indulgence he found from the authorities when he made similar statements against the Ottoman Greeks and Armenians from 1912 to 1914.

117 The type of economic policies Celal Nuri advocated between 1909 and 1911 are reminiscent of Prince Sabahaddin's liberal economic views. For a detailed discussion of this topic, see Chapter 2, footnote 12.

118 Mustafa Nuri, *Abede-i İblis*; Sırrı Giridi, *Âra-i Milel*.

119 Djelal Noury, *Le Diable*; Celal Nuri, *İttihad-ı İslam*, 164–5.

120 Celal Nuri, *Tarih-i Tedenniyat-ı Osmaniye; Mukadderat-ı Tarihiye*, 84–5, 87–93; Celal Nuri, *İttihad-ı İslam*, 220–4, 231; *İttihad-i İslam ve Almanya: İttihad-i İslam'a Zeyl* (İstanbul: Yeni Osmanlı Matbaası ve Kütüphanesi, h.1333 [1914–15]), 17–19; Dželal Nuri; Salih Bakamović, "Panislamizam: Islam u Prošlosti, Sadašnjosti i Budućnosti," *Biser: List za Širenje Islamske Prosvjete* (Mostar): Godine III: Broj 13 i 14 (July 1 and 15, 1918), 196–7; *Tarih-i İstikbal: Mesail-i Siyasi* (İstanbul: Yeni Osmanlı Matbaası, h.1331 [1913]), 167–75.

121 Celal Nuri, *Tarih-i Tedenniyat-ı Osmaniye; Mukadderat-ı Tarihiye*, 396–8; Celal Nuri, *Tarih-i İstikbal: Mesail-i Siyasi*, 130, 136–7.

122 Celal Nuri, *Tarih-i İstikbal: Mesail-i Siyasi*, 181–2.

123 Celal Nuri, *Tarih-i Tedenniyat-ı Osmaniye; Mukadderat-ı Tarihiye*, 296; Celal Nuri, *Devlet ve Meclis Hakkında Müsahabeler* (Ankara: TBMM Matbaası, 1932), 82.

124 Celal Nuri, *Tarih-i İstikbal: Mesail-i Fikriye* (İstanbul: Yeni Osmanlı Matbaası, h.1331 [1912–13]), 23–53.

125 Demir, *Aydınlarının İslam'a Bakışı*, 83–4, 88–90.

126 Celal Nuri, *Havaic-i Kanuniyyemiz*, 77, 82.

127 Celal Nuri, *Kadınlarımız*.

128 Ziya Gökalp, *Türk Ahlakı* (İstanbul: Bilgeoğuz, 2013), 159–60.

129 Afet İnan, *Tarih Boyunca Türk Kadınının Hak ve Görevleri* (İstanbul: Milli Eğitim Bakanlığı, 1975), 179.

130 Celal Nuri, *Türkçemiz* (Konstantiniye: Cemiyyet Kütüphanesi, 1917), 21.

131 Celal Nuri, *Türk İnkılabı* (İstanbul: Sühulet Kütüphanesi Semih Lütfi, 1926), 141–201, 269–301.

132 *Birinci Dil Kurultayı: Tezler, Müzakere Zabıtları* (İstanbul: Devlet Matbaası, 1933), 274–9.

Chapter 2

1. Celâl Nuri, *Kara Tehlike* (Dersaadet: Cemiyyet Kütüphanesi, r.1334 [1918]), 37.
2. Celâl Nuri, *Tarih-i Tedenniyat-ı Osmaniye; Mukadderat-ı Tarihiye. İki eser tevhid ve baz-ı fasl ve fıkralar ilave edilerek musahhah bir surette ikinci defa tab edilmiştir* (Yeni Osmanlı Matbaası ve Kütüphanesi, 1915), 114–25.
3. Gustave Le Bon, *The Psychology of Peoples: Its Influence on Their Evolution* (New York: Macmillan, 1898), 56–7.
4. Celâl Nuri, *Rum ve Bizans* (Konstantiniye: Cemiyyet Kütüphanesi, 1917), 49.
5. Djelal Noury, *Cauchmar? Roman de Temps Hamidiens* (Pera: Edition du "Jeune-Turc," 1911).
6. Celâl Nuri, *Havaic-i Kanuniyyemiz* (İstanbul: Matbaa-yı İctihad, h.1331 [1912–13]), 23.
7. Celâl Nuri, *Havaic-i Kanuniyyemiz*, 17–18.
8. Djelal Noury, *Problèmes Sociaux* (Constantinople: Imprimerie du "Courier d'Orient," 1909), 5–34, 49–68.
9. Djelal Noury, *Problèmes Sociaux*, 68–79; Celâl Nuri, *Havaic-i Kanuniyyemiz*, 65–72, 83–98.
10. Djelal Noury, *Une Année de Liberté Istanbul* (Constantinople: Imprimerie du "Courier d'Orient," 1909), 19–29; Celâl Nuri, *Havaic-i Kanuniyyemiz*, 13–63. It should be noted that the CUP did implement much of this program in 1916–17, by seriously reducing the power of the ulema establishment in the *şeyhülislamlık* by not only removing the pious foundations, *medrese*s and Islamic law courts from their jurisdiction, but even removing the *şeyhülislamlık* from the cabinet of ministers. Erik Jan Zürcher, *Turkey: A Modern History*, third edition (London; New York: I.B. Tauris, 2010), 121–2; M. Hakan Yavuz, "Turkey without Sharia?" in: *Sharia Politics: Islamic Law and Society in the Modern World* (Bloomington, IN: Indiana University Press, 2011), 157–8.
11. Djelal Noury, *Problèmes Sociaux*, 35–47. The Unionists expanded the mission of the Agricultural Bank to provide greater loans for landowners in 1914 and 1916 and founded a pious foundation bank in order to support Muslim artisans entrepreneurial efforts in Istanbul and other urban centers in 1914. Zafer Toprak, *Türkiye'de "Milli İktisat": 1908–1918* (Ankara: Yurt Yayınları, 1982), 138, 149–50.
12. Şerif Mardin has gone so far as to categorize Celal Nuri as a liberal. He compares Celal Nuri to Prince Sabahaddin (1879–1948), the famous Ottoman intellectual and founder of the Free Enterprise and Decentralization Association, the archrival of the CUP. Celal Nuri indeed pushed for reforming provincial laws and credit practices in the expectation that it would help develop agrarian commerce led by Ottoman provincial elites. Şerif Mardin, "İktisadi Düşünce: Tanzimat'tan Cumhuriyet'e İktisadi Düşüncesi Gelişmesi (1838–1918)," in: Murat Belge et al.,

Tanzimat'tan Cumhuriyet'e Türkiye Ansiklopedisi, Cilt: 3 (İstanbul: İletişim Yayınları, 1985), 631. The hope was that these reforms would stimulate the empire's economic development in a way that would minimize governmental interference. Prince Sabahaddin would likely have agreed with that particular argument. Djelal Noury, *Problèmes Sociaux*, 3–62. After the Italian invasion of Libya, Celal Nuri distanced himself from Prince Sabahaddin by attacking his primary source of inspiration, namely Edmond Demolins (1852–1907), a French sociologist who glorified the ideal of individualism in his work *What Makes the Anglo-Saxons Superior* (*A Quoi Tient la Superiorite des Anglo-Saxons*) (1897). Edmond Demolins; Louis Bert Lavigne, translator, *Anglo-Saxon Superiority: To What Is It Due* (Toronto: The Musson Book Company, 1899).

Demolins argued that the Anglo-Saxon was superior to all others because:

> it is the Anglo-Saxon element which has developed to the highest degree individual initiative,…[and] has restricted within the narrowest limits the action of the public powers, the intervention of the state. Demolins, *Anglo-Saxon Superiority*, 208.

Demolins went on to postulate:

> The more a man obeys an inclination to rely on help from others, from the community or the state, the less is his force of initiative developed, the less is he inclined to exert himself personally to make a livelihood. On the other hand, the more he is expected to rely on himself alone and his personal work, the more is his force of initiative developed, the more he is inclined to exert himself, not with merely making a living, but also of rising higher and higher. Demolins, *Anglo-Saxon Superiority*, 209.

For Demolins, the Anglo-Saxons were the pinnacle of all the Western nations, having been most true to the Roman recognition of private property rights. Demolins, *Anglo-Saxon Superiority*, 207. This distinguished the Anglo-Saxons and their ancient predecessors from communistic societies among the nomads of "the Asiatic steppes, amidst those enormous tracts of grassland where humanity started its evolution." While these nomads migrated elsewhere over the centuries, their tendency toward collectivist inaction and social stagnancy persisted. Demolins, *Anglo-Saxon Superiority*, 207. Thus, Demolins hoped that the French and other Western nations would emulate the Anglo-Saxons, who have "raised … the power of work in human worth … so prodigously high." The East, in contrast, was doomed to be "enwrapped in deep slumber for many centuries." Demolins, *Anglo-Saxon Superiority*, 208.

Demolins's main fear, however, was the rise of socialist parties in Europe. By the time Demolins wrote in 1897 the Second Socialist International was functioning smoothly, and the Anti-Socialist Ban in Germany was lifted. Demolins rightly predicted the German Social Democratic Party would eventually come to power. He also decried the rise of similar movements in Scandinavia, Russia, and of course in his native France. These parties' common program was:

> the necessity of having all social questions resolved by the action of the law, or state. All dream of a society in which the state should regulate and organize more or less labor, property, salaries, and should take upon itself to make happy one and all by playing the role of a great universal employer. The state is the new providence found by socialism. Demolins, *Anglo-Saxon Superiority*, 189.

Celal Nuri took issue with Demolins, denouncing him as "having noisily proclaimed to the world that the English are individualist and do not need socialism." Celal Nuri noted that wildcat strikes first took off in England and then spread to Germany: "[Such] events contradict this author in a jarring manner." Celâl Nuri, *İttihad-ı İslam: İslamın Mazisi, Hali, İstikbali* (İstanbul: Yeni Osmanlı Matbaası, h.1331 [1912–13]), 286–7.

The reasons for its spread were clear. Nordau, whom Celal Nuri cited at length, wrote about "the great economic lie" that promised Europe's citizens an ever happier and more prosperous life. This was based on the false notion:

> All good and happiness lay in the extreme exertions of man's laboring faculties … Their doctrine can be condensed into two commandments: thou shalt consume as much as possible, no matter whether the consumption is justified by actual necessity or not; thou shalt produce as much as possible no matter whether the productions are needed or not. Max Nordau, *The Conventional Lies of Our Civilization*, Translated from the German (Chicago: Laird & Lee, 1895), 249. The original German edition was published in 1883.

Indeed, the rapid rise of industrial capitalism, and the ensuing growth of towns, led to an enormous division in society between the toiling working classes, who were always in constant danger of starvation, and a parasitical group of speculators, who either consumed the profits or reinvested them to further their web of exploitation both at home and abroad through international corporations.

The greatest reason for this social malaise, in Nordau's mind, was the demise of the free-holding farmer:

> The son of the soil forsakes his plow, the freedom of the country and nature and the pure, abundant sunshine and air, to force his way into that fatal prison, the factory, and take up his abode in some pestilential tenement house in the big city in obedience to a kind of suicidal instinct. The same instinct seems to impel the human race as a whole, to abandon the food producing soil and cast themselves into the slop of manufacturing industry where they suffocate and starve. Nordau, *The Conventional Lies*, 241.

Nordau despaired that the rush toward industrial production led to the loss of a country's true wealth, its agricultural products. Governments needed to compensate for this loss by promoting the "solidarity of the community" through state-subsidized compulsory primary school education, universal male conscription, and, most radically, the abolishment of the right of inheritance. This last measure would in effect nationalize all property which would then be dispersed only for a single lifetime to the individual. Nordau, *The Conventional Lies*, 229, 264–8.

Celal Nuri agreed with Nordau that something drastic needed to be done: "The status quo in Europe cannot continue ... Yes! The social condition in Europe became intolerable and we are on the eve of a revolution." Celâl Nuri, *Tarih-i İstikbal: Mesail-i İçtimai* (İstanbul: Yeni Osmanlı Matbaası, h.1332 [1913–14]), 91. But he cast doubt on whether the solidarist program that Nordau advocated would prevent a full-blown socialist revolution. Celal Nuri thought that the European socialist movement was indeed a "formidable and awesome force" given their political parties, social organizations, trade unions, and networking among the seemingly endless stream of workers pouring into the cities: "This ... [movement] has gained so much power that if ... [they] declared a general strike throughout the world they could topple a number of governments." Celâl Nuri, *İttihad-ı İslam*, 288–9. They were in a developmental stage, seemingly ready to give birth to a new era: "Socialism will become extraordinarily important in the first half of the twentieth century. It will establish a national sultanate of Europe, and even spread to America five to ten years after that." Celâl Nuri, *İttihad-ı İslam*, 287.

Although Celal Nuri noted that there were socialists "even in Turkey," he saw no real chance for them "since there is no industry." Celâl Nuri, *İttihad-ı İslam*, 287. It was here, ironically enough, that Celal Nuri pushed for agricultural reform. Unlike Western Europe and America, Ottoman Turkey had not industrialized, and therefore might be in a position to promote a prosperous, entrepreneurial agrarian class of producers. Changes in the land law to allow for capital accumulation for these enterprises were a form of liberalization. In short, such measures facilitated a gradualist economic course of development.

13 Djelal Noury, *La Droit Publique et l'Islam* (Constantinople: Imprimerie du "Courier d'Orient," 1909), 3–4, 7.
14 Djelal Noury, *La Droit Publique*, 10–11.
15 Djelal Noury, *La Droit Publique*, 20.
16 Djelal Noury, *Une Année de Liberté*, 8.
17 Celâl Nuri, *Muhtıra*, 55.
18 Celâl Nuri, *Muhtıra*, 39; Celâl Nuri, *Tarih-i Tedenniyat-ı Osmaniye; Mukadderat-ı Tarihiye*, 485.
19 Celâl Nuri, *Tarih-i Tedenniyat-ı Osmaniye; Mukadderat-ı Tarihiye*, 485.

20 Ş. Tufan Buzpınar "Celal Nuri's Concepts of Westernization," *Middle Eastern Studies*, Vol. 43, No. 2 (March 2007), 248–9; M. Şükrü Hanioğlu, "Garbcılar: Their Attitudes toward Religion and Their Impact on the Official Ideology of the Turkish Republic," *Studia Islamica*, Vol. 86, No. 2 (August 1997), 136.
21 Celâl Nuri, *Kendi Nokta-i Nazarımdan Hukuk-ı Düvel* (İstanbul: Osmanlı Şirketi Matbaası, h.1330 [1911–12]), 4.
22 Celâl Nuri, *Hukuk-ı Düvel*, 9–11.
23 Celâl Nuri, *Hukuk-ı Düvel*, 4.
24 Celâl Nuri, *Hukuk-ı Düvel*, 6.
25 Abdullah Cevdet; Mustafa Gündüz, translator, *İctihad'ın İctihadı: Abdullah Cevdet'ten Seçme Yazılar* (Ankara: Lotus, 2008), 195. Buzpınar, "Westernization," 250–2; Hanioğlu, "Garbcılar," 145.
26 Abdullah Cevdet, *İctihad'ın İctihadı*, 195.
27 Abdullah Cevdet, *İctihad'ın İctihadı*, 190–1.
28 Celâl Nuri, *Müslümanlara, Türklere Hakaret, Düşmanlara Riayet ve Muhabbet* (İstanbul: "Kadir" Matbaası), 1332 [1913–14]), 13–26, 32.
29 Celâl Nuri, *Hakaret*, 32.
30 Celâl Nuri, *Hakaret*, 31.
31 Celâl Nuri, *Hakaret*, 24.
32 Celâl Nuri, *Hukuk-ı Düvel*, 4, 12, 63, 77.
33 Andreas Müller, "Friederich F. Martens on the Office of the Consul and Consular Jurisdiction in the East," *European Journal of International Law*, Vol. 25, No. 3 (August 2014), 872–3.
34 Müller, "Martens," 875–7, 881–2.
35 James Lorimer, *The Institutes of the Law of Nations: A Treatise of the Jural Relations of Separate Political Communities*, vol. 1 (Edinburgh; London: William Blackwood and Sons, 1883), 102–3, footnote 1.
36 Lorimer, *Institutes*, 123.
37 Müller, "Martens," 883, footnote 57.
38 Lorimer, *Institutes*, 177.
39 Celâl Nuri, *Hukuk-ı Düvel*, 22–4.
40 Celâl Nuri, *Hukuk-ı Düvel*, 91–2.
41 Celâl Nuri, *Hukuk-ı Düvel*, 91; Celâl Nuri, *İttihad-ı İslam*, 212.
42 Feroz Ahmad, *The Young Turks and the Ottoman Nationalities: Armenians, Greeks, Albanians, Jews and Arabs, 1908–1918* (Salt Lake City: University of Utah Press, 2014), 38–9.
43 Celâl Nuri, *Hukuk-ı Düvel*, 29, 113–16.
44 Celâl Nuri, *Tarih-i Tedenniyat-ı Osmaniye; Mukadderat-ı Tarihiye*, 237, 370–7; Celâl Nuri, *Tarih-i İstikbal: Mesail-i Siyasi* (İstanbul: Yeni Osmanlı Matbaası, h.1331 [1912–13]), 67–9.
45 Celâl Nuri, *Hukuk-ı Düvel*, 91.

46 Celâl Nuri, *Tarih-i İstikbal: Mesail-i Siyasi*, 59–80.
47 Celâl Nuri, *Tarih-i İstikbal: Mesail-i Siyasi*, 83–6.
48 Celâl Nuri, *İttihad-ı İslam ve Almanya: İttihad-ı İslam'a Zeyl* (İstanbul: Yeni Osmanlı Matbaası ve Kütüphanesi, h.1333 [1914–15]), 12–13; York Norman, "Beyond Jihad: Alexander Helphand Parvus, Musa Kazim, and Celal Nuri on the Ottoman-German Alliance," in: Hakan Yavuz with Feroz Ahmed, editors, *War & Collapse: World War I and the Ottoman State* (Salt Lake City: The University of Utah Press, 2016), 275.
49 Celâl Nuri, *Almanya*, 59.
50 Celâl Nuri, *Almanya*, 53–4.
51 Celâl Nuri, *Almanya*, 61–2.
52 Gustave Le Bon; Robert K. Stevenson, translator and editor, "Algeria and the Ideas Prevailing in France concerning Colonization," *Revue Scientifique*, October 2, 1887, 18.
53 Le Bon, "Algeria," 18–19.
54 Celâl Nuri, *İttihad-ı İslam*, 185–210.
55 Celâl Nuri, *Almanya*, 63–4.
56 York Norman, "Beyond Jihad," 269–78.
57 Such selfish behavior came to be known by the term "Yan Geldizam" in the propaganda and intellectual discourse of the final years of empire. Celâl Nuri, *İlel-i Ahlâkiyyemiz* (İstanbul: Yeni Osmanlı Matbaası ve Kütüphanesi, h.1332 [1913–14]), 90.
58 Celâl Nuri, *Ahlâkiyyemiz*, 70.
59 Celâl Nuri, *Ahlâkiyyemiz*, 21–31, 35–9.
60 Celâl Nuri, *Ahir Zaman* (Dersaadet, 1335 [1919]). Mustafa Kurt notes that the novel was written by 1918. Mustafa Kurt, *Celâl Nuri İleri'nin Romanları Bir İnceleme* (Ankara: Kurgan Edebiyat, 2012), 155.
61 Zürcher, *Turkey*, 125–6; Toprak, 138.
62 Mevlüt Çelebi, "Mütareke İstanbul'unda Bir İtalyan Dostu: Celâl Nuri," *Tarih ve Toplum*, Vol. 18, No. 108 (Aralık 1992), 45–6. Tarik Zafer Tunaya, *Türkiye'de Siyasal Partiler Cilt 2: Mütareke Dönemi*, fourth edition (İstanbul: İletişim, 2012), 252.
63 Recep Duymaz, "Celâl Nuri İleri," in: *İslam Ansiklopedisi*, vol. 7 (İstanbul: Türkiye Diyanet Vakfı, 1993), 242–3; Mustafa Kemal Atatürk, *Atatürk'ün Bütün Eserleri*, fifth edition (İstanbul: Kaynak Yayınları, 2015), vol. 4, 242; Bilal. Şimşir, *Malta Sürgünleri*, 2. baskı (Ankara: Bilgi Yayınları, 1985), 180.
64 *Meclis-i Mebusan Zabit Ceridesi (İçtima-i Fevkalade), Devre: 4, Cild: 1, İçtima Senesi: 1, Onüçüncü İnikad: 23 Şubat 1336 (1920), Pazartesi*, 186.
65 Şimşir, *Malta Sürgünleri*, 180.
66 Şimşir, *Malta Sürgünleri*, 404.
67 Giridi Ahmed Saki. *Celâl Nuri Bey ve Cezri Fikirleri* (Dersaadet: Hukuk Matbaası, 1335–8 [1919–22]), 20, 26–8. Zürcher notes that documents such as these were

part constitutional proposals and part party platforms. Zürcher, *Young Turk Legacy*, 198. Giridi Ahmed Saki's tract, which included Celal Nuri's constitutional proposal, was part of a party proposal for a small Unionist breakaway faction of the Radical Party (*Cezri Fırkası*). For information on the larger liberal Radical Party (*Radikal Avam Fırkası*) at the time, see Tarik Zafer Tunaya, *Türkiye'de Siyaset Partiler Cilt 2: Mütareke Dönemi 1918-1922, 4. Baskı* (İstanbul: İleteşim Yayinlari, 2010), 105-8.
68 Saki, *Cezri Fikirleri*, 37-8.
69 Celâl Nuri, *Taç Giyen Millet* (İstanbul: Cihan Biraderler Matbaası, h.1339/r.1341 [1923]), 183-4.
70 Celâl Nuri, *Taç Giyen Millet*, 90-1.
71 Erik Jan Zürcher, *Political Opposition in the Early Turkish Republic* (Leiden: Brill Academic Publishers, 1991), 56, 63, 110; Zürcher, *Turkey*, 159-60.
72 Celâl Nuri, *Taç Giyen Millet*, 68-70.
73 Celâl Nuri, *Taç Giyen Millet*, 183-4.
74 Celâl Nuri, *Taç Giyen Millet*, 68-70, 103-17.
75 Celâl Nuri, *Taç Giyen Millet*, 125-9.
76 Celâl Nuri, *Taç Giyen Millet*, 111-12. In his own 1919 proposal for a full-scale revision of the existing Ottoman constitution, Celal Nuri had called for a similar "public sultanate" (*saltanat-i umumiye*). He proposed at the time that parliament have legislative sovereignty but that the Ottoman dynasty and caliph remain a symbolic head of state under military guardianship. Saki, *Cezri Fikirleri*, 19-20.
77 Celâl Nuri, *Taç Giyen Millet*, 204-7.
78 Edward Mead Earle, "The New Constitution of Turkey," *Political Science Quarterly*, Vol. 40, No. 1 (March 1925), 89.
79 Filiz Karaca, editor, *Osmanlı Anayasası: Kanun-ı Esasî* (İstanbul: Doğu Kitabevi, 2009), 37. Here I would respectfully disagree with Dr. Zürcher who claims that "Islam became the state religion with the 1924 Constitution. The old Ottoman constitution made no reference to a state religion." Zürcher, *Turkey*, 350 ft. 14.
80 Celal Nuri also wanted to define Turkish ethnicity in a way that privileged Sunni Islam and the Turkish language as key identifiers. When leading the parliamentary discussion about Article 88, which defined citizenship in the new republic, he argued that a true citizen was a Hanefi Sunni Muslim and spoke Turkish. He shared the sentiments of Hamdullah Suphi (Tanrıover), a renowned poet and longtime head of the Turkish Hearths (*Türk Ocağı*), that citizenship should not be granted to those who either were loyal to a foreign power or refused to speak Turkish and adapt the national culture. Nonetheless, the actual article defined "all citizens of the Turkish Republic without distinction of, or reference to, race or religion." The Lausanne Treaty had required this open definition of citizenship so that Armenians and Greeks who still lived in the country would be granted equal rights. *Türk Büyük Milli Meclis Zabit Ceridesi, Devre: II, Cild: 8/1, İçtima Senesi: II, Kırkikinci*

İçtima: 20.4. 1340 (1924), Pazar: 910; İlhan Unat, *Türk Vatandaşlık Hukuku: Metinler, Mahkeme Kararları* (Ankara: Sevinç Maatbası, 1966), 41; Howard Eissenstat, "Metaphors of Race and Discourse of Nation: Racial Theory and State Nationalism in the First Decades of the Turkish Republic," in: Paul Spickard, editor. *Race and Nation: Ethnic Systems in the Modern World* (New York and London: Routledge, 2005), 249; Marc David Baer, *The Dönme: Jewish Converts, Muslim Revolutionaries, and Secular Turks* (Stanford: Stanford University Press, 2010), 240; Söner Çağaptay, *Islam, Secularism and Nationalism in Modern Turkey: Who Is a Turk?* (London; New York: Rutledge, 2006), 14–15, 171.

81   Utkan Kocaturk, *Atatürk ve Türkiye Cumhuriyeti Tarihi Kronolojisi, 1918–1938* (Ankara: Türk Tarih Kurumu Basımevi, 2000), 476; Tarık Zafer Tunaya, *İslamcılık Cereyanı II* (İstanbul: Yeni Gün Haber Ajansı, 1998), 105; Taha Parla, *Türkiye'de Anayasalar*, genişletmiş yeni baskı, üçüncü baskı (İstanbul: İletişim, 2002), 22.

82   Parla, *Türkiye'de Anayasalar*, 25.

Chapter 3

1   Celâl Nuri, *Ahir Zaman* (Dersaadet, h.1335 [1916–17]).

2   See, for example, Yakub Kadri Karaosmanoğlu's *Sodom ve Gomore* (1926) and Ömer Seyfettin's "Cabi Efendi," "Niçin Zengin Olmamış," and "Zeytin Ekmek" (1919); Erol Köroğlu, *Ottoman Propaganda and Turkish Identity Literature in Turkey during World War I* (London; New York: I.B. Tauris, 2007), 168–71; Jan Erik Zürcher, *The Young Turk Legacy and Nation Building: From the Ottoman Empire to Atatürk's Turkey* (London; New York: I.B. Tauris, 2013), 194, 331 footnote 14. I also want to thank Toygun Altıntaş of the University of Chicago for mentioning the relevance of Ömer Seyfettin in this regard.

3   Dželal Nuri [İleri]; Salih Bakamović, "Panislamizam: Islam u Prošlosti, Sadašnjosti i Budućnosti," in: *Biser: List za Širenje Islamske Prosvjete* (Mostar): Godine III: Broj 13 i 14 (July 1 and 15, 1918), 196.

4   Celâl Nuri, *Havaic-i Kanuniyyemiz* (İstanbul: Matbaa-yı İctihad, h.1331 [1912–13]), 39–44; Celâl Nuri, *Tarih-i İstikbal: Mesail-i Siyasi* (İstanbul: Yeni Osmanlı Matbaası, h.1331 [1912–13]), 167–75; Celâl Nuri, *İttihad-i İslam ve Almanya: İttihad-i İslam'a Zeyl* (İstanbul: Yeni Osmanlı Matbaası ve Kütüphanesi, h.1333 [1914–15]), 17–21.

5   Djelal Noury, *Cauchmar? Roman de Temps Hamidiens* (Pera: Edition du "Jeune-Turc," 1911), 212–16.

6   Celâl Nuri, *Tarih-i İstikbal: Mesail-i Siyasi*, 176–83; Celâl Nuri, "Ermeniler ve Cezri Siyaset," *Ati*, No. 315, 23 Teşrin-i Sani 1334 [October 23, 1928].

7   Ayandan Nuri (Mustafa Nuri), *Abede-i İblis: Yezidi'nin Taifesinin İtikadı Adatı Evsafı* (İstanbul: Matbaa-i İctihad, h.1328 [1910–11]).

8   It should be noted that Şeyh Adi bin Misafir was a Sufi who was associated with Abdulkadir Gilani, founder of the Kadiri order.
9   Djelal Noury, *Le Diable Promu Dieu* (Constantinople: Imprimerie du "Jeune-Turc," 1910), 31; Ayandan Nuri Mustafa Nuri, *Abede-i İblis*, 69–70, 81–2.
10 The following section summarizes Celal Nuri and his father's prejudicial views of the Yezidis. For actual scholarly work on this minority, see Birgül Açıkyıldız, *The Yezidis: The History of a Community, Culture and Religion* (London; New York: I.B. Tauris, 2010); Philip G. Kreyenbroek, *Yezidism—It's Background, Observances and Textual Tradition* (Lewiston: E. Mellon Press, 1995).
11 Yezidis do not worship "gods" or the "devil" but instead a Heptad—a series of seven angels sent by God.
12 Djelal Noury, *Le Diable*, 53; Mustafa Nuri, *Abede-i İblis*, 100. Meleki Tavous was the greatest of the seven angels (or Hass) of the Heptad.
13 Djelal Noury, *Le Diable*, 30; Mustafa Nuri, *Abede-i İblis*, 79–80. For a definitive account of actual Yezidi beliefs, see Açıkyıldız, *The Yezidis*, 71–90; Kreyenbroek, *Yezidism*, 45–124, 145–69.
14 Djelal Noury, *Le Diable*, 33, 60; Mustafa Nuri, *Abede-i İblis*, 77, 118–20.
15 Djelal Noury, *Le Diable*, 33–5; Mustafa Nuri, *Abede-i İblis*, 83–6. For an accurate description of hierarchies in Yezidi society, see Açıkyıldız, *The Yezidis*, 1–32, 91–8; Kreyenbroek, *Yezidism*, 125–44.
16 Djelal Noury, *Le Diable*, 48–50; Mustafa Nuri, *Abede-i İblis*, 97–8, 107–8.
17 Djelal Noury, *Le Diable*, 62–3; Mustafa Nuri, *Abede-i İblis*, 81–2.
18 Sırrı Giridi, *Âra-i Milel* (İstanbul: Bab-ı Ali Caddesinde Numero 52, h.1303 [1885–86]), 171; Djelal Noury, *Le Diable*, 52–3.
19 For the debate on the actual origins of the name Yezidi, see Açıkyıldız, *The Yezidis*, 82; Kreyenbroek, *Yezidism*, 3, 95.
20 Sunni Muslim authorities would argue that the Meleki Tavous's refusal to God's command to bow down before man was identical to Iblis's refusal to bow down before Adam. Iblis is of course referred to as *şeytan* or a devil. Kreyenbroek, *Yezidism*, 3, 46, 147; Açıkyıldız, *The Yezidis*, 73–4, 79, 161.
21 Mustafa Nuri, *Abede-i İblis*, 120–2.
22 Mustafa Nuri, *Abede-i İblis*, 122; Abdullah Yusuf Ali, translator, *The Meaning of the Holy Quran*, newly revised ninth edition (Beltsville: Amana Publications, 1997), 19.
23 Djelal Noury, *Le Diable*, 32, 61–2; Mustafa Nuri, *Abede-i İblis*, 124–30, 140–1.
24 Djelal Noury, *Le Diable*, 37–8; Mustafa Nuri, *Abede-i İblis*, 88–9. For the use of the terms *kaval* and *kiutchek* in a sexual sense, see Danielle von Dobbs, *Dancing Modernity: Gender, Sexuality and the State in the Ottoman Empire and Early Turkish Republic* (unpublished Ph.D. Dissertation, University of Arizona, 2008), 29–53.
25 Djelal Noury, *Le Diable*, 49; Mustafa Nuri, *Abede-i İblis*, 89–91, 97.
26 Djelal Noury, *Le Diable*, 41–2; Mustafa Nuri, *Abede-i İblis*, 90, 96.

27 Djelal Noury, *Le Diable*, 44–5; Mustafa Nuri, *Abede-i İblis*, 92.
28 Djelal Noury, *Le Diable*, 3.
29 Djelal Noury, *Le Diable*, 3.
30 Djelal Noury, *Le Diable*, 23; Mustafa Nuri, *Abede-i İblis*, 110–11.
31 Djelal Noury, *Le Diable*, 40, 46, 54; Mustafa Nuri, *Abede-i İblis*, 93.
32 Djelal Noury, *Le Diable*, 31–2; Mustafa Nuri, *Abede-i İblis*, 81.
33 Philip G. Keyenbroek, *Yezidism*, 6–7.
34 Djelal Noury, *Le Diable*, 20–2; Mustafa Nuri, *Abede-i İblis*, 105–9, 115–16, 132–4. Also see Birgül Açıkyıldız, *The Yezidis*, 56–7.
35 Many Yezidis were in fact repressed in Eastern Anatolia in 1915 along with the Armenians and Suriyanis. Açıkyıldız, *The Yezidis*, 57.
36 Birsen Bulmuş, *Plague, Quarantines and Geopolitics in the Ottoman Empire* (Edinburgh: Edinburgh University Press, 2012), 152–76.
37 Djelal Noury, *Le Diable*, 55–8; Mustafa Nuri, *Abede-i İblis*, 68–9. Celal Nuri and his father were no doubt disturbed by reports of American missionaries trying to evangelize among the Yezidis and therefore more than willing to denounce the "heretics" as a potential fifth column. Amed Gökçen, *Osmanlı ve İngiliz Arşiv Belgelerinde Yezidiler* (İstanbul: Bilgi Üniversitesi Yayınları, 2012), 318–20, 424–5. This was a common line of arguments among Hamidian governing circles and also struck a chord with Unionists, such as in 1915 when the Ottoman government suspected that the Yezidis would join the Dashnak revolt against them. Açıkyıldız, *The Yezidis*, 57.
38 Celâl Nuri, *İttihad-ı İslam: İslamın Mazisi, Hali, İstikbali* (İstanbul: Yeni Osmanlı Matbaası, h.1331 [1912–13]), 207–8.
39 Celâl Nuri, *Almanya*, 53.
40 Celâl Nuri, *İttihad-ı İslam*, 207–8.
41 Celâl Nuri, *İttihad-ı İslam*, 197.
42 Celâl Nuri, *Tarih-i Tedenniyat-ı Osmaniye; Mukadderat-ı Tarihiye. İki eser tevhid ve baz-ı fasl ve fıkralar ilave edilerek musahhah bir surette ikinci defa tab edilmiştir* (Yeni Osmanlı Matbaası ve Kütüphanesi, h.1331 [1914–15]), 85–8; Celâl Nuri, *İttihad-ı İslam*, 160.
43 Celâl Nuri, *İttihad-ı İslam*, 160.
44 Celâl Nuri, *İttihad-ı İslam*, 161. For an article on Unionist diplomatic and political tensions with Persia, see M. Volkan Atuk, "İttihat-ı Terakki Cemiyeti'nin İran Politikası," *Belleten* 83/269 (2019), 261–88. Fariba Zarinebaf also makes a useful comparison and contrast between the CUP and the Iranian constitutionalists. Fariba Zarinebaf, "From Istanbul to Tabriz: Modernity and Constitutionalism in the Ottoman Empire and Iran," *Comparative Studies of South Asia, Africa and the Middle East*, Vol. 28, No. 1 (2008): 154–69.
45 Celâl Nuri, *Tarih-i İstikbal: Mesail-i Siyasi*, 183–4.

46 Celâl Nuri, *Tarih-i İstikbal: Mesail-i Siyasi*, 183, 185. Again such statements are in sync with the integrationist approach the Ottoman central government often had toward the Kurds since the formation of the Hamidiye regiments in 1891. Celal Nuri and the CUP briefly flirted with the idea of giving Eastern Anatolian districts more local autonomy in 1910 but did not give up on using the regiments (albeit with a different name). Celal Nuri, *Havaic-i Kanuniyyemiz*, 37–9; David McDowall, *A Modern History of the Kurds, Third Edition* (London; New York: I.B. Tauris, 2004), 59–63, 95, 99; Robert Olson, *The Emergence of Kurdish Nationalism and the Sheikh Said Rebellion, 1880–1925* (Austin: University of Texas Press, 1989), 1, 7–14.

47 Celâl Nuri, *İttihad-ı İslam*, 164.

48 Celâl Nuri, *İttihad-ı İslam*, 164.

49 Celâl Nuri, *İttihad-ı İslam*, 165. Celal Nuri, like Baha Sait and, frankly, the policies of the previous Hamidian regime, feared the Alevis might revolt alongside the non-Muslim Anatolian minorities, stirred presumably by American missionary activity beginning in the mid-to-late nineteenth century. Zürcher, *Young Turk Legacy*, 120, 318, footnotes 26 and 27; Yalçın Çakmak, *Sultan'ın Kızılbaşları: II. Abdülhamid Dönemi Alevi Algısı ve Siyaseti* (İstanbul: İletişim, 2019), 16–47, 379–85.

50 Sırrı Giridi, *Âra-i Milel*, 59.

51 Sırrı Giridi, *Âra-i Milel*, 68–9, 108.

52 Sırrı Giridi, *Âra-i Milel*, 140–9.

53 Celâl Nuri, *Tarih-i Tedenniyat-ı Osmaniye; Mukadderat-ı Tarihiye*, 87–8; Dželal Nuri, "Panislamizam," 196. This is reminiscent of the views of Al-Afghani and Namık Kemal. York Norman, "Disputing the Iron Circle: Renan, Afghani, and Kemal on Islam, Science, and Modernity," *Journal of World History*, Vol. 22, No. 4 (December 2011), 693–714; Jamal a'd-din Al-Afghani (Nikki R. Keddie, translator and editor), "Answer to Renan," in: Nikki R. Keddie, editor, *An Islamic Response to Imperialism: Political and Religious Writings of Sayyid Jamal a'd-din Al-Afghani* (Berkeley: University of California Press, 1968).

54 Celâl Nuri, *Tarih-i Tedenniyat-ı Osmaniye; Mukadderat-ı Tarihiye*, 360–1; Glorifying Andalusians was very popular among the Unionist readers as seen from the popularity of Ziya Paşa's History of Andalusia (*Endelüs Tarihi*). Atatürk for example took copious notes on his copy. Recep Cengiz et al., *Atatürk'ün Okuduğu Kitaplar, 5. Cilt* (Ankara: Anıtkabir Derneği, 2001), 1–277.

55 Celâl Nuri, *Tarih-i Tedenniyat-ı Osmaniye; Mukadderat-ı Tarihiye*, 364–7.

56 Celâl Nuri, *Tarih-i İstikbal: Mesail-i Siyasi*, 167–9.

57 Celâl Nuri, *Tarih-i İstikbal: Mesail-i Siyasi*, 175.

58 Gustave Le Bon; Robert K Stevenson, translator and editor, "Algeria and the Ideas Prevailing in France concerning Colonization." *Revue Scientifique*, October 2, 1887, 14–15.

59 Celâl Nuri, *İttihad-ı İslam*, 185–210.

60 Le Bon, "Algeria," 6.
61 Bulmuş, 146–9, 153–4, 162–72, 179.
62 Dželal Nuri, "Panislamizam," *Biser*, 196–7; Celâl Nuri, *Tarih-i İstikbal: Mesail-i Siyasi*, 170.
63 Celal Nuri certainly was aware of Blunt's views, having translated a thirty-page letter in which Blunt later retracted *The Future of Islam*'s thesis. Celâl Nuri, *İttihad-ı İslam*, 211–32.
64 Cyril Glasse, *The New Encyclopedia of Islam*, third edition (Lanham: Rowman & Littlefield, 2013), 384. Bedri Gencer, *Islâm'da Modernleşme 1839-1939*, 4. Baskı (İstanbul: Doğu Batı, 2017), 13–15, 44–8, 244–50, 284–308, 441–5, 541–8.
65 Wilfrid Scawen Blunt, *The Future of Islam* (London: Kegan, Paul, Trench & Co., 1882), 204.
66 Celâl Nuri, *İttihad-ı İslam*, 231.
67 Celâl Nuri, *İttihad-ı İslam*, 220–4.
68 Celâl Nuri, *Almanya*, 18.
69 Celâl Nuri, *Almanya*, 17–18.
70 Celâl Nuri, *Almanya*, 19. As Feroz Ahmad illustrates, the Unionists did hope that Egypt and the other Arab provinces would, alongside the Turkish dominated provinces, constitute an Ottoman "dual monarchy." Ahmad, *The Young Turks and the Ottoman Nationalities: Armenians, Greeks, Albanians, Jews and Arabs, 1908-1918* (Salt Lake City: University of Utah Press, 2014), 118–19.
71 Celâl Nuri, *Tarih-i İstikbal: Mesail-i Siyasi*, 172–4.
72 Celâl Nuri, *İttihad-ı İslam*, 115–24. Celal Nuri did not discuss the Albanians at length in his works, somewhat surprising given the importance of Albanian nationalists in supporting initial 1908 uprising. For further information on this issue, consult Ahmad, *Ottoman Nationalities*, 56–65 and James Tallon's recent dissertation, "The Failure of Ottomanism: The Albanian Rebellions of 1909–1912" (Unpublished Ph.D. Dissertation, University of Chicago, 2012).
73 Hasan Kayalı, *Arabs and Young Turks: Ottomanism, Islamism and Arabism in the Ottoman Empire, 1908–1918* (Berkeley: University of California Press, 1997), 192–6.
74 Celâl Nuri, *Rum ve Bizans* (Konstantiniye: Cemiyyet Kütüphanesi, 1917), 19. Celal Nuri claimed the elite were known as the "blues." This name originally came from a team of chariot riders who raced in the Hippodrome of Constntinople. The urban poor were likewise known as the "greens"—the name of another chariot team.
75 Celâl Nuri, *Rum*, 19–22, 28–9.
76 Celâl Nuri, *Rum*, 36–7.
77 Celâl Nuri, *Rum*, 25–33.
78 Celâl Nuri, *Rum*, 40–50. One can also see this nationalistic perspective in Halil İnalcık's "Istanbul: An Islamic City," *Journal of Islamic Studies*, Vol. 1 (1990), 1–23.

79 For an analysis of the Greek patriarchate in the early- to mid-nineteenth century, see Christine Philliou, *Biography of an Empire: Governing Ottomans in an Age of Revolution* (Berkeley: University of California Press, 2010), 65–81.
80 Celâl Nuri, *Rum*, 6–9.
81 Celâl Nuri, *İlel-i Ahlâkiyyemiz* (İstanbul: Yeni Osmanlı Matbaası ve Kütüphanesi, h.1332 [1913–14]), 102.
82 Celâl Nuri, *Rum*, 6–13.
83 Celâl Nuri, *Rum*, 14–16. For more recent critical analysis of the Fallmerayer thesis, see Sathis Gourgouris, *Dream Nation: Enlightenment and the Colonization Of Modern Greece* (Stanford: Stanford University Press, 1996), 142–7; Giorgos Veloudis, *Jakob Phillip Fallmerayer and the Birth of Greek Historicism* (Athens: Mnimon, 1982); George Stamatoyannopoulos, Aritra Bose, Athanasios Teodosiadis, Fotis Tsetsos, Anna Platinga, Nikoletta Psatha, Nikos Zogas, Evangelia Yannaki et al., "Genetics of the Peloponnesian Populations and the Theory of Extinction of the Medieval Peloponnesian Greeks," *European Journal of Human Genetics* (2018).
84 Celâl Nuri, *Ahlâkiyyemiz*, 103.
85 Celâl Nuri, *Ahlâkiyyemiz*, 103.
86 Celâl Nuri, *Tarih-i Tedenniyat-ı Osmaniye; Mukadderat-ı Tarihiye*, 131–6. Also see Ahmad, *the Ottoman Nationalities*, 44–5.
87 Celâl Nuri, *Tarih-i Tedenniyat-ı Osmaniye; Mukadderat-ı Tarihiye*, 396.
88 Celâl Nuri, *Tarih-i Tedenniyat-ı Osmaniye; Mukadderat-ı Tarihiye*, 398.
89 Celâl Nuri, *Tarih-i İstikbal: Mesail-i Siyasi*, 130, 136–7.
90 Abdullah Yusuf Ali, translator, *The Meaning of the Holy Quran*, newly revised ninth edition (Beltsville: Amana Publications, 1997), Surah 109, 1708; Celâl Nuri, *Tarih-i İstikbal: Mesail-i Siyasi*, 142.
91 Ahmad, *Ottoman Nationalities*, 44–5.
92 Celâl Nuri, *Rum*, 12. For the historical context of the Greek annexation of Crete, see Barbara Jelavich, *History of the Balkans Volume 2: 20th Century* (New York; London: Cambridge University Press, 1983), 40–5.
93 Adum; S. Sirenes, translator. *Osmanlı İmparatorluğu'nun Tarih-i Tedennisi Celâl Nuri Bey'in Tarih-i Tedenniyat-ı Osmaniyyesi'ni Tenkiden Azad Emarid Gazetesinde Münderic Silsile-i Makalat* (Der Saadet: Bâb-ı Âli Sadaret Kapusı Karşısında «Edeb» Matbaası, 1331 [1912–13]), 97.
94 Ahmad, *Ottoman Nationalities*, 8–9; Zürcher, *Turkey: A Modern History*, third edition (London; New York: I.B. Tauris, 2010), 83; Erickson, *Ottomans and Armenians*, 7–37.
95 Edward J Erickson, *Ottomans and Armenians: A Study in Counterinsurgency* (New York: Palgrave Macmillan, 2013), 30–2.
96 Adum, *Celâl Nuri Bey'in Tarih-i Tedenniyat-ı Osmaniyyesi*, 78.
97 Djelal Noury, *Cauchmar?*, 212–16.

98   Celâl Nuri, *Tarih-i İstikbal: Mesail-i Siyasi*, 178.
99   Celâl Nuri, *Tarih-i İstikbal: Mesail-i Siyasi*, 181.
100 Raymond Kévorkian, *The Armenian Genocide: A Complete History* (London; New York: I.B. Tauris, 2011), 65, 109, 210, 830 n.115. Bedross Der Matossian, *Shattered Dreams of Revolution: From Liberty to Violence in the Late Ottoman Empire* (Stanford: Stanford University Press, 2014), 177–8.
101 Celâl Nuri, *1327 Senesinde Selanik'te Mün'akid İttihad ve Terakki Kongresine Celâl Nuri Bey Tarafından Takdim Kılınan Muhtıradır* (İstanbul: Osmanlı Şirketi Matbaası, h.1327 [1909–10]), 48.
102 Celâl Nuri, *Muhtıra*, 48.
103 Celâl Nuri, *Muhtıra*, 50.
104 Zürcher, *Young Turk*, 215–18, 230–1.
105 Adum, *Celâl Nuri Bey'in Tarih-i Tedenniyat-ı Osmaniyyesi*, 97–9.
106 Ahmad, *Ottoman Nationalities*, 37–9.
107 Celâl Nuri, *Havaic-i Kanuniyyemiz*, 39–42; Celâl Nuri, *Tarih-i İstikbal: Mesail-i Siyasi*, 176–82.
108 Ahmed Emin cited by Ahmad, *Ottoman Nationalities*, 39.
109 Celâl Nuri, *Tarih-i İstikbal: Mesail-i Siyasi*, 182.
110 Celâl Nuri, *Tarih-i İstikbal: Mesail-i Siyasi*, 178–9.
111 Celâl Nuri, *Tarih-i İstikbal: Mesail-i Siyasi*, 181–2.
112 Ahmad, *Ottoman Nationalities*, 28–9.
113 Adum, *Celâl Nuri Bey'in Tarih-i Tedenniyat-ı Osmaniyyesi*, 81, 93.
114 Celâl Nuri, *Tarih-i İstikbal: Mesail-i Siyasi*, 178.
115 Ahmad, *Ottoman Nationalities*, 74.
116 Kévorkian, *The Armenian Genocide*, 830 n. 115.
117 Celâl Nuri, "Ermeniler ve Ermenistan," *Edebiyat-ı Umumiye Mecmuası*, Vol. 3, No. 44, 6 Temmuz 1918 [July 6, 1918], 838; Gustave Le Bon, *The Crowd: Study of the Popular Mind* (Lexington: Aristeus Books, 2012), 101.
118 Celâl Nuri, "Ermeniler ve Ermenistan," 833, 838.
119 Giridi Ahmed Saki, *Celâl Nuri Bey ve Cezri Fikirleri* (Dersaadet-Hukuk Matbaası, 1335–8 [1919–22]), 29.
120 Celal Nuri was a member of the Turkish Wilsonian League which had written a letter as early as December 5, 1919, requesting that the Americans "should lend its aid and experience for the solution of the problem of the heterogeneous religions and races in Turkey." Tarik Zafer Tunaya, *Türkiye'de Siyaset Partiler Cilt 2: Mütareke Dönemi 1918–1922*, 4. Baskı (İstanbul: İletişim Yayinlari, 2010), 252, 260–70.
121 George L. Mosse, "Max Nordau and his Degeneration," in: Max Nordau, *Degeneration* (Translated from the second edition of the German Edition) (Lincoln; London: University of Nebraska Press, 1993), XV.
122 Max Nordau, *Paradoxes*, English edition (Chicago: L. Schick, 1886), 344–77.

123 Max Nordau, "Address at the Sixth Zionist Congress." Accessed June 28, 2015: https://www.jewishvirtuallibrary.org/source/Zionism/nordau2.html.

124 Nordau, Anna, and Maxa, *Max Nordau: A Biography* (New York: Nordau Committee, 1943), 193-4.

125 Israel Cohen, *The Zionist Movement: Its Aims and Achievements* (London: W. Speaight & Sons, 1912), 25.

126 Ozan Özavcı, "A Jewish 'liberal' in Istanbul: Vladimir Jabotinsky, the Young Turks and the Zionist Press Network, 1908-1911," in: Abigail Green, Simon Levis Sullam, editors, *Jews, Liberalism, Anti-Semitism: A Global History* (New York: Palgrave Macmillan, 2020), 304-9; Özgür Türesay, "Antisionism eet antisémitisme dans la presse ottoman d'Istanbul à l'époque jeune turque (1909-1912). L'exemple d'Ebüziyya Tevfik," *Turcica: Revue d'études turques*, Vol. 41 (2009), 165-72; Israel Cohen, *The Zionist Movement*, 25-6. Julia Phillips Cohen notes that Moiz Cohen wrote privately after the empty speech that he feared "the rise of anti-Jewish sentiment in the empire." Julia Phillips Cohen, *Becoming Ottomans: Sephardi Jews and Imperial Citizenship in the Modern Era* (New York; London: Oxford University Press, 2014), 106.

127 Cohen, *Becoming Ottomans*, 104.

128 Celâl Nuri, *Tarih-i İstikbal: Mesail-i İçtimai* (İstanbul: Yeni Osmanlı Matbaası, h.1332 [1913-14]), 106-7.

129 Celâl Nuri, *Hatemül-Enbiya* (İstanbul: Yeni Osmanlı Matbaası ve Kütüphanesi, h.1332 [1913-14]), 266-8.

130 Celâl Nuri, "Yahudi." *İkdam* (14 Teşrin-i Evvel 1929 [October 14, 1929]).

131 Celâl Nuri, *Şimâl Hatıraları* (İstanbul: Matbaa-i İctihad, h.1330 [1912-13]), 45-51. Celâl Nuri, *Kutup Müsahabeleri: Müşahedat, Muhakemat, Mukayesat, Hikayat, İstiğrakiyat, Nisaiyat* (İstanbul: Yeni Osmanlı Matbaa ve Kütüphanesi h.1331 [1912-13]), 155-8. This was the phrase that he typically used for Jews throughout his works.

132 Celâl Nuri, *Kutup Müsahabeleri*, 155-8.

133 Celâl Nuri, *Şimâl Hatıraları*, 48.

134 Celâl Nuri, *Devlet ve Meclis Hakkında Musahabeler* (Ankara: TBMM Matbaası, 1932), 82. In 1929 he argued that the Jews of Palestine may have been hopeful for a new state but their claims "hurt the legitimate, historical and fundamental rights of the Arabs." Celâl Nuri, "Yahudi."

135 Celâl Nuri, *Devlet*, 82.

136 Celâl Nuri, *Devlet*, 79-80.

137 Celâl Nuri, *Tarih-i Tedenniyat-ı Osmaniye; Mukadderat-ı Tarihiye*, 296.

138 *Türk Büyük Milli Meclis Zabit Ceridesi, Devre: II, Cild: 8/1, İçtima Senesi: II, Kırkikinci İçtima: 20.4. 1340 (1924), Pazar*: 910; İlhan Unat, *Türk Vatandaşlık Hukuku: Metinler, Mahkeme Kararları* (Ankara: Sevinç Maatbası, 1966), 41; Howard Eissenstat, "Metaphors of Race and Discourse of Nation: Racial Theory

and State Nationalism in the First Decades of the Turkish Republic," in: Paul Spickard, editor, *Race and Nation: Ethnic Systems in the Modern World* (New York; London: Routledge, 2005), 249; Marc David Baer, *The Dönme: Jewish Converts, Muslim Revolutionaries, and Secular Turks* (Stanford: Stanford University Press, 2010), 240.

139   *Türk Büyük Milli Meclis Zabit Ceridesi, 20.4. 1340 (1924)*, 910.
140   Celâl Nuri, *Devlet*, 82.
141   Söner Çağaptay, *Who Is a Turk?* 26–7. Rıfat N. Bali, *Bir Günah Keçisi: Munis Tekinalp Cilt 1: Yahudi, Yurtsever ve Kemalist Bir Fikir Adamının Öyküsü* (İstanbul: Libra, 2012), 17–95. Also see Avram Galanti, *Vatandaş Türkçe Konuş* (Ankara: Kebikeç, 2000); Munis Tekinalp; Yıldız Akpolat, *Tekin Alp ve Türkleştirme* (İstanbul: Fenomen, 2005).
142   Celâl Nuri, *Tarih-i Tedenniyat-ı Osmaniye; Mukadderat-ı Tarihiye*, 393.
143   Celâl Nuri, "Rumlar ve Siyaset-i Cezri," *Ati*, numero: 313, 21 Teşrin-i Sani (October) 1334 (1918).
144   Celâl Nuri, *Tarih-i Tedenniyat-ı Osmaniye; Mukadderat-ı Tarihiye*, 395–400.
145   Başak İnce, *Citizenship and Identity in Turkey: From Ataturk's Republic to the Present Day* (London; New York: I.B. Tauris, 2012), 74–5.
146   Celâl Nuri, "Ermeniler ve Cezri Siyaset"; Saki, *Cezri Fikirleri*, 29–30.
147   Ahmed Emin Yalman, *Yakın Tarihte Gördüklerim ve Geçirdiklerim*, 2 vols. (İstanbul: Rey, 1970), 932–52.
148   Christoph Herzog, *Geschichte und Ideologie: Mehmed Murad und Celal Nuri über die historischen Ursachen des osmanischen Niedergangs* (Berlin: Klaus Schwarz Verlag, 1996), 94. Turan Akkoyun, "1924'de Kılıç Ali'nin Celal Nuri'ye Saldırısı ve İzmir Basınının Tavrı," *Tarih ve Toplum 17/99* (Mart 1992), 54–6.
149   They feared that the moderate Unionist opposition might use this rhetoric to delegitimize their own Kemalist nationalist credentials. It also did not wish to shed light on the ongoing process of expropriation and/or purchasing of the former states of the outgoing non-Muslim population—key to achieving the goal of establishing a "national economy."
150   Söner Çağaptay, "Race, Assimilation, and Kemalism: Turkish Nationalism and the Minorities in the 1930s," *Middle Eastern Studies*, Vol. 40, No. 3 (2007): 87–90.
151   Max Nordau, *The Conventional Lies of Our Civilization*, translated from the seventh edition of the GermanWork (London: William Heinemann, 1895), 318–19.

Chapter 4

1   Şükrü Hanioğlu, "Abdullah Cevdet, Turkey, 1869–1932," in: Charles Kurtzman, editor, *Modernist Islam, 1840–1940: A Sourcebook* (Oxford; New York: Oxford University Press, 2002), 172. Celâl Nuri, *Tarih-i İstikbal: Mesail-i İçtimai*

(İstanbul: Yeni Osmanlı Matbaası, h.1332 [1913–14]), 21; Christoph Herzog, *Geschichte und Ideologie: Mehmed Murad und Celal Nuri über die historischen Ursachen des osmanischen Niedergangs* (Berlin: Klaus Schwarz Verlag, 1996), 113.

2   Mehmet Akgün, *Materializmin Türkiye'ye Girişi ve İlk Etkileri* (Ankara: Turizm ve Kültür Bakanlığı, 1988), 11–57.

3   Sevan Nişanyan, *Yanlış Cumhuriyet: Atatürk ve Kemalizm Üzerine 51 Soru* (İstanbul: Kırmızı Yayınlar, 2008), 155–6. This is a rough estimate because the first census that specifically surveyed the percentage of literate and illiterate citizens was in 1927, three years after the establishment of the Republic of Turkey.

4   For the most thorough examination of Ottoman vulgar materialists, see Mehmet Akgün, *Materializmin Türkiye'ye Girişi*. Cemal Kutay is seemingly inspired by both Celal Nuri and Abdullah Cevdet. Besides translating Celal Nuri's *Hatemül-Enbiya* (İstanbul: Yeni Osmanlı Matbaası, h. 1331 [1912–13]) into Modern Turkish, Kutay names five of the titles of his chapters "Hit! ... But Listen" (*"Vur! ... Fakat Dinle!"*), a reference to an article Abdullah Cevdet wrote in April 1913. Abdullah Cevdet; Mustafa Gündüz, translator. *İctihad'ın İctihadı: Abdullah Cevdet'ten Seçme Yazılar* (Ankara: Lotus, 2008), 157–65; Celal Nuri; Cemal Kutay, translator, *Tarih Önünde İslam Peygamberi* (İstanbul: Aksoy Yayıncılık, 1998), 262–6, 333–94.

5   Ludwig Büchner. *Force and Matter or Principles of the Natural Order of the Universe. With a System of Morality Based Thereon* (New York: Truth Seeker Company, 1950).

6   I have used a Turkish translation of this work: Reinhart Pieter Anne Dozy; Abdullah Cevdet and Vedat Atila, translators, *İslam Tarihi* (İstanbul: Gri Yayınları, 2006).

7   Thomas Carlyle, *On Heroes, Hero Worship and the Heroic in History* (New York: Thomas Y. Crowell & Co., 1891), 58–104.

8   Ernest Renan, "Muhammad and the Origins of Islam," in: Ibn Warraq, editor and translator, *The Quest for the Historical Muhammad* (Amherst, NY: Prometheus Books, 2000), 127–66.

9   Ibn Warraq, 130; Renan cited the original number as 20,000; Celal Nuri believed it was 600,000; Celâl Nuri, *Hatem ül-Enbiya*, 22–3.

10 Celâl Nuri, *Hatemül-Enbiya*, 22–3.

11 Also see Ş. Tufan Buzpınar, "Celal Nuri's Concepts of Westernization and Religion," *Middle Eastern Studies*, Vol. 43, No. 2 (March 2007), 252–3.

12 Celal Nuri drew much personal inspiration from a long dead figure in Islamic intellectual history: Averroes or Ibn Rushd (1126–98). Averroes was a highly controversial polymath whom Celal Nuri deemed to be an Islamic precursor of vulgar materialism. Averroes envisioned that there was no separate spiritual world apart from material reality and that one could understand it through logical explanation and natural law. Individual spirits, which were tied to the body, eventually died with it. Only the collective world spirit, which emanated in matter, would survive.

Averroes faced opposition from traditional Islamic scholars, who retorted that Averroes rational view of the world was inaccurate, since God created and destroyed matter at will, and that the underlying spiritual reality had to be considered first and foremost. These scholars, who dominated Islamic thought until the nineteenth century, dismissed Averroes's teachings is fundamentally non-Islamic, because he demeaned God by seeing him in material as well as spiritual terms. To them it was sacrilege to assert that those who examine natural law were seeking God's presence just as much as theologians were when they contemplated spiritual writings and principles. Celal Nuri lamented that their dogmatism suppressed all hints of scientific inquiry. This suppression ironically signaled the decline of Islamic civilization just at the point when Averroes's ideas were about to revive the West. (These arguments are reminiscent of Al-Ghazali (1058–1111), a scholar who lived shortly before Averroes.) Herzog, *Geschichte und Ideologie*, 117; Celâl Nuri, *Tarih-i İstikbal: Mesail-i Fikriye* (İstanbul: Yeni Osmanlı Matbaası, h.1331 [1912–13]), 84–5, 72–105; Dželal Nuri; Salih Bakamović, "Panislamizam: Islam u Prošlosti, Sadašnjosti i Budućnosti," *Biser: List za Širenje Islamske Prosvjete* (Mostar): Godine III: Broj 9 i 10 (May 1 and 15, 1918), 130.

Celal Nuri urged his Ottoman readers to have no illusions that their own great thinkers, such as Ebussuud Efendi (1490–1574) or Zembelli Ali Cemali Efendi (d. 1526), famous *şeyhülislam*s under Süleyman the Magnificent (r.1520–66), could vaguely compare to such an intellectual giant as Averroes: "They … [were] snails next to this lion." Celâl Nuri, *Tarih-i İstikbal: Mesail-i Fikriye*, 75.

It was only after the Young Turk Revolution that the sultanate could hope to pick up where Averroes had left off, in Celal Nuri's eyes:

> Right now we are restoring the freedom of thought that has been forbidden in the Islamic world for six centuries … I hope that matters of thought will be discussed in our mosques with complete freedom as it was in Cordoba … [As a result] the reign of Mehmet V will come closer to the reign of al-Mamun and Islam will strengthen. Celâl Nuri, *Tarih-i İstikbal: Mesail-i Fikriye*, 76.

Celal Nuri faced deep skepticism from Şehbenderzade, who saw Averroes as a questionable model for emulation. While Şehbenderzade realized there was value in re-examining non-Islamic scholarship, he absolutely disagreed with the notion that the material and spiritual worlds could not be disassociated from each other. Rather, Şehbenderzade seconded the *Ashari* view that God and the spiritual world preceded and succeeded the material one, and that science was limited in its ability to discern truth in a way spiritual contemplation was not.

Like the older generation of Ottoman *Tanzimat* reformers, Şehbenderzade saw scientific innovation as necessary in counteracting the threat of European colonialism, but only if it preserved the moral and fundamental integrity of the faith. He was also shocked by Celal Nuri's dismissive attitude toward earlier

Ottoman thinkers and statesmen. To Şehbenderzade, it was not fair to dismiss the likes of Ebussuud and Zembelli—who were religious thinkers, and not philosophers—or to totally disregard Ottoman and other Islamic scholars on the life of Muhammad and the role of science, such as himself or Ahmet Cevdet Pasha before him.

13 Ahmet İshak Demir, *Cumhuriyet Dönemi Aydınlarının İslam'a Bakışı* (İstanbul: Ensar Neşriyatı, 2004), 118–19; Kutay, *Tarih Önünde İslam Peygamberi*, 108–10.

14 Celâl Nuri, *Hatemül-Enbiya*, 22–3.

15 Perhaps the most tangible contribution Celal Nuri made toward putting such scientific concepts into practice was in the field of law. Contrary to the thought that Islam was bound to traditional interpretations that highlighted the importance of not only the Quran, but also the sayings of Muhammad, the commentary of Muhammad's companions, and that of other legal scholars, Celal Nuri contended that Islam was always open to new principles. As such, it would allow for empirical knowledge and rationality to take a more central role. This was the true meaning of *ictihad*, the term most often used by Islamic scholars for fundamental judicial reinterpretation of Islamic law. Whereas the famous claim that "the gates of *ictihad* had closed" led Orientalists to conclude that Islamic law had become retrogressive after the mid-ninth century, Celal Nuri believed that "Islam was in no way against new judicial interpretations of free thought." Dželal Nuri; Bakamović, "Panislamizam," 130. Buzpınar also discusses the issue at length. Buzpınar, "Celâl Nuri's Concepts of Westernization and Religion," 253–4. Joseph Schacht, *An Introduction to Islamic Law* (Oxford: Clarendon Press, 1964), 70–2.

This did not mean Celal Nuri believed in working within the context of an amalgamated version of Islamic law that would accept both traditional and modern sources. His argument was confirmed by the thirty-ninth article of the *Mecelle*—the Ottoman civil code in force since 1877—which stated that "the terms of law vary with the change in times." Celâl Nuri, *Havaic-i Kanuniyyemiz* (İstanbul: Matbaa-yı İctihad, h.1331 [1912–13]), 108, 114; Celâl Nuri, *Hatem ül-Enbiya*, 250–1. This foundational principle commanded that different criteria be used when needed for the good of the Islamic community. Article 21 of the *Mecelle* provided further justification: "Necessity renders prohibited things permissible." Dželal Nuri, "Panislamizam," 131. Celal Nuri undoubtedly was sympathetic to the general argument among *Hanefi*s, the dominant traditional Islamic denomination among Ottoman Turks, that innovations and modernization as a whole were acceptable as long as they were necessary for the welfare and survival of the Islamic community.

Ahmed Cevdet Pasha's *Mecelle* was undoubtedly important. This code was intended to be a systematically abridged form of basic noncommercial contract law for implementation throughout the empire. Rejecting the argument by the French ambassador and Ali and Fuat Pashas that the civil law should be adapted for verbatim from the Code Napoleon, Ahmed Cevdet Pasha instead believed that he could systematize existing Hanefi legal principles in a way that would meet the demands of modern life. This was critical, in his opinion, to preserve his country's leading role within Islamic civilization. Mehmet Akif Aydın, "Mecelle-i Ahkam-ı Adliyye," *İslam Ansiklopedisi*, Cilt: 28 (Ankara: Diyanet İşleri Bakanlığı, 2003), 231–5. Indeed, he would highlight the enduring power of Islamic law in his own history of Muhammad, where the Prophet exclaimed that he bequeathed Islamic law on the basis of the Quran, his sayings and actions to his followers, and that "they would not be corrupted at any time" if they remained true to them. Ahmed Cevdet Paşa; Mustafa Kasadar, translator, *Hatemül-Enbiya, Son Peygamber HZ. MUHAMMED: Sallallahu Aleyhi Sellem* (İstanbul: Ravza Yayınları, 2006), 277–8.

Celal Nuri, nonetheless, asserted that the *Mecelle* was painfully out of date. He pointed out that the *Mecelle*, like the Napoleonic Code, was written during a time of despotism, and therefore did not conform to the virtues of the Young Turk regime, which he styled as a constitutional monarchy. Celâl Nuri, *Havaic-i Kanuniyyemiz*, 77, 82. This could be seen in Ahmet Cevdet Pasha's history of Muhammad, where he claimed that the Quraysh were the rightful rulers of the Arabs and were not required to consult with the people. Ahmed Cevdet Paşa, *Son Peygamber*, 284, 293. Celal Nuri, in contrast, believed that the sultan was subject to constitutional rule.

But Celal Nuri's political differences with Ahmed Cevdet Pasha also extended to the international arena. When crafting the *Mecelle*, Ahmed Cevdet Pasha refused to adopt the entire Napoleonic Code. This decision was made in defiance of the French, who were the leading foreign creditor to the Ottomans and who could use the debts to undermine the empire's sovereignty. The argument for adopting a Western law code wholesale often boiled down to international demands for equality between the empire's Muslims and non-Muslims. This was evident in the Gülhane Noble Rescript (*Hatt-ı Şerif*) of 1839, where the sultan, pressed by the British for reforms, guaranteed all subjects "perfect security for life, honor, and fortune" regardless of religion. J.C. Hurewitz, *Diplomacy in the Near and Middle East: A Documentary Record, Volume I: 1535–1914* (Princeton: Van Nostrand Company, 1956), 114. The Imperial Rescript (*Hatt-ı Hümayun*) of 1856, issued at the end of the Crimean War after a successful British and French intervention on their behalf, expanded on this principle by granting non-Muslims equality before the law in commerce, fines, and criminal suits. It also extended in theory to civil law, although family law was reserved for the religious courts of the respective communities. Hurewitz, *Diplomacy in the Near and Middle East: Volume I*, 151.

Ahmed Cevdet's *Mecelle* therefore represented an Ottoman attempt to modernize Islamic law. The *Mecelle* would be confirmed in Article 87 of the 1876 Ottoman Constitution, along with Islamic law, which was reserved again for the Muslim community's family matters.

Celal Nuri's criticisms notwithstanding, the *Mecelle* remained in force until 1926, when it was replaced wholesale by a translated version of the 1914 Swiss

Civil Code. While there was talk in 1917 about revising or replacing the *Mecelle* when debating the family law of that year, no action was taken. Şerafettin Turan, *Türk Devrimi Tarihi, 3. Kitap (Birinci Bölüm), Yeni Türkiye'nin Oluşumu (1923–1938)*, third edition (İstanbul: Bilgi Yayınları, 2013), 218, 221. The 1921 Turkish Constitution, promulgated during the Independence War, did not mention the *Mecelle* specifically, but implied its continuation, given the fact that Articles 7 and 11 confirmed Islamic legal courts for family law.

But Celal Nuri may have helped lay the legal groundwork for revising or even replacing the *Mecelle* in the 1924 Constitution when it states in Article 26 that "the Grand National Assembly itself executes the holy law *(ahkâm-i şeriye)*." Edward Mead Earle, "The New Constitution of Turkey," *Political Science Quarterly*, Vol. 40, No. 1 (March 1925), 91. He confirms these views in a 1923 pamphlet *The Crown Wearing Nation (Taç Giyen Millet)* where he says that Islamic jurisprudence is the purview of the constitution and parliament. Celal Nuri, *Taç Giyen Millet* (İstanbul: Cihan Biraderler Matbaası, h.1339/r.1341 [1923]), 209.

Celal Nuri, the rapporteur for the parliamentary constitutional committee, was no doubt aware that his government had also signed the Lausanne Treaty (1923), which again specified the rights of legal equality for Muslims and non-Muslims both in civil and family law. This decision would justify adopting the Swiss Civil Code, which would eliminate the need for both the *Mecelle* and the Islamic family courts. Şerafettin Turan, *Yeni Türkiye'nin Oluşumu*, 218–23. Moreover, adopting such a code would no longer be grounds for inciting local Greeks, Armenians, Jews, and other non-Muslim minorities to revolt, since the new state was roughly 97 percent Muslim. Söner Çağaptay, *Islam, Secularism and Nationalism in Modern Turkey: Who Is a Turk?* (London; New York: Rutledge, 2006), 16. (Çağaptay cites the 1927 census for the Republic of Turkey where Muslims made up 97.36 percent of the population.)

Mahmut Esat (Bozkurt), the minister of justice in 1926 who supervised the adoption of the new Swiss Civil Code, went one step further. He claimed that secularizing the last remaining elements of Islamic law would also provide the cultural impetus to guarantee independence: "It is obligatory for national sovereignty that the law code should be cut from … [Islam]." Turan, *Yeni Türkiye'nin Oluşumu*, 222.

Atatürk of course had no regrets about such a "fiat accompli":

> I adhere to the reality that "every revolution is *sui generis* by nature" … [I admit with] total sadness … that the Turkish nation has wasted 300 years facing … [the]sorrowful and painful barriers [that the old law represented]. Turan, *Yeni Türkiye'nin Oluşumu*, 220.

While Celal Nuri certainly played a part in secularizing the law code, he may have disagreed with how the government took the new code wholesale from

Europe without considering the national spirit. Celal Nuri had long believed that laws by themselves could not be imposed to shape society. Celâl Nuri, *Havaic-i Kanuniyyemiz*, 3. Although he was silent about the topic in 1926, one can surmise that he did not believe the reform had the power to transform Turks into a European people without profound cultural change. This process could only occur by first introducing the vulgar materialistic philosophy to the elite, and then over time spreading its values to the masses by transforming Islam into a faith that encouraged scientific thought.

16 Celâl Nuri, *Tarih-i İstikbal: Mesail-i Fikriye*, 33.
17 Celâl Nuri, *Tarih-i İstikbal: Mesail-i Fikriye*, 23–53.
18 Celâl Nuri, *Tarih-i İstikbal: Mesail-i Fikriye*, 106.
19 Celâl Nuri, *Tarih-i İstikbal: Mesail-i Fikriye*, 17.
20 Celâl Nuri, *Tarih-i İstikbal: Mesail-i Fikriye*, 20, 30–2, 34–5, 71.
21 Namık Kemal, *Renan Müdafaanamesi*, edited by Ali Ekrem Bulayır, Külliyat-ı Kemal (Birinci Tertip Istanbul: Selanik Matbaası, h.1326 [1910–11]), 58.
22 Celal Nuri began his volume on vulgar materialism with a satirical introduction of himself meeting the mysterious soothsayer Titmes who sought to be his spiritual guide to the world beyond, a likely jab at Şehbenderzade's character of Miror Dede in his work *Awakened Dreams* (*Âmak-i Hayâl*). Mirror Dede, a Sufi master, guided Raji, a befuddled young man in search of the true meaning of life. Celâl Nuri, *Tarih-i İstikbal: Mesail-i Fikriye*, 3–16. Ahmet Hilmi [Şehbenderzade]; translated from Âmak-i Hayâl and edited by Refik Algan and Camille Helminski, *Awakened Dreams: Raji's Journeys with the Miror Dede* (Putney, VT: Threshold Books, 1993).
23 Ahmet Hilmi Şehbenderzade, *Huzur-ı Akl ü Fende Maddiyun Meslek-i Delaleti* (Darülhilafe: Matbaa-ı İslamiyye, 1332 [1914–15]), 3–103; Ömer Ceran, *Şehbenderzade Filibeli Ahmed Hilmi'nin Dini ve Felsefi Görüşleri* (Bursa: Sır Yayıncılık, 2013), 35–7.
24 Şehbenderzade, *Huzur-ı Akl ve Fende Maddiyun*, 3–16, 134–51.
25 Hüseyin Rahmi Yananlı, "Sunuş," in: Ahmet Hilmi Şehbenderzade; Hüseyin Rahmi Yananlı translator, *İslam Tarihi* (İstanbul: Huzur Yayınları, 2011), 25–7.
26 Ahmet Hilmi, *Awakened Dreams*.
27 Celâl Nuri, *Perviz* (İstanbul: Zarafet Matbaası, h.1332 [1914–15]). Mustafa Kurt, *Celâl Nuri İleri'nin Romanları Bir İnceleme* (Ankara: Kurgan Edebiyat, 2012), 35–50.
28 Ivan Turgenev; translated and edited by Richard Freeborn, *Fathers and Sons* (New York: Oxford University Press, 2008).
29 Besides the Şehbenderzade translations already cited in this chapter, see Ahmet Hilmi; Ahmet Almaz, translator, *Allah'ı İnkar Mümkün Müdür? Atatürk'ü Değiştiren Kitap* (İstanbul: Yakamoz, 2008); Şehbenderzade Filibeli Ahmet Hilmi; M. Şevket Eygi, translator, *Müslümanlar Uyanın!* (İstanbul: Bedir Yayınevi, 1966).
30 Celâl Nuri, *Hatemül-Enbiya*, 238–51.

31 Celâl Nuri, *Hatemül-Enbiya*, 259–60.
32 Celâl Nuri, *Hatemül-Enbiya*, 261–4.
33 Celâl Nuri, *Hatemül-Enbiya*, 265–72.
34 Celâl Nuri, *Hatemül-Enbiya*, 274.
35 Celâl Nuri, *Hatemül-Enbiya*, 285–6.
36 Celâl Nuri, *Hatemül-Enbiya*, 75–6, 83.
37 But such denunciations could only be done in theological terms. Both Luther and Muhammad preached the message that all believers were equal, based on divine revelation, the only language that the popular masses understood. Celal Nuri referenced Le Bon, who "talks about the necessary beliefs of the common people throughout his works. He is right a thousand times!" A religion can change but will always remain in one form or another. Celâl Nuri, *Hatemül-Enbiya*, 59.

Friedrich Nietzsche believed instead that Luther destroyed the chance that Renaissance humanism could spread from Italy to Europe as a whole:

> At a moment when a higher order of values, values that were noble, that say yea to life, and that guaranteed a future, had succeeded in triumphing over the opposite values, the values of degeneration, in the very seat of Christianity itself—*and even in the hearts of those sitting there,*—Luther, that cursed monk, not only restored the church, but, what was 1000 times worse, restored Christianity, and at a time too when it lay defeated. Christianity, *The Denial of the Will to Live*, exalted to a religion! Luther … attacks the church, and in so doing restored it! Catholics would be perfectly justified in celebrating these in honor of Luther, and in producing festival plays … Luther and the "rebirth of morality"! Friedrich Nietzsche; translated by Anthony Ludovici, *Ecco Hommo*, in: Oscar Levy, editor, *The Complete Works of Friedrich Nietzsche* (New York: The Macmillan Company, 1911), 124–5; Celâl Nuri, *Tarih-i Osmani ve Keşfiyyat, Rönesans ve Reform Harekatı* (Cemiyet Kütüphanesi, 1917), 50.

Celal Nuri retorted that: "Luther was not a 'cursed monk.' He did well, and in my opinion, his coming to the world was a pure goodness for mankind." Celâl Nuri, *Tarih-i Osmani ve Keşfiyyat*, 51. This could be seen for instance when he denounced academics' overreliance on scholasticism: "What are the benefits of these libraries filled with volumes of books explaining in detail so many traditions and legends no one ever heard of? Even the authors never understood what they meant." Celâl Nuri, *Tarih-i Osmani ve Keşfiyyat*, 40.

Luther's writings opened the way for scholars to examine natural phenomena without having to consider what earlier philosophers had said. The caveat, however, was that the new learning should never conflict with the teachings of the holy book. Celâl Nuri, *Tarih-i Osmani ve Keşfiyyat*, 40. On these grounds, Luther disapproved of Copernicus's theory that the Earth revolved around the Sun. Jean Calvin, whose own systematic version of Protestantism arguably surpassed Luther's, had Michael Servet, a natural geographer, executed for allegedly betraying the faith. Servet had fled to Calvin with the mistaken belief that he would grant him asylum from Catholic persecution. Theodore Beze, a close friend of Calvin, also condemned those like Servet who differed with Aristotle. Celâl Nuri, *Tarih-i Osmani ve Keşfiyyat*, 40–1. Thus, Luther and Calvin's reforms alone were not enough to usher in the modern age of scientific experiment and intellectual freedom.

38 Herzog, *Geschichte und Ideologie*, 108–9; Celâl Nuri, *Tarih-i Osmani ve Keşfiyyat*, 48.
39 Celâl Nuri, *Tarih-i İstikbal: Mesail-i Fikriye*, 72.
40 Celâl Nuri, *Tarih-i İstikbal: Mesail-i Fikriye*, 72.
41 Celâl Nuri, *Hatemül-Enbiya*, 308–17.
42 Renan, "Muhammad," 132.
43 Carlyle, *On Heroes*, 72.
44 Carlyle, *On Heroes*, 78.
45 Carlyle, *On Heroes*, 132–3.
46 Carlyle, *On Heroes*, 100.
47 Carlyle, *On Heroes*, 85–6.
48 Carlyle, *On Heroes*, 103–4.
49 Carlyle, *On Heroes*, 99.
50 Renan, "Muhammad," 157.
51 Renan, "Muhammad," 141.
52 Celâl Nuri, *Hatemül-Enbiya*, 64.
53 Celâl Nuri, *Hatemül-Enbiya*, 171.
54 Celâl Nuri, *Hatemül-Enbiya*, 176–7.
55 Celâl Nuri, *Hatemül-Enbiya*, 65–8; Demir, *İslam'a Bakışı*, 275.
56 Celâl Nuri, *Hatemül-Enbiya*, 51–4.
57 Celâl Nuri, *Hatemül-Enbiya*, 81–2. Yet another Frenchman Celal Nuri singled out for criticism was Napoleon Bonaparte. He acknowledged his military genius but simply exploited those whom he conquered. This could be seen in 1798, for instance, when Napoleon invaded Egypt. He dishonestly proclaimed himself a Muslim in order to pacify his new subjects, but quickly pillage Cairo and also favored the local Coptic Christians over the majority Muslim population—setting up a pattern Western imperialists would use to subjugate the Ottomans and turn them into colonies. Celâl Nuri, *Hatemül-Enbiya*, 82–3, 312.
58 Celâl Nuri, *Hatemül-Enbiya*, 309–17.
59 Celâl Nuri, *Hatemül-Enbiya*, 127.
60 Gustave Le Bon, *The Psychology of Peoples: its Influence on their Evolution* (New York: Macmillan, 1898), 198.
61 George L. Mosse, "Machiavelli," from History 119, European Cultural History, 1500–1815, recorded audio lecture originally broadcast in Fall 1969 for WHA

Radio series' "University of the Air." Accessed December 15, 2015: http://mosseprogram.wisc.edu/audio_history119.htm.
62 Şehbenderzade Filibeli Ahmed Hilmi, *Tarih-i İslâm*, I. Cild (Kostantiniyye: Hikmet Matbaası, h.1326 [1908–9]), 128–30.
63 Şehbenderzade Filibeli Ahmed Hilmi, *Tarih-i İslâm*, II. Cild (Kostantiniyye: Hikmet Matbaası, h.1327 [1909–10]), 540.
64 Milli Kütüphane Genel Müdürlüğü, *Atatürk'ün Özel Kütüphanesi'nin Kataloğu* (Ankara: Başbakanlık Basımevi, 1973), 100, entries 584–5.
65 Recep Cengiz et al., *Atatürk'ün Okuduğu Kitaplar* (Ankara: Anıtkabir Derneği, 2001), vol. 7: 481–5; vol. 11: 457–70; vol. 16: 257–73; vol. 19: 79–157; vol. 20: 279–354; vol. 23: 122–240.
66 Hanioğlu, *Atatürk: An Intellectual Biography* (Princeton: Princeton University Press, 2011), 153.

Chapter 5

1 Deniz Kandiyoti, "End of Empire: Islam, Nationalism, and Women in Turkey," in: Reina Lewis and Sara Mills, editors, *Feminist Postcolonial Theory* (New York: Routledge, 2003), 33.
2 Celâl Nuri, *Kadınlarımız. Umumiyeti İtibariyle Kadın Meselesi ve Tarihi. Müslüman ve Türk Kadınları* (İstanbul: Matbaa-i İctihad, h.1331 [1912–13]).
3 Nilüfer Göle, *The Forbidden Modern: Civilization and Veiling* (Ann Arbor: University of Michigan Press, 1996), 39.
4 Kandiyoti, "End of Empire," 32.
5 Zafer Toprak, "The Family, Feminism, and the State during the Young Turk Period, 1908–1918," in: *Première Recontre Internationale sur l'Empire Ottoman et la Turquie Moderne* (İstanbul; Paris: Éditions ISIS, 1991), 441–52.
6 Erik J. Zürcher, *The Young Turk Legacy and Nation Building* (London; New York: I.B. Tauris, 2010), 216 referring to Niyazi Berkes, *The Development of Secularism in Modern Turkey* (Montreal: McGill University Press, 1964), 337–66.
7 Deniz Kandiyoti noted that Celal Nuri "[argued] that Islam was in no way inimical to the equality of women." Deniz Kandiyoti, "End of Empire," 272.
   Fatma Aliye (Topuz) (1862–1936), the first Ottoman woman to openly publish her own thoughts on the topic in 1892, viewed polygamy, marriage laws, and issues regarding women's rights in the professions and education as legitimized by Islamic legal sources—the Quran, and the sayings of Prophet Muhammad, his companions, and later Muslim judicial authorities. Fatma Aliye; Orhan Sakin, translator, *Osmanlı'da Kadın: Cariyelik, Çokeşlilik, Moda* (İstanbul: Ekim, 2012). Fatma Aliye was not the first Ottoman to write on women's rights in the empire.

Earlier works on the topic include Şinasi's *Şair Evlenmesi* (1870); Namık Kemal's "Terbiye-i Nisvân Hakkında Bir Layiha" (1867), "Aile" (1872), and *İtibah* (1876); Ahmet Midhat's *Felsefe-i Zenan* (1870), *Eyvah* (1870), and *Diplomalı Kız* (1890); Sami Paşazade Sezai's *Sergüzeşt* (1888); and Şemsettin Sami's *Kadınlar* (1880). Other works before the Young Turk Revolution include Nabizade Nazım's *Zehra* (1896) and Selahattin Asım's *Türk Kadınlığının Tereddisi* (1905). Fatma Aliye, Mahmud Esad; Firdevz Canbaz, translator, *Çok Eşlilik: Taaddüd-i Zevcat* (Ankara: Hece İnceleme, 2007), 13.

Fatma Aliye's view was not surprising, given the fact that she was the daughter of Ahmet Cevdet Pasha (1822–95), the greatly influential *Tanzimat* reformer, who helped compile the *Mecelle* (1877), the empire's new codification of civil law that combined Islamic and Western legal concepts and innovations. The *Mecelle* did not cover family law. Deniz Kandiyoti, "End of Empire," 267–8.

Some scholars, such as the prominent French feminist Odette Laguerre (1860–1956), highlighted one particular phrase in the *Mecelle*: "If a work is necessary, a space opens." This statement, she argued, was an indication that both the Ottomans and the Islamic world writ large were open to women's rights. Odette Laguerre; Baha Tevfik, Kemal Bakır, and Ali Utku, translators, *Feminizm: Âlem-i Nisvân* (Konya: Çizgi Yayınları, 2015), 103. Laguerre said that Islamic law also provided an excellent foundation for feminism, the movement to gain equality in every respect with men. She would go on to provide concrete examples from the Quran and Muhammad's sayings to illustrate that women in Islamic societies enjoyed greater legal rights than women in the Christian West. She even concluded that "Islam is feminism," a powerful statement apparently intended to spark a movement in the Middle East. Laguerre; Tevfik, *Feminizm: Âlem-i Nisvân*, 115.

8   For further information on Ahmet Cevdet and the *Mecelle*, see pages 108–9, ft. 15.
9   Much of Gökalp's work on this subject was originally written as journal articles in the months and weeks leading to the passage of the Ottoman Law on October 25, 1917. A list of these articles is given in Zoprak, "Family, Feminism, and the State," 437–8. The articles were compiled as part of an anthology after Gökalp's death edited by Mustafa Görgen. Ziya Gökalp; Mustafa Görgen, *Türk Ahlakı* (İstanbul: Türk Kültür Yayını, 1975). I have used a later edition of this same volume: Ziya Gökalp; Mehmet Celal Atgın, editor, *Türk Ahlakı* (İstanbul: Bilgeoğuz, 2013).
10 Cenab Şehabeddin, "Yarınki Efkâr-ı İslamiye," *Peyâm-Sabah*, 13 Kanunusâni 1337 [January 13, 1921]; Cenab Şehabeddin, "Hâtime-i Münazara," *Peyâm-Sabah*, 17 Kanunusâni 1337 [January 17, 1921]; Cenab Şehabeddin, "Muhterem Muarrızlara," *Peyâm-Sabah*, 24 Kanunusâni 1337 [January 24, 1921]; Cenab Şehabeddin, "Mahfel'e Cevab," *Peyâm-Sabah*, 24 Şubat 1337 [February 24, 1921]; Halil Hamid, *İslamiyette Feminizm yahud Alem-i Nisvanda Musavat-ı Tamme* (Dersaadet: Keteon Matbaası, 1328 (1910–11)); Halil Hamid, *Dünkü, Bügünkü, Yarınkı Kadın* (İstanbul: Necm-i İstikbal Matbaasi, 1334 (1915–16)); Halil Hamit, *İslam'da Feminizm:*

Fakir Bir Hürriyet Zengin Bir Esaretten Evladı (İstanbul: Okumuş Adam Yayınları, 2001); Salahaddin Asım, *Osmanlı'da Kadınlığın Durumu* (İstanbul: Arba, 1989); Salahaddin Asım, *Türk Kadınlığının Tereddisi yahud Karılaşmak* (İstanbul: Resimli Kitap Matbaası, no date).

11 Nilüfer Göle concluded: "For Western thinkers [like Celal Nuri] the liberation of women corresponded to their attainment of the status of human being. What is interesting is that by this reasoning, women would not reach the status of human being for their own sakes but would be serving society in its attempt to rise to the level of 'civilized.' According to this outlook, equality between the sexes emerges as a necessary condition and the formation of modern families and the actualization of this requires the training of both sons and daughters in this direction." Nilüfer Göle, *The Forbidden Modern*, 39.

12 Celâl Nuri, *Kadınlarımız*, 130–8.

13 Ludwig Büchner, *Am Sterbelager des Jahrhunderts* (Geißen: Verlag von Emil Roth, 1900), 299–336; Charles Letourneau, *The Evolution of Marriage and of the Family* (London; New York: Charles Scribner's Sons, 1895); Max Nordau, *The Conventional Lies of Our Civilization*, Translated from the German (Chicago: Laird & Lee, 1895), 269–323.

14 Qasim Amin; Samiha Sidhom Peterson, translator, *The Liberation of Women and the New Woman* (Cairo; New York: The American University in Cairo Press, 2000).

15 Ziya Gökalp; Atgın, *Türk Ahlakı*.

16 Hilmi Ziya Ülken, moreover, draws attention to the importance of comparing Celal Nuri to Ziya Gökalp: "The work of Celal Nuri had a serious impact on [the question of women] and resolved the disputes [among Unionist writers] long before Gökalp touched this issue. [His work not only] ... addresses the question in terms of Islamic and Western laws and their comparison, [but] it [also] touches upon the evolution of women in society sociologically, and it examines how the question of women was put into practice in ancient civilizations and religions." Hilmi Ziya Ülken, *Türkiye'de Çağdaş Düşünce Tarihi* (İstanbul: Ülken Yayınları, 1992), 401–2.

17 Erik Jan Zürcher, *Turkey: A Modern History*, third edition (London; New York: I.B. Tauris, 2010), 122. Mehmet Akif Aydın, "Hukuk-ı Aile Kararnamesi," in: *İslam Ansiklopedisi*, 18. Cilt (İstanbul: Türkiye Diyanet Vakfı, 1998), 314–18. The Unionists who passed this code were intent on eliminating the need for non-Muslim minorities and foreign citizens to have separate family courts as they did prior to this decree. They also presumably did not want to provoke further discontent in the Arab provinces, which were affected by the Arab Revolt and the British expeditionary forces at the time it was promulgated. For a feminist critique of the law, see Judith E. Tucker, "Revisiting Reform: Women and the Ottoman Law of Family Rights, 1917," *The Arab Studies Journal*, Vol. 4, No. 2 (1996), 4–17.

18 Celâl Nuri, *Kadınlarımız*, 14–30. Halil Hamid also devoted considerable space in his work to deal with women's history in ancient civilizations. Hamid praised the ancient Greeks, Egyptians, and Chaldeans for elevating women's status in society, unlike Celal Nuri. Halil Hamit, *İslam'da Feminizm*, 31–5, 42–3.
19 Celâl Nuri, *Hatemül-Enbiya* (İstanbul: Yeni Osmanlı Matbaası ve Kütüphanesi, h.1332 [1913–14]), 238–64.
20 Celâl Nuri, *Kadınlarımız*, 41–7.
21 Celâl Nuri, *Kadınlarımız*, 48–9.
22 Celâl Nuri, *Kadınlarımız*, 53–4.
23 Celâl Nuri, *Kadınlarımız*, 53–4.
24 Celâl Nuri, *Kadınlarımız*, 55–6.
25 Celâl Nuri, *Kadınlarımız*, 58–9.
26 Celâl Nuri, *Kadınlarımız*, 59.
27 Celâl Nuri, *Kadınlarımız*, 59–62.
28 Celâl Nuri, *Kadınlarımız*, 61–2.
29 Gaspard Gourgoud, *The St. Helena Journal of General Baron Gourgaud* (January 9, 1817); as quoted in *The St. Helena Journal of General Baron Gourgaud, 1815–1818: Being a Diary written at St. Helena during a Part of Napoleon's Captivity* (1932) as translated by Norman Edwards, a translation of *Journal de Sainte-Hélène 1815–1818* (London: John Lane, 1932), 73.
30 Abdülhak Hamid Tarhan, "Duhter-i Hindu," in: Abdülhak Hamid Tarhan; İnce Enginün, editor, Abdülhak Hamid Tarhan Tiyatroları 3, 35–149.
31 Abdülhak Hamid Tarhan, "Duhter-i Hindu," 65–6.
32 Abdülhak Hamid Tarhan, "Duhter-i Hindu," 65.
33 Abdülhak Hamid Tarhan, "Duhter-i Hindu," 142–9.
34 Abdülhak Hamid Tarhan, "Duhter-i Hindu," 103.
35 Celâl Nuri, *Kadınlarımız*, 65.
36 Celâl Nuri, *Kadınlarımız*, 142–3.
37 Celâl Nuri, *Hatemül-Enbiya*, 56–7.
38 Celâl Nuri, *Hatemül-Enbiya*, 56–7.
39 Celâl Nuri, *Kadınlarımız*, 169–70.
40 Celâl Nuri, *Kadınlarımız*, 158–61.
41 Celâl Nuri, *İttihad-ı İslam: İslamın Mazisi, Hali, İstikbali* (İstanbul: Yeni Osmanlı Matbaası, h.1331 [1912–13]), 207.
42 Celâl Nuri, *Hatemül-Enbiya*, 45–9.
43 Celâl Nuri, *Kadınlarımız*, 26.
44 Celâl Nuri, "Osmanlılar'dan Evvel (II)," *Edebiyat-ı Umumiye Mecmuası*, Vol. 2, No. 31, 2 Haziran 1917 [June 2, 1917], 88.
45 Celâl Nuri, *İttihad-ı İslam ve Almanya: İttihad-ı İslam'a Zeyl* (İstanbul: Yeni Osmanlı Matbaası ve Kütüphanesi, h.1333 [1914–15]), 60–1.

46 Celâl Nuri, "Osmanlılar'dan Evvel (II)," 89.
47 Celâl Nuri, *Rum ve Bizans* (Konstantiniye: Cemiyyet Kütüphanesi, 1917), 49.
48 Celâl Nuri, *Rum*, 49.
49 Celâl Nuri, *Rum*, 49.
50 Celâl Nuri, *Rum*, 49.
51 Djelal Noury, *Cauchmar? Roman de Temps Hamidiens* (Pera: Edition du "Jeune-Turc," 1911).
52 Djelal Noury, *Cauchmar?* 1–112.
53 Djelal Noury, *Cauchmar?* 143–51.
54 Djelal Noury, *Cauchmar?* 152–98.
55 Djelal Noury, *Cauchmar?* 222–8.
56 Djelal Noury, *Cauchmar?* 229–48.
57 Djelal Noury, *Cauchmar?* 249–51.
58 Djelal Noury, *Cauchmar?* 88.
59 *Cauchmar* was published very shortly before Halide Edib's *Yeni Turan* (1912), which bears distinct resemblances to *Cauchmar*. Kaya, the heroine of *Yeni Turan*, like Müghri İrem of *Cauchmar*, sacrificed herself for the good of the country. Both novels also are relatively liberal in outlook, particularly celebrating the cultural diversity of the empire. This attitude changed quickly for Celal Nuri and most CUP members after the devastating losses of the Balkan Wars. Halide Edib [Adıvar], *Yeni Turan* (İstanbul: Can Sanat Yayınları, 2014).
60 Djelal Noury, *Cauchmar?* 151–86.
61 This contrasts again with Abdulhak Hamid's *Duhter-i Hindu*. Surucuyi, unlike Mughri Irem, never really acted on behalf of her own people, but instead was hopelessly in love with Thompson, her colonial lover. While she consented to marrying Torramtor, a seventy-five-year-old Indian elder who wedded her to protect her honor, she did not necessarily share Torramtor's willingness to sacrifice himself for another. When Torromtor then led a rebellion against the British and gets killed, she married Thompson to avoid being burned on Torramtor's funeral pyre. Abdülhak Hamid Tarhan, "Duhter-i Hindu," 75–142.
62 Celal Nuri indeed often highlighted on the plight of the Kazan Tatar Turks, of whom there were a number of prominent Unionist emigres, such as Yusuf Akçura, Sadri Maksudi, and Halim Sabit. The Kazan Tatar Turks were located near the Ural Mountains on the Volga River, approximately 450 miles east of Moscow, a geography Celal Nuri claimed "could join Asia to Europe … [like] a second America." The town of Kazan on the shore of the river greatly impressed him when he visited:

> Praise be to God that many of the merchants are Muslims. The signs above are in Turkish. It is as if I am in my country … Daily life is full of trade and industry, and the place attracts people from the surrounding cities. What a strange

Babylon! Here it is possible to run into all sorts from Central Asia. During market times it resembles an ethnographical museum. Celâl Nuri, *Şimâl Hatıraları* (İstanbul: Matbaa-i İctihad, h.1330 [1911–12]), 104–6; 121–4.

He was equally impressed with the people he met there:

> [The Kazan Tatar Turks are] indefatigable, wise, able, progressive and practical. Although there previously were no schools and intellectual life on the banks of the Volga, now the Kazan Tatars have a written language, literature, and press culture. Celâl Nuri, *Şimâl Hatıraları*, 22.

They also built their religious schools (*medrese*) and mosques without even a "kopek" of Russian financial support, and "paid their own salaries for their employees out of the purse of patriotism." Celâl Nuri, *Şimâl Hatıraları*, 22–3. As a result of this intense communal moral and entrepreneurial activity, "they are not addicted to alcohol, vodka, prostitution, and foolish squandering … like the Russians." Celâl Nuri, *Şimâl Hatıraları*, 24. Soon their activities, he predicted, would integrate other nearby Turkish peoples, such as the *Çerimiş(?)*, *Çuvaş*, *Murued(?)*, and then expand to Bukhara, Khiva, and all of Turkistan: "They will enter Central Asia like quicksilver." Celâl Nuri, *Şimâl Hatıraları*, 105; Celâl Nuri, *İttihad-ı İslam*, 106, 108.

The Kazan Tatar Turks' relationship with the Russians was a curious one. As descendants of the Mongol Golden Horde, the Kazan Tatar Turks had unified Russia in the mid-thirteenth century under the Prince of Moscow, whose title was the "faithful slave." Celal Nuri claimed that the first of these princes was a Tatar Turk. Their problem, however, was that they simply were too tolerant of their Russian subjects:

> The Tatar Turks looked benevolently towards religious difference. Muslims and shamans could perform their rituals without any interruption … And there was even a Christian chapel in the palace. Kubilay Khan could be found in the church with the bishops. He too wanted to establish an Orthodox Church at Saray [on the Volga]. Celâl Nuri, *Tarih-i Tedenniyat-ı Osmaniye; Mukadderat-ı Tarihiye*, 407.

The Tatar Turks' failure to capitalize on their military victory and establish a vibrant faith community under Islam led to a cultural vacuum that the Russian and Greek Orthodox Church filled: "The numbers of churches and monasteries increased … and … [the Russian people] grew." Celâl Nuri, *Tarih-i Tedenniyat-ı Osmaniye; Mukadderat-ı Tarihiye. İki eser tevhid ve baz-ı fasl ve fıkralar ilave edilerek musahhah bir surette ikinci defa tab edilmiştir* (Istanbul: Yeni Osmanlı Matbaası ve Kütüphanesi, h.1331 [1912–13]), 407–8.

The Kazan Tatar Turks, a fragment of the former ruling class, escaped persecution from the emerging Muscovite Russian czarist state until the mid-sixteenth century:

Russia took over Kazan several centuries ago. When they conquered the place they forced the population to convert [to Orthodox Christianity] or they slaughtered them. Naturally the Kazan Tatar Turks left town and took refuge in the forests and deserts. The town [of Kazan] remained Russian for centuries, but recently the Kazan Tatar Turks have dominated several urban districts through their practical minds, commerce and endeavours. They now make up 40% of the population. This trend continues, as Kazan Tatar Turks have taken over more and more property from the Russians through their industriousness. Celâl Nuri, *Şimâl Hatıraları*, 24.

The Anatolian Turks, as the leading nationality, or "race" of the Ottoman Empire could learn invaluable lessons from the Kazan Tatar Turks, Celal Nuri contended. Mehmed II, the conqueror of Constantinople, was very much like Kubilay Khan and the Golden Horde. He was militarily successful, but he sat on his laurels after he and his cohort had engaged in pillaging, and drunken orgies. Mehmed II compounded his error by granting substantial toleration to the Orthodox Christian Church and other non-Muslim minorities, again echoing what the Tatar Turks had done with the Russian Orthodox:

We saw the same developments in Tataristan and Turkey. Just as the Russian nation was able to save itself, so too the Balkan nations [like Greece] reached their goal. The Turks, the dear brothers of the Tatar Turks, repeated their mistakes, despite their foreknowledge of this history. Celâl Nuri, *Tarih-i Tedenniyat-ı Osmaniye; Mukadderat-ı Tarihiye*, 407–10.

Celal Nuri once again highlighted the nature of conquest itself as the pivotal moment where a people had to adapt to changing circumstances, and shift from a warlike, nomadic people to a civilized, urbane and pious folk. Here he was no doubt reminded of Taine's words:

I mean that after some centuries they bring the nation into a new condition, religious, literary, social, economic; a new condition which, combined with their renewed effort, produces another condition, sometimes good, sometimes bad, sometimes slowly, sometimes quickly and so forth; so that we may regard the whole progress of each distinct civilization as the effect of a permanent force which, at every stage, varies its operation by modifying the circumstances of its action. Hippolyte Taine, *History of English Literature*, vol. 1 (New York: Frederick Unger Publishing Company, republished 1965 from 1883 edition), 16.

Accordingly, the Anatolian Turks had reached a critical fork in the road regarding their own historical evolution. If they could reform themselves morally and economically into an emerging Islamic bourgeoisie, they could act in time to revitalize their empire and transform it into a vibrant, modern state. But if their empire collapsed around them, as happened to the Golden Horde in Muscovy, they would have no choice but to belatedly advance under a hostile regime.

For further discussion on this topic, see York Norman, "The Historical Importance of Kazan Tatar Turks to the Late Ottoman Empire and the Ideas of Celal Nuri," in: Muhammad Savaş Kafkasyalı, editor, *Islam in Central Asia*, vol. 3 (Türkistan, Kazakhstan: Ahmet Yesevi University, 2013), 417–28.

63 Celâl Nuri, *Şimâl Hatıraları*, 25, 28.
64 Celâl Nuri, *Şimâl Hatıraları*, 25.
65 Celâl Nuri, *Şimâl Hatıraları*, 27.
66 Celâl Nuri, *Tarih-i Tedenniyat-ı Osmaniye; Mukadderat-ı Tarihiye*, 250–2; Celâl Nuri, *Şimâl Hatıraları*, 24–5.
67 Celâl Nuri, *Tarih-i Tedenniyat-ı Osmaniye; Mukadderat-ı Tarihiye*, 254–6; Celâl Nuri, *Kadınlarımız*, 171–4.
68 Celâl Nuri, *Kadınlarımız*, 139–48.
69 Celâl Nuri, *Havaic-i Kanuniyyemiz* (İstanbul: Matbaa-yı İctihad, h.1331 [1912–13]), 19.
70 Celâl Nuri, *Kadınlarımız*, 135–8, 149–64.
71 Celâl Nuri, *Kadınlarımız*, 135–8.
72 Celâl Nuri, *Kadınlarımız*, 197–205.
73 Celâl Nuri, *Havaic-i Kanuniyyemiz*, 48–54.
74 Celâl Nuri, *İlel-i Ahlâkiyyemiz* (İstanbul: Yeni Osmanlı Matbaası ve Kütüphanesi, h.1332 [1913–14]), 33.
75 Celâl Nuri, *Kadınlarımız*, 118–28.
76 İhsan Sabri Balkaya, "Afife Fikret'e Göre Feminizm," *Atatürk Üniversitesi Türkiyat Enstitüsü Dergisi*, Sayı, Vol. 4 (1996), 106.
77 Balkaya, "Afife Fikret," 106. Also see pages 68, 76, and 193.
78 Mustafa Kurt, *Celâl Nuri İleri'nin Romanları Bir İnceleme* (Ankara: Kurgan Edebiyat, 2012), 155–69.
79 Two more famous examples of such literature are Yukub Kadri Karaosmanoğlu's *Nur Baba* (1915) and Halide Edib Adıvar's *Ateşten Gömlek* (1922). Yukub Kadri [Karaosmanoğlu], *Nur Baba* (İstanbul: İletişim, 2014); Halide Edib [Adıvar], *Ateşten Gömlek* (İstanbul: Can Sanat Yayınları, 2007).
80 Nordau, *The Conventional Lies of Our Civilization*, 321–3.
81 Djelal Noury, *Cauchmar?*, 58–60, 64–71, 173–4, 194, 198.
82 Letourneau, *The Evolution of Marriage*, 356. Both Nordau and Letourneau went so far in their arguments as to argue that the modern nuclear family might be abandoned in the future in favor of free love, since men by nature are promiscuous, and need different sexual partners to achieve their happiness. Children hence would see the state itself as their "parents." Celal Nuri alluded to Nordau at the very end of his pamphlet on women, noting that the Turks were not ready for his arguments. I would contend, however, that Celal Nuri, an intellectual who firmly believed in classical liberal bourgeois family values and character-building, likely saw this as an utopian vision utterly unconnected with his own society. Celâl Nuri, *Kadınlarımız*, 225.

83   Ziya Gökalp; Atgın, *Türk Ahlakı*, 85.
84   Ziya Gökalp; Atgın, *Türk Ahlakı*, 56–60.
85   Ziya Gökalp; Atgın, *Türk Ahlakı*, 82.
86   Ziya Gökalp; Atgın, *Türk Ahlakı*, 173–4.
87   Ziya Gökalp; Atgın, *Türk Ahlakı*, 96.
88   Ziya Gökalp; Atgın, *Türk Ahlakı*, 116–17.
89   Ziya Gökalp; Atgın, *Türk Ahlakı*, 135–8.
90   Ziya Gökalp; Atgın, *Türk Ahlakı*, 146.
91   Ziya Gökalp; Atgın, *Türk Ahlakı*, 139.
92   Ziya Gökalp; Atgın, *Türk Ahlakı*, 160.
93   Emile Durkheim; Edward Saragin, Translator, *Incest: The Nature and Origin of the Taboo* (New York: Lyle Stuart, 1963), 11–119.
94   Ziya Gökalp; Atgın, *Türk Ahlakı*, 82, 86, 132–3, 180, 183.
95   Celâl Nuri, *Kadınlarımız*, 210.
96   Abdullah Yusuf Ali, translator, *The Meaning of the Holy Quran*, newly revised ninth edition (Beltsville: Amana Publications, 1997), 1075; Celâl Nuri, *Kadınlarımız*, 201–2.
97   Abdullah Yusuf Ali, translator, *The Meaning of the Holy Quran*, 1066; Qasim Amin, *The Liberation of Women*, 43; Celâl Nuri, *Kadınlarımız*, 201–2.
98   Qasim Amin; Peterson, *The Liberation of Women*, 45; Celâl Nuri, *Kadınlarımız*, 203–4.
99   Celâl Nuri, *Kadınlarımız*, 199.
100 Qasim Amin; Peterson, *The Liberation of Women*, 134.
101 Ahmet İshak Demir, *Cumhuriyet Dönemi Aydınlarının İslam'a Bakışı* (İstanbul: Ensar Neşriyatı, 2004), 264; Qasim Amin, *The Liberation of Women*, 46.
102 Qasim Amin; Peterson, *The Liberation of Women*, 47. These opinions were confirmed by Fatma Aliye. She argued that while the face-veil was excessive, the headscarf was lovingly embraced by the women who wore it. She thus did not see the headscarf as an obstacle to a woman participating in public life. Fatma Aliye, *Osmanlı'da Kadın*, 61–5. These views contrasted sharply with those of Salahattin Asım, a radical westernizer who wished to ban the headscarf as well as the face-veil. Salahaddin Asım, *Osmanlı'da Kadınlığın Durumu* (İstanbul: Arba, 1989), 27–78.
103 Abdullah Yusuf Ali, translator, *The Meaning of the Holy Quran*, 184.
104 Abdullah Yusuf Ali, translator, *The Meaning of the Holy Quran*, 227.
105 Demir, *İslam'a Bakışı*, 277.
106 Celâl Nuri, *Kadınlarımız*, 142–5.
107 Cenab Şehabeddin, "Mahfel'e Cevab."
108 Cenab Şehabeddin, "Hâtime-i Münazara."
109 Cenab Şehabeddin, "Hâtime-i Münazara." İskilipli Mehmet Atıf (1875–1926), an outspoken Islamic theologian (*ulema*), asserted that the Quran did indeed sanction polygamist marriage. He again cited verses 3 and 129 from *Al-Nisa*. In his opinion, the first of these verses allowed polygamy on condition that the husband

can afford it, and the second verse he took as a warning to a husband to be fair to all of his wives, and not evidence that the institution was fundamentally unjust. Moreover, he mentioned *Al-Furqan* verse 74, which awards the highest place in heaven to those who pray to "grant unto us wives and offspring [that] will be the comfort of our eyes." İskilibli Mehmed Atıf, "Cenab Şehabeddin Bey'e Birinci Cevab" [Taaddüd-i Zevcât], *Mahfel*, No: 8 Cemaziyelahir 1339 [February–March, 1921], 130–3. Abdullah Yusuf Ali, translator, *The Meaning of the Holy Quran*, 906. Here, the word "wives" is mentioned in the plural form. Finally, İskilipli Mehmet Atıf disputed Cenab Şahabettin's account of Prophet Muhammad's discussion with Fatimah about Ali's plan to marry Jehl. He clarified that Muhammad did not allow the marriage because of Jehl's hostility toward Islam, not because he thought that Fatima would be treated unfairly if Ali took a second wife. İskilibli Atıf, "Üçüncü Cevab," *Mahfel*, Şaban 1339 [April–May 1921], 161–4.

Fatma Aliye, writing roughly a generation before the other writers, took a much more nuanced position. She, like İskilipli Mehmet Atıf, agreed that polygamy was valid according to Islamic sources. She pointed to Muhammad's marriages to Aisha, Zaynab, and certain other companions of the Prophet. These marriages were done, she maintained, during a time of warfare and other hardships, and should be seen as humane acts done to preserve the dignity of the women. She also saw this practice as continuing to her own day, although largely confined to the countryside, where large clans still predominated. Having many children under one household suited their society and economy. Nevertheless, she frankly admitted that a member of the urban elite like herself would not choose such a marriage. The implication here was that the practice of polygamy would gradually end as the country modernized. Fatma Aliye, *Osmanlı'da Kadın*, 49–59.

110 Abdullah Yusuf Ali, translator, *The Meaning of the Holy Quran*, 190.
111 Abdullah Yusuf Ali, translator, *The Meaning of the Holy Quran*, 226–7.
112 Celâl Nuri, *Kadınlarımız*, 151.
113 Celâl Nuri, *Kadınlarımız*, 151–7.
114 Ziya Gökalp; Atgın, *Türk Ahlakı*, 121–2.
115 Fatma Aliye took a more liberal line. Pointing to the customary practice of women in Antakya initiating a divorce with her husband by wearing a blue face-veil, she thought that the Ottoman court should move beyond the traditional Islamic interpretation of women divorcing only because of the husband's cruelty and desertion. In effect, she was arguing for reform regarding divorce much in the same way that Celal Nuri favored it for abolishing polygamy. Fatma Aliye, *Osmanlı'da Kadın*, 101–6.
116 Celâl Nuri, *Kadınlarımız*, 162–3.
117 Fatma Aliye argued in her own work that men who married were obliged to hire servants to do the household cleaning, and could not ask their wives to do so unless they were too impoverished. Here she looked at an example from Islamic

history. Someone from the companions and disciples of the Prophet Muhammad comes to Caliph Umar to complain about his wife. Umar replies to him that men should not protest about their wives hiring maids since the wives take care of the children. Bluntly, he stated: "It [cleaning] is not their burden, and if we bring these issues up we [husbands] will wind up losing." Fatma Aliye, *Osmanlı'da Kadın*, 118.

Fatma Aliye, herself a famous writer, and intellectual, asserted that women must have the time and space necessary to cultivate their own minds. Ahmet Midhat, who wrote a short biography of her, talked about her voracious appetite for knowledge, and her mastery of not only Ottoman Turkish but also French, a language she learned at a very young age. He also was aware that Fatma's marriage had its difficulty. Her husband initially prohibited her from reading books in French, supposedly because he feared that it would lead to her own moral corruption. Ahmet Mithat Efendi; Bedia Ermat, translator, *Fatma Aliye: Bir Osmanlı Kadınının Doğuşu* (İstanbul: Sel Yayınları, 2011). This must have deeply disturbed Ahmet Midhat, as he had earlier written the novel *Felsefe-i Zenan* (1870), which focused on the tragic death of Zekiye, a wealthy, bright young woman. Zekiye had originally lived in a house in an upscale district of Istanbul with her sister, Akile. Life in that house, which was run by her sister, servants, and fellow female acquaintances, was happy, educational, and cosmopolitan. But Zekiye, when asked by Muhsin Pasha, an Ottoman official, to join his retinue as he was being appointed governor to Aleppo, decided to leave. A short time later, she met Sıtkı Efendi, a young secretary of the general, who took a liking to her and asked her to marry him. She accepted, greatly frustrating Akile, who then corresponded by letter to convince her to return to Istanbul. But Akile lost contact with her shortly after Zekiye had a child, and she traveled to Aleppo to see what happened. She was shocked to find out that Sıtkı had killed her as a result of reading her letters. Ahmet Mithat Efendi; S. Emrah Arlıhan, translator, *Felsefe-i Zenan* (İstanbul: Sel Yayınları, 2011). The moral of the story, namely that marriage meant the death of women's independence, no doubt had Fatma Aliye's sympathetic ear.

118 Zürcher, *Turkey*, 122.
119 Aydın, "Hukuk-ı Aile Kararnamesi," 314–18.
120 Kandiyoti, "End of Empire," 22–3.

Chapter 6

1 Celal Nuri, *Ahir Zaman* (Dersaadet: Atî Matbaası, h.1335 [1916–17]), 95–9. The novel was written under the pseudonym "Afife Fikret." Mustafa Kurt, *Celal Nuri İleri'nin Romanları Bir İnceleme* (Ankara: Kurgan Edebiyat, 2012), 155, 164.

2 Murat Şefkatlı, editor, *Türk Yurdu*, 1. Cilt (1–2) (Ankara: Tutibay Yayınları, 1998), 86.
3 Nail Tan, *Atatürk ve Türk Dil Kurumu* (Ankara: Türk Dil Kurumu Yayınları, 2011), 7–9; Agâh Sırrı Levend, *Türk Dilinde Gelişme ve Sadeleştirme Evreleri* (Ankara: Ankara Üniversitesi Basımevi, 1972), 391–5.
4 Celal Nuri, *Türkçemiz* (Konstantiniye: Cemiyyet Kütüphanesi, 1917), 21–2; Celal Nuri, *Türk İnkılabı* (İstanbul: Sühulet Kütüphanesi Semih Lütfi, 1926), 148–50.
5 Geoffrey Lewis, *The Turkish Language Reform: A Catastrophic Success* (Oxford; New York: Oxford University Press, 1999), 6–7.
6 Lewis, *A Catastrophic Success*, 27; Nurettin Gülmez, *Tanzimat'tan Cumhuriyet'e Harfler Üzerine Tartışmalar* (Bursa: Alfa Aktüel, 2006), 130–3; Bilal Şimşir, *Türk Yazı Devrimi* (Ankara: Türk Tarih Kurumu Basımevi, 1992), 1–2.
7 Lewis, *A Catastrophic Success*, 28; Şimşir, *Türk Yazı Devrimi*, 18–28, 41; Levend, *Türk Dilinde Gelişme*, 113–77, 255–7. Ahuntzade Mirza Fethali (1812–78), a prominent Azerbaijani intellectual, also played a prominent role in these discussions when he came to Istanbul in 1863 with a proposal to add new letters to indicate vowels.
8 Şimşir, *Türk Yazı Devrimi*, 33–5, 369.
9 Erik J. Zürcher, *The Young Turk Legacy and Nation Building* (London; New York: I.B. Tauris, 2010), 112–13.
10 Celal Nuri, "Okunacak Kitab, Tenevvüre Çare," *İkdam*, No. 11168, 25 Mayıs 1928 [May 25, 1928].
11 Celal Nuri, *Türk İnkılabı* (İstanbul: Sühulet Kütüphanesi Semih Lütfi, 1926), 245–6.
12 Celal Nuri, *Kara Tehlike* (Dersaadet: Cemiyyet Kütuphanesi, r.1334 [1918]), 67.
13 Sevan Nişanyan, *Yanlış Cumhuriyet: Atatürk ve Kemalizm Üzerine 51 Soru* (İstanbul: Kırmızı Yayınları, 2008), 155–6. Nişanyan speculates that Ottoman illiteracy rates may well have declined from the 89.7 percent 1927 figure to 70 percent had the war not devastated the educational system.
14 Sadri Maksudi, *Türk Dili İçin* (Ankara: Türk Ocakları İlim ve Sanat Heyeti, 1930), 13. For further discussion of Maksudi's work, see Umut Uzer, *An Intellectual History of Turkish Nationalism: Between Turkish Ethnicity and Islamic Identity* (Salt Lake City: The University of Utah Press, 2016), 51–2.
15 Şimşir, *Türk Yazı Devrimi*, 97–8; 116–23.
16 Levend, *Türk Dilinde Gelişme*, 409–12.
17 Max Müller, *Lectures on the Science of Language, volume 1* (London: Longmans, Greene & Co., 1885); Max Müller, *Letter to Chevalier Bunsen on the Classification of the Turanian Languages* (London: A. & P.A. Spottiswoode, 1854).
18 Celal Nuri, *Türkçemiz* (Konstantiniye: Cemiyyet Kütüphanesi, 1917), 46.
19 Müller, *Turanian Languages*, 222–3.
20 Müller, *Turanian Languages*, 217.
21 Celal Nuri, "Harf İnkılabından Sonra Edebiyatda, İrfanda (Hangi) İstikameti Tutacağız?" *İkdam*, No. 11282, 19 Eylül 1928 [September 19, 1928].

22 Celal Nuri, "Harf İnkılabında Sonra." This statement provides an interesting contrast to Celal Nuri's claim in 1926 that the Turks should "imitate ... methods of progress ... that brought Europe to its present level of development," an argument that Buzpınar stresses in his seminal article about Celal Nuri's Westernist tendencies. Ş. Tufan Buzpınar, "Celal Nuri's Concepts of Westernization," *Middle Eastern Studies*, Vol. 43, No. 2 (March 2007), 252. Celal Nuri apparently saw a literary culture as separate and distinct from the more universal process of secularization. This is roughly consistent with Celal Nuri's 1913 distinction between the technological (*sinai*) and the real (*hakiki*) aspects of civilization. As Buzpınar argues, Celal Nuri "held that the technological civilization of the West was value free and it did not involve cultural, social and spiritual values. Any underdeveloped nation that wishes to achieve progress can only do so by adopting this civilization completely." Buzpınar, "Celal Nuri's Concepts of Westernization," 250.
23 Celal Nuri, "Irk," *Edebiyat-ı Umumiye Mecmuası*, Vol. 2, No. 26, 28 Nisan 1917 [April 28, 1917], 5–11; Celal Nuri, "Muhit ve Türkler (I)," *Edebiyat-ı Umumiye Mecmuası*, Vol. 2, No. 28, 12 Mayıs 1917 [May 12, 1917], 33–6; Celal Nuri, "Muhit ve Türkler (II)," *Edebiyat-ı Umumiye Mecmuası*, Vol. 2, No. 29, 19 Mayıs 1917 [May 19, 1917], 49–52; Celal Nuri, "Zaman," *Edebiyat-ı Umumiye Mecmuası*, Vol. 2, Nos. 4–35, 29 Eylül 1917 [September 29, 1917], 157–9; Celal Nuri, *Türk İnkılabı*, 19–71.
24 Sadri Maksudi, *Türk Dili İçin*, 21.
25 Müller, *Science of Language*, 354–5.
26 Sadri Maksudi, *Türk Dili İçin*, 8.
27 Sadri Maksudi, *Türk Dili İçin*, 5.
28 Lewis, *A Catastrophic Success*, 57. Zürcher, *Turkey: A Modern History*, third edition (London; New York: I.B. Tauris, 2010), 190.
29 Celal Nuri, *Kara Tehlike* (Dersaadet: Cemiyyet Kütüphanesi, r.1334 [1918]), 5. Both the *gazel* and *kaside* were Ottoman forms of poetry. Ziya Gökalp's article, also entitled "Kara Tehlike" or "black danger," is printed in full in Celal Nuri's book. Celal Nuri, *Kara Tehlike*, 5–7.
30 Celal Nuri, *Kara Tehlike*, 5.
31 Celal Nuri, *Kara Tehlike*, 7–8.
32 Celal Nuri, *Türkçemiz*, 9–10.
33 Celal Nuri, *Kara Tehlike*, 20.
34 Celal Nuri, *Kara Tehlike*, 19.
35 Celal Nuri, *Kara Tehlike*, 20.
36 Celal Nuri, *Kara Tehlike*, 20.
37 Celal Nuri, *Türkçemiz*, 81.
38 Celal Nuri, *Türkçemiz*, 90. *Revani* is a type of sweet made with semolina. *Muhalebbi* is a sweet pudding made with milk and rice flour. *Kadayıf* is a sweet pastry with shredded wheat and syrup. *Keşgül* is also a dessert made with sweetened milk or custard with almonds and pistachio.

39 This was another type of Ottoman poetry.
40 Celal Nuri, *Türkçemiz*, 21.
41 Celal Nuri, *Kara Tehlike*, 72.
42 Abdülhak Hamid Tarhan; İnce Enginün, editor, *Bütün Şiirleri*, vol. 2 (İstanbul: Dergah Yayınları, 1882), 179–81.
43 Abdülhak Hamid Tarhan; İnce Enginün, editor, *Bütün Şiirleri*, vol. 2, 183–7.
44 Abdülhak Hamid; Enginün, editor, *Bütün Şiirleri*, vol. 2, 188.
45 Abdülhak Hamid; Enginün, editor, *Bütün Şiirleri*, vol. 2, 179–80.
46 Celal Nuri, *Kara Tehlike*, 13.
47 Celal Nuri, *Kara Tehlike*, 84.
48 Celal Nuri, *Kara Tehlike*, 84.
49 Celal Nuri, *Kara Tehlike*, 85.
50 Celal Nuri, *Kara Tehlike*, 85.
51 Celal Nuri, *Kara Tehlike*, 84.
52 Celal Nuri, *Kara Tehlike*, 82–6.
53 Celal Nuri, *Kara Tehlike*, 21.
54 Celal Nuri, *Kara Tehlike*, 14, 34.
55 Celal Nuri, *Kara Tehlike*, 91–3.
56 Celal Nuri, *Kara Tehlike*, 65.
57 Celal Nuri, *Türkçemiz*, 11–12.
58 *Türk Yurdu*, 1. Cilt (1–2), 86.
59 Celal Nuri, *Kara Tehlike*, 94.
60 Celal Nuri, *Kara Tehlike*, 94–6.
61 Celal Nuri, *Kara Tehlike*, 3. It should be noted that Ziya Gökalp's protest was also supported by Ahmet Ağaoğlu, Celal Sahir (Erozan), Mehmet Fuat (Köprülü), and Yahya Kemal (Beyatlı).
62 Celal Nuri, *Kara Tehlike*, 16–18.
63 Ziya Gökalp; Kemal Bek, editor, *Türkleşmek, İslamlaşmak, Muasırlaşmak* (İstanbul: Bordo Siyah, 2005), 35–6, 25–6.
64 Lewis, *A Catastrophic Success*, 32.
65 Celal Nuri, *Tarih-i Tedenniyat-ı Osmaniye; Mukadderat-ı Tarihiye. İki eser tevhid ve baz-ı fasl ve fıkralar ilave edilerek musahhah bir surette ikinci defa tab edilmiştir* (Yeni Osmanlı Matbaası ve Kütüphanesi, h.1331 [1912–13]), 33, 182.
66 Celal Nuri, *Tarih-i Tedenniyat-ı Osmaniye; Mukadderat-ı Tarihiye*, 183.
67 Celal Nuri, *Türk İnkılabı*, 245–6.
68 Celal Nuri, *Türk İnkılabı*, 177–8; Celal Nuri, *Tarih-i Tedenniyat-ı Osmaniye; Mukadderat-ı Tarihiye*, 43, 183.
69 Zeynep Korkmaz, *Atatürk ve Türk Dili Belgeler* (Ankara: Türk Dil Kurumu, 1992), 7.
70 Lewis, *A Catastrophic Success*, 34.
71 Celal Nuri, "Fransızcanın Güçlüğü, Türkçenin Kolaylığı," *İkdam*, No. 11283, 20 Eylül 1928 [September 20, 1928], 42–3.

72 Celal Nuri, "Yeni Harflere Alışgınlık," *İkdam*, 31 Ağustos 1928 [August 31, 1928].
73 Celal Nuri, "Latin Harflerinin Türkçeye Tatbiki," *İkdam*, No. 11236, 4 Ağustos 1928 [August 4, 1928]; Celal Nuri, "Dil Encümenin Yeni Elifbası," *İkdam*, nr. 11243, No. 11243, 11 Ağustos 1928 [August 11, 1928]; Celal Nuri, "Ahenkten Mürekkeb Bir Dil 2," *İkdam*, no. 11276, 13 Eylül 1928 [September 13, 1928]; 175-6, 185. Celal Nuri, *Türk İnkılabı*, 179-86.
74 Celal Nuri, "Latin Harfleri."
75 Celal Nuri, "Latin Elifbasının Kabulüne Doğru Hüsn-i Hat, Latince Kaligrafi," *İkdam*, No. 11254, 22 Ağustos 1928 [August 22, 1928].
76 Celal Nuri, "Harf İnkılabından Sonra."
77 Ziya Gökalp, *Türkçülüğün Esasları (Günümüz Türkçesiyle)*, eleventh edition, translated from the Ottoman Turkish by Mahir Ünlü and Yusuf Çotuksöken (İstanbul: İnkılap, 2011), 93.
78 Sadri Maksudi, *Türk Dili İçin*, 474.
79 Sadri Maksudi, *Türk Dili İçin*, 198.
80 Sadri Maksudi, *Türk Dili İçin*, 242, 270-1.
81 Sadri Maksudi, *Türk Dili İçin*, 305.
82 It should be noted that Atatürk himself avidly read all three of these works, as seen in his copious notes in them. Recep Cengiz et al., *Atatürk'ün Okuduğu Kitaplar*, vol. 7 (Ankara: Anıtkabir Derneği, 2001), 193-279, 173-92, 99-166.
83 Sadri Maksudi, *Türk Dili İçin*, 371-4.
84 Celal Nuri, *Kara Tehlike*, 77.
85 Celal Nuri, "Türkçenin İfade Kabiliyeti," *İkdam*, No. 11198, 27 Haziran 1928 [June 27, 1928]; Celal Nuri, *Türkçemiz*, 96.
86 Celal Nuri, "Fransızcanın Güçlüğü"; Celal Nuri, *Türk İnkılabı*, 144.
87 Celal Nuri, "Türkçenin İfade Kabiliyeti"; Celal Nuri, "Ahenkten Mürekkeb Bir Dil 2."
88 Celal Nuri, *Türk İnkılabı*, 145-7.
89 Celal Nuri, *Türk İnkılabı*, 157-8.
90 Celal Nuri, "Osmanlıcadan Türkçeye Tercüme," *İkdam*, No. 11295, 2 Teşrin-i Evvel 1928 [October 2, 1928].
91 Celal Nuri, *Türk İnkılabı*, 287-9.
92 Celal Nuri, *Türk İnkılabı*, 160-1.
93 *Birinci Dil Kurultayı: Tezler, Müzakere Zabıtları* (İstanbul: Devlet Matbaası, 1933), XIV.
94 *Birinci Dil Kurultayı*, 274, 279.
95 *Birinci Dil Kurultayı*, 275-6.
96 *Birinci Dil Kurultayı*, 279.
97 *Birinci Dil Kurultayı*, 279.
98 *Birinci Dil Kurultayı*, 276.
99 Celal Nuri, *Kara Tehlike*, 47-52.
100 *Birinci Dil Kurultayı*, 277.
101 *Birinci Dil Kurultayı*, 322.

102 Sadri Maksudi, *Türk Dili İçin*, 489.
103 Ziya Gökalp; Ünlü & Çotuksöken, *Türkçülüğün Esasları*, 103.
104 *Birinci Dil Kurultayı*, 284.
105 *Birinci Dil Kurultayı*, 317.
106 *Birinci Dil Kurultayı*, 316.
107 This term means "productivity" in modern Turkish.
108 Another participant, Namdar Rahmi (Karatay) (1896–1953), a philosopher, also gave an interesting speech denouncing Huseyin Cahit's evolutionary position. He argued that evolution often occurred in leaps and bounds. Namdar Rahmi cited Henri Bergson's theory of creative evolution among others. *Birinci Dil Kurultayı*, 284, 303–4.
109 *Birinci Dil Kurultayı*, 284.
110 *Birinci Dil Kurultayı*, 315.
111 Nail, *Atatürk ve Türk Dil Kurumu*, 33.
112 Zeynep Korkmaz, *Türk Dilin Tarihi Akışı İçinde Atatürk ve Dil Devrimi* (Ankara: Ankara Üniversitesi Basımevi, 1963), 59. This is far higher than Celal Nuri's estimate of 20,000 words in Ottoman Turkish, as mentioned earlier in this chapter.
113 Lewis, *A Catastrophic Success*. The quote comes from the title of this book.

Chapter 7

1 Geoffrey Lewis, *The Turkish Language Reform: A Catastrophic Success* (Oxford; New York: Oxford University Press, 1999), 34.
2 Celal Nuri, *Türkçemiz* (Konstantiniye: Cemiyyet Kütüphanesi, 1917), 11–12; Celal Nuri, *Türk İnkılabı* (İstanbul: Sühulet Kütüphanesi Semih Lütfi, 1926), 245–6.
3 Celâl Nuri, *Hatemül-Enbiya* (İstanbul: Yeni Osmanlı Matbaası, h.1331 [1912–13]), 176–7.
4 Şehbenderzade Filibeli Ahmed Hilmi, *Huzur-ı Akl ve Fende Maddiyun*, 3–16, 134–51; Şehbenderzade Filibeli Ahmed Hilmi, *Meslek-i Dalâleti*, 123–30, 197–206.
5 Celâl Nuri, *Tarih-i Tedenniyat-ı Osmaniye; Mukadderat-ı Tarihiye*, 396, 398.
6 Ahmed Emin Yalman, *Yakın Tarihte Gördüklerim ve Geçerdiklerim*, Cilt: 2 (İstanbul: Rey, 1970), 932–52.
7 Celâl Nuri, *Devlet ve Meclis Hakkında Musahabeler* (Ankara: TBMM Matbaası, 1932), 79–80, 82.
8 *Türk Büyük Milli Meclis Zabit Ceridesi, Devre: II, Cild: 8/1, İçtima Senesi: II, Kırkikinci İçtima: 20.4. 1340 (1924), Pazar*: 910.
9 Afet İnan, *Türk Kadınının Hak ve Görevleri, Tarih Boyunca Türk Kadınının Hak ve Görevleri*, üçüncü basılış (İstanbul: Milli Eğitim Bakanlığı, 1975), 145–62, 179–81.

10 Erik J. Zürcher, *Turkey: A Modern History*, third edition (London; New York: I.B. Tauris, 2010), 169–72.
11 Erik Jan Zürcher, *Political Opposition in the Early Turkish Republic* (Leiden: Brill Academic Publishers, 1991), 17–31.
12 Zürcher, *Turkey*, 179.
13 Celâl Nuri, *Havaic-i Kanuniyyemiz Havaic-i Kanuniyyemiz* (İstanbul: Matbaa-yı İctihad, h.1331 [1912–13]), 23, 118.

Bibliography

Primary Sources

Abdullah Cevdet; Mustafa Gunduz, translator. *İctihad'ın İctihadı: Abdullah Cevdet'ten Seçme Yazılar* (Ankara: Lotus, 2008).
Abdullah Yusuf Ali, translator. *The Meaning of the Holy Quran*, newly revised ninth edition (Beltsville: Amana Publications, 1997).
Ahmed Cevdet Paşa; Mustafa Kasadar, translator. *Hatemül Enbiya, Son Peygamber HZ. MUHAMMED: Sallallahu Aleyhi Sellem* (İstanbul: Ravza Yayınları, 2006).
[Adıvar], Halide Edib. *Ateşten Gömlek* (İstanbul: Can Sanat Yayınları, 2007).
[Adıvar], Halide Edib. *Ateşten Gömlek: Sakarya Ordusuna* (İstanbul: Teşebbüs Matbaası, 1339 [1923]).
[Adıvar], Halide Edib. *Memoirs of Halidé Edib* (New York; London: The Century, 1926).
[Adıvar], Halide Edib. *Yeni Turan* (İstanbul: Can Sanat Yayınları, 2014).
[Adıvar], Halide Edib. *Yeni Turan* (İstanbul: Tanın Matbaası, 1329 [1913]).
Adum; S. Sirenes, translator. *Osmanlı İmparatorluğu'nun Tarih-i Tedennisi Celal Nuri Bey'in Tarih-i Tedenniyat-ı Osmaniyyesi'ni Tenkiden Azad Emarid Gazetesinde Münderic Silsile-i Makalat* (Der Saadet: Bâb-ı Âli Sadaret Kapusı Karşısında "Edeb" Matbaası, h. 1331 [1912–13]).
Ahmed Şuayb. *Hayat ve Kitablar* (İstanbul: Tetebbuat Edebiye ve Tarihiye, 1318 [1902–3]), 1–196.
Ahmet Mithat Efendi; Bedia Ermat, translator. *Fatma Aliye: Bir Osmanlı Kadının Doğuşu* (İstanbul: Sel Yayınları, 2011).
Ahmet Mithat Efendi; S. Emrah Arlıhan, translator. *Felsefe-i Zenan* (İstanbul: Sel Yayınları, 2011).
Ahmet Mithat Efendi. *Fatma Âliye Hanım Yahut Bir Muharirre-yi Osmaniye'nin Neşeti* (İstanbul: Kırk Anbar 1311 [1893–4]).
Arsal, Sadri Maksudi, *Türk Dili İçin* (Ankara: Turk Ocakları İlim ve Sanat Heyeti, 1930).
Atatürk, Mustafa Kemal. *Atatürk'ün Bütün Eserleri*, fifth edition (İstanbul: Kaynak Yayınları, 2015).
Ayandan Nuri (Mustafa Nuri). *Abede-i İblis: Yezidi'nin Taifesinin İtikadı Adatı Evsafı* (İstanbul: Matbaa-i İctihad, h.1328 [1910]).
Birinci Dil Kurultayı: Tezler, Müzakere Zabıtları (İstanbul: Devlet Matbaası, 1933).
Blunt, Wilfrid Scawen. *The Future of Islam* (London: Kegan, Paul, Trench & Co., 1882).
Büchner, Ludwig. *Force and Matter or Principles of the Natural Order of the Universe. With a System of Morality Based Thereon* (New York: Truth Seeker Company, 1950).

Carlyle, Thomas. *On Heroes, Hero Worship and the Heroic in History* (New York: Thomas Y. Crowell & Co., 1891).

Cenab Şehabeddin. "Hâtime-i Münazara," *Peyâm-Sabah*, 17 Kanunusâni 1337 [January 17, 1921].

Cenab Şehabeddin. "Mahfele Cevab," *Peyâm-Sabah*, 24 Şubat 1337 [February 24, 1921].

Cenab Şehabeddin. "Muhterem Muarızlara," *Peyâm-Sabah*, 24 Kanunusâni 1337 [January 24, 1921].

Cenab Şehabeddin. "Yarınki Efkâr-ı İslamiye," *Peyâm-Sabah*, 13 Kanunusâni 1337 [January 13, 1921].

Fatma Aliye, Mahmud Esad; Firdevz Canbaz, translators. *Çok Eşlilik: Taaddüd-i Zevcat* (Ankara: Hece İnceleme, 2007).

Fatma Aliye; Mahmud Esad. *Letaif-i Rivayat* (İstanbul: Malumat Kutuphanesi 1316 [1898–9]).

Fatma Aliye; Orhan Sakin, translator. *Osmanlı'da Kadın: Cariyelik, Çokeşlilik, Moda* (İstanbul: Ekim, 2012).

Demolins, Edmond; Louis Bert Lavigne, translator, *Anglo-Saxon Superiority: To What Is It Due* (Toronto: The Musson Book Company, 1899).

Dozy, Reinhart Pieter Anne; Abdullah Cevdet and Vedat Atila, translators. *İslam Tarihi* (İstanbul: Gri Yayınları, 2006).

Dozy, Reinhart Pieter Anne; Abdullah Cevdet, translator. *Tarih-i İslamiyet* (Mısır: Matbaa-yı İctihad, 1908).

Durkheim, Émile; Edward Saragin, translator. *Incest: The Nature and Origin of the Taboo* (New York: Lyle Stuart, 1963).

Galanti, Avram. *Vatandaş Türkçe Konuş* (Ankara: Kebikeç, 2000).

Galanti, Avram. *Vatandaş Türkçe Konuş: Yahut, Türkçe'nin Tâmimi Meselesi* (İstanbul: Hasan Tabiat Matbaası, 1928).

Gourgoud, Gaspard. *The St. Helena Journal of General Baron Gourgaud* (January 9, 1817); as quoted in *The St. Helena Journal of General Baron Gourgaud, 1815–1818: Being a Diary Written at St. Helena during a Part of Napoleon's Captivity* (1932) as translated by Norman Edwards, a translation of *Journal de Sainte-Hélène 1815–1818* (London: John Lane, 1932).

Gövsa, Alaettin. *Türk Meşhurları Ansiklopedisi* (İstanbul: Yedigün Neşriyatı, 1946).

Güntekin, Reşat Nuri. *Çalıkuşu* (İstanbul: İnkılâp, 2014).

Halil Hamit, *İslam'da Feminizm: Fakir Bir Hürriyet Zengin Bir Esaretten Evladır* (İstanbul: Okumuş Adam Yayınları, 2001).

Ibn Khaldun; Franz Rosenthal, translator, *The Muqadimmah: An Introduction to History*, 3 vols. (New York: Pantheon Books, 1958).

[İleri], Celal Nuri; Cemal Kutay, translator, "Son Peygamber." In: *Tarih Önünde İslam Peygamberi* (İstanbul: Aksoy Yayıncılık, 1998), 116–261.

[İleri], Celal Nuri; İbrahim Demirci, translator. *Kutub Musâhabeleri* (İstanbul: Mavi Yayıncılık, 1997).

[İleri], Celal Nuri; İbrahim Demirci, translator, *Şimâl Hâtıraları* (İstanbul: Mavi Yayıncılık, 1997).

[İleri], Celal Nuri; Mahir Aydın, translator, *Uygarlık Çatışmasında Türkiye* (İstanbul: Ulus Yayınları, 2004).

[İleri], Celal Nuri; Özer Ozankaya, translator, *Kadınlarımız* (Ankara: T.C. Kültür Bakanlığı, 1993).

[İleri], Celal Nuri; Özer Ozankaya, translator. *Türk Devrimi: İnsanlık Tarihinde Türk Devriminin Yeri* (Ankara: Kültür Bakanlığı, 2002).

[İleri], Celal Nuri; Şennur Şenel, translator, *Taç Giyen Millet* (İstanbul: Berikan Yayınları, 2008).

[İleri], Celâl Nuri. *1327 Senesinde Selanik'te Mün'akid İttihad ve Terakki Kongresine Celal Nuri Bey Tarafından Takdim Kılınan Muhtıradır* (İstanbul: Osmanlı Şirketi Matbaası, h.1327 [1909]).

[İleri], Celâl Nuri. "Ahenkten Mürekkeb Bir Dil 2," *İkdam*, no. 11276, 13 Eylül 1928 [September 13, 1928].

[İleri], Celâl Nuri. *Ahir Zaman* (Dersaadet, h.1335 [1916–17]).

[İleri], Celâl Nuri. *Coğrafya-yı Tarihi Mülk-i Rum* (Konstantiniye: Cemiyyet Kütüphanesi, 1918).

[İleri], Celâl Nuri. *Devlet ve Meclis Hakkında Musahabeler* (Ankara: TBMM Matbaası, 1932).

[İleri], Celâl Nuri. "Dil Encümenin Yeni Elifbası," *İkdam*, No. 11243, 11 Ağustos 1928 [August 11, 1928].

[İleri], Celâl Nuri. "Ermeniler ve Cezri Siyaset," *Ati*, No. 315, 23 Teşrin-i Sani 1334 [October 23, 1928].

[İleri], Celâl Nuri. "Ermeniler ve Ermenistan," *Edebiyat-ı Umumiye Mecmuası*, Vol. 3, No. 44, 6 Temmuz 1918 [July 6, 1918], 833–9.

[İleri], Celâl Nuri. "Fransızcanın Güçlüğü, Türkçenin Kolaylığı," *İkdam*, No. 11283, 20 Eylül 1928 [September 20, 1928].

[İleri], Celâl Nuri. "Harf İnkılâbında Sonra Edebiyatda, İrfanda (Hangi) İstikameti Tutacağız?," *İkdam*, No. 11282, 19 Eylul 1928 [September 19, 1928].

[İleri], Celâl Nuri. *Harp'ten Sonra Türkleri Yükseltelim* (Konstantiniye: Cemiyyet Kütüphanesi, 1917).

[İleri], Celâl Nuri. *Hatemül-Enbiya* (İstanbul: Yeni Osmanlı Matbaası, h.1331 [1912–13]).

[İleri], Celâl Nuri. *Havaic-i Kanuniyyemiz* (İstanbul: Matbaa-yı İctihad, h.1331 [1912–13]).

[İleri], Celâl Nuri. *İlel-i Ahlâkiyyemiz* (İstanbul: Yeni Osmanlı Matbaası ve Kütüphanesi, h.1332 [1913–14]).

[İleri], Celal Nuri. "Irk," *Edebiyat-ı Umumiye Mecmuası*, Vol. 2, No. 26, 28 Nisan 1917 [April 28, 1917], 5–11.

[İleri], Celâl Nuri. *İttihad-ı İslam: İslamın Mazisi, Hali, İstikbali* (İstanbul: Yeni Osmanlı Matbaası, h.1331 [1912–13]).

[İleri], Celâl Nuri. *İttihad-i İslam ve Almanya: İttihad-i İslam'a Zeyl* (İstanbul: Yeni Osmanlı Matbaası ve Kütüphanesi, h.1333 [1914–15]).

[İleri], Celâl Nuri. *İştirak Etmediğimiz Harekat* (İstanbul: Cemiyyet Kütuphanesi, 1917).

[İleri], Celâl Nuri. *Kadınlarımız. Umumiyeti İtibariyle Kadın Meselesi ve Tarihi. Müslüman ve Türk Kadınları* (İstanbul: Matbaa-i İctihad, h.1331 [1912-13]).

[İleri], Celâl Nuri. *Kara Tehlike* (Dersaadet: Cemiyyet Kütüphanesi, r.1334 [1918]).

[İleri], Celâl Nuri. *Kendi Nokta-i Nazarımdan Hukuk-ı Düvel* (İstanbul: Osmanlı Şirketi Matbaası, h.1330 [1911-12]).

[İleri], Celâl Nuri. *Kutub Musahabeleri* (İstanbul: Yeni Osmanlı Matbaası, h.1331 [1912-13]).

[İleri], Celâl Nuri. "Latin Elifbasının Kabulüne Doğru Hüsn-i Hat, Latince Kaligrafi," *İkdam*, No. 11254, 22 Ağustos 1928 [August 22, 1928].

[İleri], Celâl Nuri. "Latin Harflerinin Türkçeye Tatbiki," *İkdam*, No. 11236, 4 Ağustos 1928 [August 4, 1928].

[İleri], Celâl Nuri. *Merhume* (Konstantiniye: Cemiyyet Kütüphanesi, 1918).

[İleri], Celâl Nuri. "Muhit ve Türkler (I)," *Edebiyat-ı Umumiye Mecmuası*, Vol. 2, No. 28, 12 Mayıs, 1917 [May 12, 1917], 33-6.

[İleri], Celâl Nuri. "Muhit ve Türkler (II)," *Edebiyat-ı Umumiye Mecmuası*, Vol. 2, No. 29, 19 Mayıs 1917 [May 19, 1917], 49-52.

[İleri], Celâl Nuri. *Müslümanlara, Türklere Hakaret, Düşmanlara Riayet ve Muhabbet* (İstanbul: "Kadir" Matbaası, h.1332 [1913-14]).

[İleri], Celâl Nuri. "Okunacak Kitab, Tenevvüre Çare," *İkdam*, No. 11168, 25 Mayıs 1928 [May 25, 1928].

[İleri], Celâl Nuri. *Ölmeyen* (Konstantiniye: Cemiyyet Kutuphanesi, 1917).

[İleri], Celâl Nuri. "Osmanlıcadan Türkçeye Tercüme," *İkdam*, No. 11295, 2 Teşrin-i Evvel 1928 [October 2, 1928].

[İleri], Celâl Nuri. "Osmanlılar'dan Evvel (II)," *Edebiyat-ı Umumiye Mecmuası*, Vol. 2, No. 31, 2 Haziran 1917 [June 2, 1917], 85-9.

[İleri], Celâl Nuri. *Perviz* (İstanbul: Zarafet Matbaası, h.1332 [1914-15]).

[İleri], Celâl Nuri. *Rum ve Bizans* (Konstantiniye: Cemiyyet Kütüphanesi, 1917).

[İleri], Celâl Nuri. "Rumlar ve Siyaset-i Cezri," *Ati*, numero: 313, 21 Teşrin-i Sani (October) 1334 (1918).

[İleri], Celâl Nuri. *Şimâl Hatıraları* (İstanbul: Matbaa-yı İctihad, h.1330 [1911-12]).

[İleri], Celâl Nuri. *Taç Giyen Millet* (İstanbul: Cihan Biraderler Matbaası, h.1339/r.1341 [1923]).

[İleri], Celâl Nuri. *Tarih-i İstikbal: Mesail-i Fikriye* (İstanbul: Yeni Osmanlı Matbaası, h.1331 [1912-13]).

[İleri], Celâl Nuri. *Tarih-i İstikbal: Mesail-i İçtimai* (İstanbul: Yeni Osmanlı Matbaası, h.1332 [1913-14]).

[İleri], Celâl Nuri. *Tarih-i İstikbal: Mesail-i Siyasi* (İstanbul: Yeni Osmanlı Matbaası, h.1331 [1913]).

[İleri], Celâl Nuri. *Tarih-i Osmani ve Keşfiyyat, Rönesans ve Reform Harekatı* (Istanbul: Cemiyet Kütüphanesi, 1917).

[İleri], Celâl Nuri. *Tarih-i Tedenniyat-ı Osmaniyye ve Mukaderrat-ı Tarihiyye* (İstanbul: Yeni Osmanlı Matbaası, h.1331 [1912-13]).

[İleri], Celâl Nuri. *Türk İnkılabı* (İstanbul: Sühulet Kütüphanesi Semih Lütfi, 1926).
[İleri], Celâl Nuri. *Türkçemiz* (Konstantiniye: Cemiyyet Kütüphanesi, 1917).
[İleri], Celâl Nuri. "Türkçenin İfade Kabiliyeti," *İkdam*, No. 11198, 27 Haziran 1928 [June 27, 1928].
[İleri], Celâl Nuri. *Vatandaşlık* (İstanbul: C. Nuri, 1931).
[İleri], Celâl Nuri. "Yahudi." *İkdam* (14 Teşrin-i Evvel 1929 [October 14, 1929]).
[İleri], Celâl Nuri. "Yeni Harflere Alışgınlık," *İkdam*, No. 11263, 31 Ağustos 1928 [August 31, 1928].
[İleri], Celâl Nuri. "Zaman," *Edebiyat-ı Umumiye Mecmuası*, Vol. 2, Nos. 4–35, 29 Eylül 1917 [September 29, 1917], 157–9.
[İleri], Djelal Noury; Archibald De Baer, translator. *The Sultan: A Romance of the Harem of Abdul Hamid* (London: Cassell, 1912).
[İleri], Djelal Noury. *Cauchmar? Roman de Temps Hamidiens* (Pera: Edition du "Jeune-Turc," 1911).
[İleri], Djelal Noury. *La Droit Publique et l'Islam* (Constantinople: Imprimerie du "Courier d'Orient," 1909).
[İleri], Djelal Noury. *Le Diable promu Dieu* (Constantinople: Imprimerie du "Jeune-Turc," 1910).
[İleri], Djelal Noury. *Problèmes Sociaux* (Constantinople: Imprimerie du "Courier d'Orient," 1909).
[İleri], Djelal Noury. *Une Année de Liberté Istanbul* (Constantinople: Imprimerie du "Courier d'Orient," 1909).
[İleri], Dželal Nuri; Salih Bakamović, translator. "Panislamizam: Islam u Prošlosti, Sadašnjosti i Budućnosti." In *Biser: List za Širenje Islamske Prosvjete* (Mostar): Godine III: Broj 1 (January 1, 1918), 1–5; Broj 2 (January 15, 1918), 1–2; Broj 3 i 4 (February 1 and 15, 1918), 33–5; Broj 7 i 8 (April 1 and 15, 1918), 97–9; Broj 9 i 10 (May 1 and 15, 1918), 129–33; Broj 11 i 12 (June 1 and 15, 1918), 165–7; Broj 13 i 14 (July 1 and 15, 1918), 196–9; Broj 15 i 16 (August 1 and 15, 1918), 225–7.
İnan, Afet et al. *Tarih I: Kemalist Eğitimin Tarih Dersleri (1931–1941)*, altıncı basım (İstanbul: Kaynak Yayınları, 2014).
İnan, Afet et al. *Tarih Boyunca Türk Kadınının Hak ve Görevleri*, üçüncü basılış (İstanbul: Milli Eğitim Bakanlığı, 1975).
İnan, Afet et al. *Türk Tarihinin Ana Hatları* (Ankara: Türk Tarih Kurumu Yayınları, 2014).
Giridi Ahmed Saki. *Celal Nuri Bey ve Cezri Fikirleri* (İstanbul: Hukuk Matbaası, 1335-8 [1919–22]).
Haydar Kemal. *Tarih-i İstikbal: Münasebetiyle Celal Nuri Bey* (İstanbul: Yeni Osmanlı Matbaası ve Kütüphanesi, h.1331 [1913]).
İskilibli Mehmed Atıf. "Cenab Şehabeddin Bey'e Birinci Cevab" [Taaddüd-i Zevcât], *Mahfel*, No. 8 Cemaziyelahir 1339 [February–March 1921], 130–3.
İskilibli Atıf. "Üçüncü Cevab," *Mahfel*, Şaban 1339 [April–May 1921], 161–4.

Le Bon, Gustave; Robert K. Stevenson, translator and editor. "Algeria and the Ideas Prevailing in France concerning Colonization." *Revue Scientifique*, October 2, 1887, 1–20.

Le Bon, Gustave. *The Crowd: Study of the Popular Mind* (Lexington: Aristeus Books, 2012).

Le Bon, Gustave. *The Psychology of Peoples: Its Influence on Their Evolution* (New York: Macmillan, 1898).

Le Bon, Gustave. *The Psychology of Revolution*, translated by Bernard Miall (London; Leipzig: T. Fisher Unwinn, 1913).

Letourneau, Charles. *The Evolution of Marriage and of the Family* (London; New York: Charles Scribner's Sons, 1895).

Lorimer, James. *The Institutes of the Law of Nations: A Treatise of the Jural Relations of Separate Political Communities*, vols. 1 and 2 (Edinburgh; London: William Blackwood and Sons, 1883).

[Karaosmanoğlu], Yukub Kadri. *Nur Baba* (İstanbul: Akşam Maatbası, 1338 [1922]).

[Karaosmanoğlu], Yukub Kadri. *Nur Baba* (İstanbul: İletişim, 2014).

Mehmed Atıf, "Diyanet-i İslamiye Efâli Beşeriye ile Ölçülemez," *Mahfel*, No. 7 Rebiülevvel 1340, 78–9.

Milli Kütüphane Genel Müdürlüğü, *Atatürk'ün Özel Kütüphanesi'nin Kataloğu* (Ankara: Başbakanlık Basımevi, 1973).

Montesquieu, Baron de. *The Spirit of the Laws*, translated by Thomas Nugent (New York: Cosimo Classics, 2011.

Müller, Max. *Lectures on the Science of Language*, vol. 1 (London: Longmans, Greene & Co., 1885).

Müller, Max. *Letter to Chevalier Bunsen on the Classification of the Turanian Languages* (London: A. & P.A. Spottiswoode, 1854).

Mustafa Sabri. "İki İzah, bir İftitah," *Alemdar*, 19 Kanunusâni 1337 [January 19, 1921].

Nietzsche, Friedrich; translated by Anthony Ludovici. *Ecco Hommo*. In: Oscar Levy, editor, *The Complete Works of Friedrich Nietzsche* (New York: The MacMillan Company, 1911).

Nordau, Max. *Degeneration*, with introduction by George L. Mosse (Lincoln and London: University of Nebraska Press, 1993).

Nordau, Max. *Paradoxes*, English edition (Chicago: L. Schick, 1886).

Nordau, Max. *The Conventional Lies of Our Civilization*, translated from the German (Chicago: Laird & Lee, 1895).

Max. Nordau. *The Conventional Lies of Our Civilization*, translated from the Seventh Edition of the German Work (London: William Heinemann, 1895).

Max. Nordau. *The Interpretation of History*, translated by M.A. Hamilton (London: Rebman Limited, 1910).

Peyami Safa. *Zavallı Celal Nuri Bey*. (İstanbul: Matbaa-yı İctihad, r.1329 [1913]).

Renan, Ernest. "Muhammad and the Origins of Islam." In: Ibn Warraq, editor and translator, *The Quest for the Historical Muhammad* (Amherst, NY: Prometheus Books, 2000), 127–66.

Renan, Ernest; with introduction by John Haynes Holmes. *The Life of Jesus* (New York: Modern Library, 1927).

Salahaddin Asım. *Türk Kadınlığının Tereddisi Yahud Karılaşmak* (İstanbul: Resimli Kitab Matbaası, no date).

[Şehbenderzade], Ahmed Hilmi. *A'mak-ı Hayâl* (İstanbul: Ahmed Saki Bey Matbaası, 1326 [1908–9]).

[Şehbenderzade], Ahmed Hilmi, translated and edited by Refik Algan and Camille Helminski. *Awakened Dreams: Raji's Journeys with the Miror Dede* (Putney, VT: Threshold Books, 1993).

[Şehbenderzade], Ahmed Hilmi. *Huzur-ı Akl ü Fende Maddiyun Meslek-i Dalâleti*. (Darülhilafe: Matbaa-ı İslamiyye, 1332 [1914–15]) in: Erdoğan Erbay and Ali Utku, translators, *Huzur-ı Akl ü Fende Maddiyun Meslek-i Dalâleti*, translated into Turkish by (Konya: Çizgi Yayınları, 2012).

[Şehbenderzade], Ahmed Hilmi, translated and edited by Cem Zorlu. *İslam Tarihi* (İstanbul: Anka Yayınları, 2005).

[Şehbenderzade], Ahmed Hilmi. *Tarih-i İslâm*, I. Cild, (Kostantiniyye: Hikmet Matbaası, h.1326 [1908–9]).

[Şehbenderzade], Ahmed Hilmi. *Tarih-i İslâm*, II. Cild (Kostantiniyye: Hikmet Matbaası, h.1327 [1909–10]).

Sırrı Giridi. *Âra-i Milel* (İstanbul: Bab-ı Ali Caddesinde Numero 52, h. 1303 [1885–6]).

Taine, Hippolyte. *History of English Literature*, vol. 1 (New York: Frederick Unger Publishing Company, republished 1965 from 1883 edition).

[Tarhan], Abdülhak Hamid; İnce Enginün, editor. "Baladan Bir Ses." In: *Bütün Şiirleri*, Cilt: 2 (İstanbul: Dergah Yayınları, 1982), 179–90.

[Tarhan], Abdülhak Hamid. *Baladan Bir Ses* (İstanbul: Yeni Osmanlı Matbaa ve Kütüphanesi, 1327 [1909–10]).

[Tarhan], Abdülhak Hamid. "Duhter-i Hindu." In: *Bütün Tiyatroları*, Cilt: 3 (İstanbul: Dergah Yayınları, 1982), 35–153.

[Tarhan], Abdülhak Hamid. *Duhter-i Hindu* (İstanbul: Tasvir-i Efkâr Matbaası, 1292 [1875–6]).

Tekinalp, Munis; Yıldız Akpolat. *Tekin Alp ve Türkleştirme* (İstanbul: Fenomen, 2005).

Turgenev, Ivan, translated and edited by Richard Freeborn. *Fathers and Sons* (New York: Oxford University Press, 2008).

Türk Büyük Milli Meclis Zabit Ceridesi, Devre: II, Cild: 8/1, İçtima Senesi: II, Kırkikinci İçtima: 20.4. 1340 (1924), Pazar: 889–944.

Türk Yurdu, 1. Cilt (1-2); Murat Şefkatlı, editor of translation team (Ankara: Tutibay Yayınları, 1998).

Qasim Amin; Samiha Sidhom Peterson, translator. *The Liberation of Women and the New Woman* (Cairo; New York: The American University in Cairo Press, 2000).

[Yalman], Ahmet Emin. *The Development of Modern Turkey as Measured by Its Press* (London: Columbia University, Studies in the Social Sciences; Longman, Green and Company, 1914).

[Yalman], Ahmet Emin. *Turkey in the World War* (New Haven: Yale University Press, 1930).
[Yalman], Ahmet Emin. *Yakın Tarihte Gördüklerim ve Geçirdiklerim*, 2 Cilt. (İstanbul: Rey, 1970).
Ziya Gokalp; Kemal Bek, editor, *Türkleşmek, İslamlaşmak, Muasırlaşmak* (İstanbul: Bordo Siyah, 2005).
Ziya Gokalp; Mehmet Celal Atgın, editor. *Türk Ahlakı* (İstanbul: Bilgeoğuz, 2013).
Ziya Gokalp; Mustafa Görgen, editor. *Türk Ahlakı* (İstanbul: Türk Kültür Yayını, 1975).
Ziya Gokalp; Niyazi Berkes, editor. *Turkish Nationalism and Western Civilization: Selected Essays of Ziya Gökalp*, translated from Ottoman Turkish by Niyazi Berkes (New York: Columbia University Press, 1959).
Ziya Gökalp. "Bugünkü Felsefe" *Genç Kalemler 2-2* (27 Nisan/10 Mayıs 1911), 110–12.
Ziya Gökalp. "İki Tehlike." In: Celal Nuri, *Kara Tehlike* (Dersaadet: Cemiyyet Kütüphanesi, r.1334 [1918]): 5–8.
Ziya Gökalp. *Kızıl Elma* (İstanbul: Hayriye ve Yeni Matbuası, r. 1330 [1914]).
Ziya Gökalp. *The Principles of Turkism*, translated from the Ottoman Turkish by Robert Devereux (Leiden: EJ Brill, 1968).
Ziya Gökalp. *Türkçülüğün Esasları* (Istanbul: Matbuat ve İstihbarat Matbaası, 1923).
Ziya Gökalp. *Türkleşmek, İslamlaşmak, Muasırlaşmak* (İstanbul: Yeni Memua, 1918).
Ziya Gökalp. *Yeni Hayat* (İstanbul: Yeni Mecmua, 1918).
Ziya Gökalp. "Yeni Hayat ve Genç Kalemler." *Genç Kalemler 2-8* (10 Ağustos 1327/23 Ağustos 1911), 110–12.

Secondary Sources

Abromeit, John. *Max Horkheimer and the Foundations of the Frankfurt School* (Cambridge, UK; New York: Cambridge University Press, 2011).
Açıkyıldız, Birgül. *The Yezidis: The History of a Community, Culture and Religion* (London; New York: I.B. Tauris, 2014).
Ahmad, Feroz. "Great Britain's Relations with the Young Turks, 1908–1918," *Middle Eastern Studies*, Vol. 2, No. 4 (1966), 304–21.
Ahmad, Feroz. *The Young Turks: The Committee of Union and Progress in Turkish Politics, 1908–14* (Oxford: Clarendon Press, 1969).
Ahmad, Feroz. *The Young Turks and the Ottoman Nationalities: Armenians, Greeks, Albanians, Jews and Arabs, 1908–1918* (Salt Lake City: University of Utah Press, 2014).
Akgun, Mehmet. *Materializmin Türkiye'ye Girişi ve İlk Etkileri* (Ankara: Turizm ve Kultur Bakanlığı, 1988).
Akın, Yiğit. *When the War Came Home: The Ottomans' Great War and the Devastation of an Empire* (Stanford: Stanford University Press, 2018).

Aksakal, Mustafa. "'Holy War made in Germany'? Ottoman Origins of the 1914 Jihad," *War in History*, Vol. 18, No. 2 (2011), 184–99.

Aksakal, Mustafa. *The Ottoman Road to War* (New York; London: Cambridge University Press, 2011).

Aksaryan, Necati. "Çağdaşlaşmaya Giden Yolu Celal Nuri ve Fikir Alanında Etkinliği" (Unpublished Ph.D. Dissertation, Hacettepe Üniversitesi, 1993).

Atuk, M. Volkan. "İttihat-ı Terakki Cemiyeti'nin İran Politikası," *Belleten*, Vol. 83, No. 269 (2019), 261–88.

Ayda, Adile. *Sadri Maksudi Arsal* (Ankara: Kültür Bakanlığı, 1981).

Aydemir, Şevket Süreyya. *Makedonya'dan Orta Asya'ya Kadar Enver Paşa*, cilt III (İstanbul: Remzi Kitabevi, 1972).

Aydın, Cemal. *The Politics of Anti-Westernism in Asia* (New York: Columbia University Press, 2007).

Aydın, Mehmet Akif. "Hukuk-ı Aile Kararnamesi." In: *İslam Ansiklopedisi*, 18. Cilt (İstanbul: Türkiye Diyanet Vakfı, 1998), 314–18.

Aydın, Mehmet Akif. "Mecelle-i Ahkam-ı Adliyye." In: *İslam Ansiklopedisi*, Cilt: 28 (Ankara: Diyanet İşler Bakanlığı, 2003), 231–5.

Baer, Marc David. *The Dönme: Jewish Converts, Muslim Revolutionaries, and Secular Turks* (Stanford: Stanford University Press, 2010).

Bali, Rıfat N. *Bir Günah Keçisi: Munis Tekinalp Cilt 1: Yahudi, Yurtsever ve Kemalist Bir Fikir Adamının Öyküsü* (İstanbul: Libra, 2012).

Balkaya, İhsan Sabri. "Afife Fikret'e Göre Feminizm," *Atatürk Üniversitesi Türkiyat Enstitüsü Dergisi*, Sayı 4 (1996), 103–14.

Bayur, Yusuf Hikmet. *Türk İnkılâbı Tarihi*, third edition (Ankara: Türk Tarih Kurumu, 1991).

Bein, Amit. "A Young Turk Islamic Intellectual: Filibeli Ahmed Hilmi and the Diverse Inteelectual Legacies of the Late Ottoman Empire," *International Journal of Middle East Studies*, Vol. 39, No. 4 (2007), 607–25.

Ben-Horin, Meir. *Max Nordau: Philosopher of Human Solidarity* (New York: Conference on Jewish Social Studies, Inc., 1956).

Berkes, Niyazi. *The Development of Secularism in Modern Turkey*. Montreal: McGill University Press, 1964.

Beyaz, Cenk. *Dersaadet'te Bir Sosyalist: Parvus Efendi* (İstanbul: Ötüken, 2013).

Bulmuş, Birsen. *Plague, Quarantines and Geopolitics in the Ottoman Empire* (Edinburgh: Edinburgh University Press, 2012).

Buzpınar, Ş. Tufan. "Celal Nuri's Concepts of Westernization," *Middle Eastern Studies*, Vol. 43, No. 2 (March 2007), 247–58.

Buzpınar, Ş. Tufan. "Öteki üzerinden hesaplaşma: Celâl Nuri ve Abdullah Cevdet'in Avrupa tartışmaları hakkında bir değirlendirme," *Dîvân: İlmî Araştırmaları*, Vol. 19 (2005/2), 251–76.

Çağaptay, Söner. *Islam, Secularism and Nationalism in Modern Turkey: Who Is a Turk?* (London; New York, Rutledge, 2006).

Çağaptay, Söner. "Race, Assimilation, and Kemalism: Turkish Nationalism and the Minorities in the 1930s," *Middle Eastern Studies*, Vol. 40, No. 3 (2007), 86–101.

Çakmak, Yalçın. *Sultan'ın Kızılbaşları: II. Abdülhamid Dönemi Alevi Algısı ve Siyaseti* (İstanbul: İletişim, 2019).

Çalen, Mehmet Kaan. "Celâl Nuri'ye Göre Muhit, Irk, Zaman Teorisi Bağlamında Eski Türkler İle Osmanlı Türkleri Arasındaki Münasebetler-1." Accessed July 16, 2015: http://www.turkyorum.com/celal-nuriye-gore-muhit-irk-zaman-teorisi-baglaminda-eski-turkler-ile-osmanli-turkleri-arasindaki-munasebetler-1/

Çavdar, Tevfik. *Türkiye'de Liberalizmin Doğuşu* (İstanbul: Uygarlık Yayınları, 1982).

Çelebi, Mevlüt. "Mütareke İstanbul'unda Bir İtalyan Dostu: Celâl Nuri, *Tarih ve Toplum*, Vol. 18, No. 108 (Aralık 1992), 45–6.

Cengiz, Recep et al. *Atatürk'ün Okuduğu Kitaplar*, Cilt: 1, 7, 11, 16, 19, 20, 23 (Ankara: Anıtkabir Derneği, 2001).

Ceran, Ömer. *Şehbenderzade Filibeli Ahmed Hilmi'nin Dini ve Felsefi Görüşleri* (Bursa: Sır Yayıncılık, 2013).

Cohen, Israel. *The Zionist Movement: Its Aims and Achievements* (London: W. Speaight & Sons, 1912).

Cohen, Julia-Phillip. *Becoming Ottomans: Sephardic Jews and Imperial Citizenship in the Modern Era* (New York; London, Oxford University Press, 2014).

Criss, Nur Bilge. *Istanbul under Allied Occupation, 1918–1923* (Leiden: E.J. Brill, 1999).

Çöpel, Hatice. "Celal Nuri İleri'nin Din Anlayışı" (Unpublished M.A. Thesis, Selçuk Üniversitesi, 2010).

Demir, Ahmet İshak. *Cumhuriyet Dönemi Aydınlarının İslam'a Bakışı* (İstanbul: Ensar Neşriyatı, 2004).

Demir, Habip. "Celâl Nuri [İleri] ve İslam Tarihçiliği (Unpublished M.A. Thesis, Ankara Üniversitesi, 2006).

Deringil, Selim. "The Ottoman Origins of Kemalist Nationalism: Namık Kemal to Mustafa Kemal," *European History Quarterly*, Vol. 23 (1993): 165–91.

Doğan, Yusuf. "Celal Nuri İleri'nin Dini ve Ictimai Hayata Bakışı" (Unpublished M.A. Thesis, Ankara Universitesi, 2003).

Duymaz, Recep. "Celâl Nuri İleri." In: *İslam Ansiklopedisi*, 7. Cilt (İstanbul: Türkiye Diyanet Vakfı, 1993), 242–5.

Duymaz, Recep. "Celâl Nuri İleri ve Âti Gazetesi" (Unpublished Ph.D. Dissertation, Marmara Üniversitesi, 1991).

Duymaz, Recep. *Dil ve Edebiyat Yazıları I: Celâl Nuri İleri* (İstanbul: Kitabevi, 1995).

Earle, Edward Mead. "The New Constitution of Turkey," *Political Science Quarterly*, Vol. 40, No. 1 (March 1925), 73–100.

Eissenstat, Howard. "Metaphors of Race and Discourse of Nation: Racial Theory and State Nationalism in the First Decades Of the Turkish Republic." In: Paul Spickard, editor. *Race and Nation: Ethnic Systems in the Modern World* (New York and London: Routledge, 2005), 239–56.

Erickson, Edward J. *Ottomans and Armenians: A Study in Counterinsurgency* (New York: Palgrave Macmillan, 2013).

Eroğlu, Nazmi. *Cavit Bey: İttihatçıların Ünlü Maliye Nazırı* (İstanbul: Ötüken, 2008).
Gencer, Bedri. *İslâm'da Modernleşme 1839-1939*, 4. Baskı (İstanbul: Doğu Batı, 2017).
Georgeon, François. *Aux Origines du Nationalisme Turc: Yusuf Akçura (1876-1935)* (Paris: Institut d'Études Anatoliennes, 1989).
Glasse, Cyril. *The New Encyclopedia of Islam*, third edition (Lanham: Rowman & Littlefield, 2013).
Gökçen, Amed. *Osmanlı ve İngiliz Arşiv Belgelerinde Yezidiler* (İstanbul: Bilgi Üniversitesi Yayınları, 2012).
Göle, Nilüfer. *The Forbidden Modern: Civilization and Veiling* (Ann Arbor: University of Michigan Press, 1996).
Gourgouris, Sathis. *Dream Nation: Enlightenment and the Colonization of Modern Greece* (Stanford: Stanford University Press, 1996).
Gülmez, Nurettin. *Tanzimat'tan Cumhuriyet'e Harfler Üzerine Tartışmalar* (Bursa: Alfa Aktüel, 2006).
Gürses, Mürsel. "Meşrutiyet Dönemi Gezi Kitaplarında Oryantalist ve Oksidentalist Söylemler," *Turkish Studies*, Vol. 7, No. 1 (2012), 1269-303.
Hanioğlu, M. Şükrü. "Abdullah Cevdet, Turkey, 1869-1932." In: Charles Kurtzman, editor. *Modernist Islam, 1840-1940: A Sourcebook* (Oxford; New York: Oxford University Press, 2002), 172-4.
Hanioğlu, M. Şukru. *Atatürk: An Intellectual Biography* (Princeton: Princeton University Press, 2011).
Hanioğlu, M. Şükrü. *A Brief History of the Late Ottoman Empire* (Princeton; Oxford: Princeton University Press, 2008).
Hanioğlu, M. Şükrü. *Bir Siyasi Düşünür Olarak: Doktor Abdullah Cevdet ve Dönemi* (İstanbul: Üçdal Nesriyat, 1981).
Hanioğlu, M. Şükrü. "Garbcılar: Their Attitudes toward Religion and Their Impact on the Official Ideology of the Turkish Republic," *Studia Islamica*, Vol. 86, No. 2 (August 1997): 153-8.
Hanioğlu, M. Şükrü. *Preparation for Revolution: The Young Turks, 1902-1908* (New York; London: Oxford University Press, 2001).
Hanioğlu, M. Şükrü. *The Young Turks in Opposition* (New York; London: Oxford University Press, 1995).
Herzog, Christoph. *Geschichte und Ideologie: Mehmed Murad und Celal Nuri über die historischen Ursachen des osmanischen Niedergangs* (Berlin: Klaus Schwarz Verlag, 1996).
Heyd, Uriel. *Foundations of Turkish Nationalism: The Life and Teachings of Ziya Gökalp* (London: Luzac & Co; Harvill Press, 1950).
Hurewitz, J. C. *Diplomacy in the Near and Middle East: A Documentary Record, Volume I: 1535-1914* (Princeton: Van Nostrand Company, 1956).
İlkin, Selim. "Cavit Bey, Mehmed." In: *İslam Ansiklopedisi*, Cilt: 7 (İstanbul: Türkiye Diyanet Vakfı, 1993), 175-6.
İnalcık, Halil. "Istanbul: An Islamic City," *Journal of Islamic Studies*, Vol. 19 (1990), 1-23.

İnce, Başak. *Citizenship and Identity in Turkey: From Ataturk's Republic to the Present Day* (London; New York: I.B. Tauris, 2012).
Jelavich, Barbara. *History of the Balkans Volume 2: 20th Century* (New York; London: Cambridge University Press, 1983).
Kandiyoti, Deniz. "End of Empire: Islam, Nationalism, and Women in Turkey." In Reina Lewis and Sara Mills, editors, *Feminist Postcolonial Theory* (New York: Routledge, 2003), 263-84.
Kansu, Aykut. *Politics in Post-Revolutionary Turkey, 1908-1913* (Leiden: Brill, 2000).
Karaca, Filiz, editor, *Osmanlı Anayasası: Kanun-ı Esasî* (İstanbul: Doğu Kitabevi, 2009).
Karaömerlioğlu, M. Asım. "Helphand-Parvus and his Impact on Turkish Intellectual Life," *Middle Eastern Studies*, Vol. 40, No. 6 (2004), 145-65.
Kayalı, Hasan. *Arabs and Young Turks: Ottomanism, Islamism and Arabism in the Ottoman Empire, 1908-1918* (Berkeley: University of California Press, 1997).
Kayaoğlu, Turan. *Legal Imperialism: Sovereignty and Extraterritoriality in Japan, the Ottoman Empire, and China* (Cambridge: Cambridge University Press, 2010).
Keddie, Nikki R. *An Islamic Response to Imperialism: Political and Religious Writings of Sayyid Jamal ad-din Al-Afghani* (Berkeley: University of California Press, 1968).
Kévorkian, Raymond. *The Armenian Genocide: A Complete History* (London; New York: I.B. Tauris, 2011).
Kırmızı, Abdulhamit. *Abdülhamid'in VALİLERİ: Osmanlı Vilayet İdaresi, 1895-1908*, üçüncü baskı (İstanbul: Klasik Yayınları, 2008), 70.
Kocatürk, Utkan. *Atatürk ve Türkiye Cumhuriyeti Tarihi Kronolojisi, 1918-1938* (Ankara: Türk Tarih Kurumu Basımevi, 2000).
Koloğlu, Orhan. "Celal Nuri'nin Jeune Turc Gazetesi ve Siyonist Bağı," *Tarih ve Toplum* (Aralık 1992), 46-8.
Korkmaz, Zeynep. *Atatürk ve Türk Dili Belgeler* (Ankara: Türk Dil Kurumu, 1992).
Korkmaz, Zeynep. *Türk Dilin Tarihi Akışı İçinde Atatürk ve Dil Devrimi* (Ankara: Ankara Üniversitesi Basımevi, 1963).
Köroğlu, Erol. *Ottoman Propaganda and Turkish Identity: Literature in Turkey during World War I* (London; New York: I.B. Tauris, 2007).
Kreyenbroek, Philip G. *Yezidism—It's Background, Observances and Textual Tradition* (Lewiston: E. Mellon Press, 1995).
Kurt, Mustafa. *Celâl Nuri İleri'nin Romanları Bir İnceleme* (Ankara: Kurgan Edebiyat, 2012).
Lewis, Geoffrey. *The Turkish Language Reform: A Catastrophic Success* (Oxford; New York: Oxford University Press, 1999).
Levend, Agâh Sırrı. *Türk Dilinde Gelişme ve Sadeleştirme Evreleri* (Ankara: Ankara Üniversitesi Basımevi, 1972).
Mango, Andrew. *Atatürk: The Biography of the Founder of Modern Turkey* (New York: Overlook Press, 1999).
Mardin, Şerif. "İktisadi Düşünce: Tanzimat'tan Cumhuriyet'e İktisadi Düşüncesi Gelişmesi (1838-1918)." In: Murat Belge et al, editors, *Tanzimat'tan Cumhuriyet'e Türkiye Ansiklopedisi*, Cilt: 3 (İstanbul: İletişim Yayınları, 1985), 618-34.

Mardin, Şerif. *The Genesis of Young Ottoman Thought: A Study in the Modernization of Turkish Political Ideas* (Syracuse: Syracuse University Press, 2000).

Matossian, Bedross Der. *Shattered Dreams of Revolution: From Liberty to Violence in the Late Ottoman Empire* (Stanford: Stanford University Press, 2014).

McDowall, David. *A Modern History of the Kurds, Third Edition* (London; New York: I.B. Tauris, 2004).

Mosse, George L. Lectures #13 and #14 from History 513, European Cultural History 1880–1930, originally broadcast in Fall 1979 for WHA Radio series' "University of the Air." Accessed December 15, 2015: http://mosseprogram.wisc.edu/audio_history513.htm

Mosse, George L. "Machiavelli," from History 119, Euopean Cultural History, 1500–1815, recorded audio lecture originally broadcast in Fall 1969 for WHA Radio series' "University of the Air." Accessed December 15, 2015: http://mosseprogram.wisc.edu/audio_history119.htm.

Mosse, George L. "Max Nordau and His Degeneration." In: Max Nordau, *Degeneration*, translated from the second edition of the German Edition (Lincoln; London, University of Nebraska Press, 1993), xiii–xxxvi.

Müller, Andreas. "Friederich F. Martens on the Office of the Consul and Consular Jurisdiction in the East," *European Journal of International Law*, Vol. 25, No. 3 (August 2014), 871–91.

Nişanyan, Sevan. *Yanlış Cumhuriyet: Atatürk ve Kemalizm Üzerine 51 Soru* (İstanbul: Kırmızı Yayınları, 2008).

Nordau, Anna and Maxa. *Max Nordau: A Biography* (New York: Nordau Committee, 1943).

Nordau, Max. "Address at the Sixth Zionist Congress." Accessed June 28, 2015: https://www.jewishvirtuallibrary.org/source/Zionism/nordau2.html

Norman, York. "Beyond Jihad: Alexander Helphand Parvus, Musa Kazim, and Celal Nuri on the Ottoman-German Alliance." In: Hakan Yavuz with Feroz Ahmed, *War & Collapse: World War I and the Ottoman State* (Salt Lake City: The University of Utah Press, 2016), 263–81.

Norman, York. "'Disputing the Iron Circle': Renan, Afghani, and Kemal on Islam, Science, and Modernity," *Journal of World History*, Vol. 22, No. 4 (December 2011), 693–714.

Norman, York. "The Historical Importance of Kazan Tatar Turks to the Late Ottoman Empire and the Ideas of Celal Nuri." In: Muhammad Savaş Kafkasyalı, editor, *Islam in Central Asia*, vol. 3 (Türkistan, Kazakhstan: Ahmet Yesevi University, 2013): 417–28.

Ochsenwald, William. *The Hijaz Railway* (Charlottesville: University of Virginia Press, 1980).

Olson, Robert. *The Emergence of Kurdish Nationalism and the Sheikh Said Rebellion, 1880–1925* (Austin: University of Texas Press, 1989).

Özavcı, Ozan. "A Jewish 'Liberal' in Istanbul: Vladimir Jabotinsky, the Young Turks and the Zionist Press Network, 1908–1911." In: Abigail Green and Simon Levis Sullam, editors, *Jews, Liberalism, Anti-Semitism: A Global History* (New York: Palgrave Macmillan, 2020), 289–314.

Pakalın, Mehmed Zeki. *Sicill-i Osmani Zeyli*, VI. Cilt (Ankara: Türk Tarihi Kurumu, 2008).

Parla, Taha. *The Social and Political Thought of Ziya Gokalp, 1876–1924* (Leiden: E.J. Brill, 1985).

Parla, Taha. *Türkiye'de Anayasalar*, genişletmiş yeni baskı, üçüncü baskı (İstanbul: İletişim, 2002).

Philliou, Christine. *Biography of an Empire: Governing Ottomans in an Age of Revolution* (Berkeley: University of California Press, 2010).

Portreler Galerisi 34. Bölüm (Aka Gündüz) TRT Diyanet (2007). Video accessed July 23, 2016: https://www.youtube.com/watch?v=R-rfPM4M21I

Schacht, Joseph. *An Introduction to Islamic Law* (Oxford: Clarendon Press, 1964).

Shaw, Stanford. *Turkey and the Holocaust: Turkey's Role in Rescuing Turkish and European Jewry from Nazi Persecution, 1933–1945* (New York: New York University Press, 1993).

Shissler, Ada Holland. *Between Two Empires: Ahmet Ağaoğlu and the New Turkey* (London: I.B. Tauris, 2002).

Stamatoyannopoulos, George; Aritra Bose, Athanasios Teodosiadis, Fotis Tsetsos, Anna Platinga, Nikoletta Psatha, Nikos Zogas, Evangelia Yannaki et al., "Genetics of the Peloponnesian Populations and the Theory of Extinction of the Medieval Peloponnesian Greeks," *European Journal of Human Genetics* (2018), 637–45.

Şimşir, Bilal. *Malta Sürgünleri*, 2. baskı (Ankara: Bilgi Yayınları, 1985).

Şimşir, Bilal. *Türk Yazı Devrimi* (Ankara: Türk Tarih Kurumu Basımevi, 1992).

Tallon, James. "The Failure of Ottomanism: The Albanian Rebellions of 1909–1912" (Unpublished Ph.D. Dissertation, University of Chicago, 2012).

Tan, Nail. *Atatürk ve Türk Dil Kurumu* (Ankara: Türk Dil Kurumu Yayınları, 2011).

Tekeli, Ilhan. "Tanzimat'tan Cumhuriyet's Eğitim Sistemindeki Değişmeler." In: *Tanzimat'tan Cumhuriyet'e Türkiye Ansiklopedisi*, Cilt 2 (İstanbul: İletişim Yayınları, 1985), 456–75.

Toprak, Zafer. "İkinci Meşrutiyet Döneminde İktisadi Düşünce." In: Murat Belge et al., editors, *Tanzimat'tan Cumhuriyet'e Türkiye Ansiklopedisi*, Cilt: 3 (İstanbul: İletişim Yayınları, 1985), 635–40.

Toprak, Zafer. "The Family, Feminism, and the State during the Young Turk Period, 1908-1918." In: *Première Recontre Internationale sur l'Empire Ottoman et la Turquie Moderne* (İstanbul; Paris: Éditions ISIS, 1991), 441–52.

Toprak, Zafer. *Türkiye'de "Milli İktisat": 1908–1918* (Ankara: Yurt Yayınları, 1982).

Tucker, Judith E. "Revisiting Reform: Women and the Ottoman Law of Family Rights, 1917," *The Arab Studies Journal*, Vol. 4, No. 2 (1996), 4–17.

Tunaya, Tarık Zafer. *İslamcılık Cereyani II* (İstanbul: Yeni Gün Haber Ajansı, 1998).

Tunaya, Tarık Zafer. *Türkiye'de Siyaset Partiler Cilt 2: Mütareke Dönemi 1918–1922*, 4. Baskı (İstanbul: İleteşim Yayinlari, 2010).

Tunçer, Polat. *İttihatçı Cavit Bey* (İstanbul: Yedi Tepe, 2010).

Turan, Şerafettin. *Türk Devrimi Tarhi, 3. Kitap (Birinci Bölüm), Yeni Türkiye'nin Oluşumu (1923–1938), Üçüncü Basım*, (İstanbul: Bilgi Yayınları, 2013).

Turesay, Özgür. "Antisionisme et antisemitisme dans la presse ottoman d'Istanbul a l'epoque jeune turque (1909-1912). L'exemple d'Ebuziyya Tevfik," *Turcica: Revue d'études turques*, Vol. 41 (2009), 147-78.

Turnaoğlu, Banu. *The Formation of the Turkish Republicanism* (Princeton; Oxford: Princeton University Press, 2017).

Ulken, Hilmi Ziya. *Türkiye'de Çağdaş Düşünce Tarihi* (İstanbul: Ülken Yayınları, 1992).

Unat, İlhan. *Türk Vatandaşlık Hukuku: Metinler, Mahkeme Kararları* (Ankara: Sevinç Maatbası, 1966), 38-44.

Uyanık, Necmi. "Batıcı Bir Aydın Olarak Celâl Nuri İleri ve Yenileşme Sürecinde Fikir Hareketlerine Bakışı," *Selçuk Üniversitesi Türkiyat Araştırmaları Dergisi*, Sayı: 15 Güz 2004: 227-74.

Uyanık, Necmi. Siyasi Düşünce Tarihimizde Batıcı Bir Aydın Olarak Celal Nuri [İleri]" (Unpublished Ph.D. Dissertation: Hacettepe Üniversitesi, 1993).

Uzer, Umut. *An Intellectual History of Turkish Nationalism: Between Turkish Ethnicity and Islamic Identity* (Salt Lake City: The University of Utah Press, 2016).

Veloudis, Giorgos. *Jakob Phillip Fallmerayer and the Birth of Greek Historicism* (Athens: Mnimon, 1982).

von Dobbs, Danielle. *Dancing Modernity: Gender, Sexuality and the State in the Ottoman Empire and Early Turkish Republic* (Unpublished Ph.D. Dissertation, University of Arizona, 2008).

Yananlı, Hüseyin Rahmi. "Sunuş." In: Ahmet Hilmi Şehbenderzade, edited and translated by Hüseyin Rahmi Yananlı, *İslam Tarihi* (İstanbul: Huzur Yayınları, 2011).

Yavuz, M. Hakan. "Turkey without Sharia?" In: *Sharia Politics: Islamic Law and Society in the Modern World* (Bloomington, IN: Indiana University Press, 2011), 146-78.

Yıldırım, Hayri. *3 Mayıs 1944 Irkçılık Turancılık Davası* (İstanbul: ToganYayıncılık, 2015).

Zarinebaf, Fariba. "From Istanbul to Tabriz: Modernity and Constitutionalism in the Ottoman Empire and Iran," *Comparative Studies of South Asia, Africa and the Middle East*, Vol. 28, No. 1 (2008): 154-69.

Zürcher, Erik Jan. *Political Opposition in the Early Turkish Republic* (Leiden: Brill Academic Publishers, 1991).

Zürcher, Erik Jan. *The Unionist Factor: The Role of the Committee of Union and Progress in the Turkish Nationalist Movement: 1905-1926* (Leiden: Brill Academic Publishers, 1984).

Zürcher, Erik Jan. *The Young Turk Legacy and Nation Building* (London; New York: I.B. Tauris, 2010).

Zürcher, Erik Jan. *Turkey: A Modern History*, third edition (London; New York: I.B. Tauris, 2010).

Index

Abdulhak Hamid (Tarhan) 10, 85, 112–13, 115, 122–3, 136n.65, 169n.61
Abdulhamid II 1–2, 10, 22–3, 25–6, 28, 30, 36, 39–41, 49–50, 53–4, 76, 88–90, 115, 128, 130n.10, 151n.49, 191
Abdullah Cevdet (Karlıdağ); Celal Nuri's break with 16, 27–8, 131n.16; early influence on Celal Nuri 7, 9–10, 18, 26–7, 65–6, 126; historians interpretations of 14–15, 157n.4
Action Army (*Hareket Ordusu*) 2
Ahmed Cevdet 66, 105, 159–60n.15, 166n.8, 166n.9
Ahmet Emin (Yalman) 60, 154n.108
Alphabet Revolution 4, 13–14, 19, 103, 104, 116–19, 125, 128, 139n.111
America 5, 25, 34, 144n.12, 169n.62
American 5, 33, 35, 57, 62, 88, 93, 124, 150 f 37, 151n.49, 154n.120
Anatolia 12, 18, 34, 62, 94, 104, 109, 130n.10, 131n.14; Central Anatolia 22, 79; Eastern Anatolia 3, 31, 44, 46, 55–6, 62, 79, 150; Western Anatolia 3, 21–2, 61
ancient Greeks 45, 71, 73, 108, 168n.18
Ankara viii, 8, 16, 22, 34, 38
anti-Semitism 38–9, 57–60
Apostle Paul 71
April 13, 1909 uprising 17, 21–6, 44–8, 53, 70
Arabs; as minority 1, 3, 18, 31, 40, 42–3, 46–9, 60, 134n.45, 152n.70; Arabic Civilization 11, 13–14, 19–20, 60, 103–5, 108–9; Arabic linguistic Influence 116, 118–24, 128, 139n.111; Islam and the Arabs 45, 72–7, 79
Armenian; community in Istanbul 39, 62, 147n.80; deportation and massacre 54, 56, 150n.35; expatriates 38, 62, 128; merchants 16, 54, 126–7, 130–1, 161n.15; support for July 1908 uprising 1–4, 12–13, 39–40, 42, 53–7, 88, 126, 128, 140n.116

Balkans 1, 9, 28, 31, 50, 134n.45, 171n.62
Balkan Wars; general impact of 2–3, 7, 10, 21; language 106, 117; minorities 49, 51, 55–6, 59, 126; reforms caused by 24, 28, 31–2
British; and the Arabs 44, 47–9, 60, 167n.13; and the Armenians 88; diplomacy 27, 29–30, 160n.15; government 27, 31, 58; and the Greeks 50, 61; and liberalism 116; and Malta 7, 17, 34, 60; occupation of Istanbul 33–4, 37, 82, 133n.31
Büchner, Ludwig 5, 8, 16, 51, 66–8, 82, 126, 128, 135n.59, 136n.60
Buddhism 70–2, 84
Buzpınar, Tufan 11, 13, 15–16, 131n.16, 136n.61, 159n.15, 177n.22
Byzantium 47, 49–50

caliphate 12, 36, 48, 51, 60, 78–9
capitulations 29–30, 37, 123
Celal Nuri (İleri); general introduction to 4–8; intellectual influences on 8–12; place in historical scholarship 14–15; reaction to the Turkish Republic 12–14; Turkish language reform 103–24; views on politics 21–38; minorities 39–63; vulgar materialism and Islam 65–79; women, family and society 81–101; conclusions about 125–30
Cenab Şahabettin 82, 96, 111, 174n.109
Christian; language 116; minorities 44–7, 55; missionaries and the Kazan Tatar Turks 170–171n.62; politics 7, 9, 12, 27; vulgar materialism 71, 75–7, 78; women 84, 166n.7
Circassian 45, 82, 89, 130n.10
Committee of Union and Progress (CUP); and the Arabs 44, 49; and the Armenians 18, 53–5, 61–2; Celal Nuri's relationship with 4, 6–8, 11–12; during the July 1908

uprising 1–3, 40; and Eastern Anatolia 151n.46 foundation of 130n.2, 130n.10; and language reform 20; politics 3–4, 21, 23–7, 36–7, 70, 150n.44; and vulgar materialism 18–19, 65–6, 78, 126, 141n.10; and women 19; and the Zionists 57–8
Communism 107, 110, 114
Confucianism 70, 74
Conservatism; and the 13 April revolt 1–2, 4, 17, 21, 26; and language 20, 119, 122; and modern historians 14 and women 90, 97, 99
Constitution; 1791 French Constitution 36; 1928 revisions of 36, 79; discussion of from 1908 to 1920 6, 10, 34, 56; Ottoman Constitution of 1876 23, 30–31, 36, 147n.79, 160; Turkish Constitution of 1921 161n.15; Turkish Constitution of 1924 13, 36, 38, 59
Crete 5, 10, 27, 153n.92

Dashnak 4, 12, 18, 40, 53–4, 61, 128
Dönme 46
Duymaz, Recep 15, 132n.19

Ebüzziya Tevfik 6, 58
elites; and language 104, 106, 125; and minorities 50–1, 54–5, 58, 152n.74; and politics 4–5, 11–12, 18–20, 23, 26, 36; on vulgar materialism and Islam 65–6, 69–70, 77, 79, 162n.15; and women 82, 90–1, 93, 174n.109
Entente 31, 33–4, 49, 61
Enver Pasha; government 113; and language reform 116–7; and Libya 28; and political Islam 60, 76–8, 126
Esperanto 12, 104

Fatma Aliye (Topuz) 165–6n.7, 173n.102, 173–4n.109, 174n.115, 174–5n.117
First World War; aftermath of 7, 11, 37; and the Arabs 3, 40, 60; and the Balkans 2; and the Bolsheviks 110; lead up to 76, 133n.31; political effect of 21, 31, 33; women 92, 100
French; attitude towards minorities 45, 54, 59; colonial ambitions 8, 27, 31–2, 47, 50, 60, 159–60n.15; government 27, 30; journalists 51–2; language 5, 7, 11, 104–06, 111, 121, 133n.30

orientalist and racist attitudes of 43, 51, 109, 133n.31; women 84–5, 96, 166, 175n.117

Georgian 89
German; anti-Semitism 13, 38, 59, 61, 126; First World War alliance with the Ottomans 4; military 26; Orientalists 51, 109; politics 142–3n.12
Greek; Balkan Wars 130n.9, 140n.116; flight from Anatolia 21; independence 10, 27–8; minority 1, 12, 17–18, 33, 49–53, 76; Orthodox Church 170n.62; Patriarchate 53, 55, 61, 128, 153n.79; participation in the struggle for Western Anatolia from 1919 to 1922 34, 37, 39, 61; under the Turkish Republic 126, 147n.80, 161n.15

Hamdullah Suphi (Tanrıöver) 59, 147n.80
Hanioğlu M. Şükrü 3, 10, 14, 16, 79, 131n.16, 139n.113
Herzog, Christoph 132n.19
Hijaz 31, 44, 47–9, 60, 98
Hitler, Adolf 13, 59, 61, 123
Hüseyin Cahit (Yalçın) 20, 107, 122–3, 180n.108

imam 23–4, 26, 51, 65, 67, 127
imperialism 10, 28, 50, 112
Islam 65–7, 70–8, 96–100
Islamic law; and political reforms 6, 11–12, 18–19, 24, 26, 33, 37, 141n.10, 159–61n.15; and women 81–4, 86, 95, 99, 166n.7, 167n.17
Istanbul; archives in viii; and language reform 103, 106, 116, 176n.7; minorities in 39, 43, 51, 54–6, 58–9, 61–2, 126, 128; politics affecting 1–3, 6, 13, 16–18, 24, 31, 33–4, 38, 133n.31, 134n.42, 141n.11; regarding vulgar materialism and Islam 76; women in 82, 89, 93, 100, 175n.117
international law 27–30, 55
Italian invasion of Libya 2, 10, 14, 21, 27, 58, 126; occupation of Anatolia 33, 37

Jews; as minority in the Ottoman Empire and Turkish Republic 57–61,

71, 75–6, 126, 155n.126, 155n.131, 155n.134; under Nazi persecution 13
Jihad 4
July 1908 uprising 1, 6, 24, 26, 39–40, 53, 76, 133n.31

Kazan Tatar Turkish; language 103, 106; society 169–172n.62; women 83, 89–92
Kurdish; language 43; people 40, 43–5, 56–7, 60, 130n.10, 151n.46

Language Revolution 104, 107, 109, 119–25
Le Bon, Gustave; influence of 8, 16, 22, 51, 134n.45–7; opinions about Islam 76–8, 163n.37; views on Algeria 28, 32, 47
Lenin, Vladimir 78, 107
Liberalism; attitude towards women 93, 174n.115; economy 17, 37, 144n.12; and language reform 115; opponents of 1, 24, 26, 33, 37, 54, 70, 120, 140n.117, 141n.12, 147n.67; political and social philosophy 24, 27, 35, 69, 169n.59; support of westernization 23, 28, 37, 49, 68, 74, 82, 112, 172n.82
Lorimer, James 28–30
Luther, Martin 71–2, 79, 114, 163–4n.37

Machiavelli, Niccolò 27, 40, 77
Malta Exile 7, 17, 34, 37, 60, 62
Mecca 47–9, 74–5, 104
Mecelle 66, 79, 159–62n.15
Medina 47, 88
Mehmed Cavit 60
Muhammad, and the Arabs 47–8; and the Shia 45–7; and vulgar materialism 65, 67, 72–9, 126, 135n.51, 159n.12, 159–60n.15, 163n.37; and women 86–7, 95, 98, 165n.7, 174n.109, 175n.117
Muslim; Alevi 40, 44–5; Hanefi 22, 38, 59, 126, 147n.80, 160n.15; Shia 18, 45–6; Sunni 5, 18, 26, 41, 46, 60, 75, 104, 122, 126, 147n.80, 149n.20
Mustafa Kemal (Atatürk); biography of 139n.113; during the early Republic 13–14, 16, 35–7, 139n.110; during the Lausanne peace negotiations 22; interest in vulgar materialism and Islam 5, 78–9; during the Turkish Independence War 8, 34; explanation of name usage x; and language reform 19–20, 104, 106–9, 116–18, 123, 125; and minorities 53, 57, 62; and the legal revolution 161n.15; secularization 3, 18; relationship with Celal Nuri 12; views on women 101, 127; and the writing of the 1924 Constitution 38
Mustafa Nuri 4–5, 40–1, 43–4

Namık Kemal 16, 105, 151n.53
National Pact (*Misak-i Milli*) 7, 12, 34
Nationalism; Armenian (see Dashnak); Greek 3, 18, 51–53, 128; Jewish (see Zionism); Muslim 4, 7–8, 12, 16–17, 21, 33–4, 36–7, 100–1, 122–6; Turkish 4, 7–8, 11, 16, 22, 33–34, 36, 38, 81–82, 89, 93, 95–96, 113–114, 120
Newspapers; *Ati* 7; *Courrier d'Orient* 6; *İkdam* 7; *İleri* 7, 88, 127
Nordau, Max; international influence of 8–9, 16, 128, 135 fs.56–7; and politics 143–4n.12; views on Jews and Zionism 57, 63; and women 82, 93, 96, 172n.82
North Pole 135n.53

Ottomanism 3, 54

Pan-Islamism 11, 14–15, 81, 131n.13
Pan-Turkism; and language reform 103, 107, 109; politics 3–4, 13, 131n.14; women 81, 83, 94–6
Parvus, Alexander Helphand 6
poetry 106, 110–16, 177n.29, 178n.39
Poland 30
populism 12, 36, 114
Prince Sabahattin 140n.117, 141–2n.12
Protestant 9, 71–2, 114, 164n.37

Quran; and the Arabs 44, 47; and politics 29, 32, 44; and vulgar materialism 66, 68, 78–9; and women 97–100, 104, 165–6n.7

Race; general views on 8–9, 30, 75, 143n.12, 147n.80; on Turks as a 83, 119–20, 171n.62
Reaction (*İrtica*) 3, 17, 35, 56, 68, 92, 128
Reform; general views on 4, 13–14; language and 103–24; political and

social 22–7, 34; vulgar materialism and 67–78; women and 89–93, 96–100
Romans 50, 163n.37
Russian; language 106, 114; minorities 50, 55, 58, 88–90; politics 9, 18, 30–31; Revolution of November 1917 106; women 170n.62
Russo-Turkish War 26

Sadri Maksudi (Arsal) 62, 106, 109, 119–21, 123, 176n.14
Sahip Bey 25, 48
Salonika (Thessaloniki) 12, 28, 54, 128
Secularism 3, 5, 14, 22, 36, 67, 79, 112, 125, 177n.22
Sedat Nuri (İleri) 132n.20
Şehbenderzade, Ahmed Hilmi 12, 14, 16, 66, 68–9, 77–9, 126, 158–9n.12, 162n.22, 162n.29
Sephardic Jews 15, 39
Sharif Husayn 49
Sharighian, Hawrutian 4, 12, 53–6, 61, 63
Sırrı Giridi 5, 41, 46
Social Darwinism 39, 57, 70, 83, 128
Socialism 68, 143–4n.12
Suphi Nuri (İleri) 7, 132n.20
Surname Law (1934) x, 127, 134n.39

Taine, Hyppolyte 8–9, 16, 75, 109, 135n.52, 171n.62
Talât Pasha 11, 60, 82, 113
Turkish; language 103–24; political identity 12–4, 34–7; Republic x, 10, 12–13, 15, 17–18, 21–2, 38–9, 57, 60, 139n.110, 157n.3, 161n.15; women 89–96

Turkish Independence War 11, 17, 39, 67, 78, 126

Unionists; general historical context of 4, 8, 10, 13; on language 109, 119, 122; on minorities 39, 56; on vulgar materialism and Islam 76; on women 82, 125; and politics 18, 21–2, 24, 26, 29, 33, 37, 127, 129
Unity of the Elements (*İttihad-i Anasir*) 54

von Martens, Friedrich Fromhold 28–9
Vulgar Materialism 9, 18, 27, 65–9, 79, 126, 157n.4, 157n.12, 162n.15, 162n.22

Westernism 3, 15–16, 27, 81, 134n.38, 177n.22

Yezidis 5, 18, 40–4, 60, 126, 149 fs. 10, 11, 13, 15, 150n.37
Young Turks; general importance of 6, 16, 130n.2, 133n.31; and language reform 105, 107, 115, 122; on minorities 40, 48, 51, 60, 63; in political discussions 26–8, 31, 36; on vulgar materialism and Islam 66, 158n.12, 160n.15; views on women 88, 90, 125, 166n.7
Yunus Nadi (Abalıoğlu) 13, 16

Zionism 9, 52, 58, 60
Ziya Gökalp; general influence of 16; and language reform 11, 19, 103–08, 110–16, 119, 122–3, 177n.29; opinions on women 19, 81–3, 93–6, 99, 101, 125, 166n.9, 167n.16
Zürcher, Erik J. 4, 12–13, 131n.16, 134n.44, 134n.45, 146–7n.67, 147n.79

www.ingramcontent.com/pod-product-compliance
Lightning Source LLC
Chambersburg PA
CBHW061829300426
44115CB00013B/2298